HANAN
ASHRAWI

A PASSION FOR PEACE

HANAN ASHRAWI

A PASSION FOR PEACE

BARBARA VICTOR

FOURTH ESTATE · *London*

First published in Great Britain in 1995 by
Fourth Estate Limited
289 Westbourne Grove
London W11 2QA

A catalogue record for this book is available from the
British Library

ISBN 1–85702–181–9

Printed in the United States of America

*In loving memory of
Abrasha and Elena Paull
and Frank Gertler*

CONTENTS

Contents

ACKNOWLEDGMENTS

THERE ARE MANY PEOPLE, both personally and professionally, who have been of enormous help throughout the writing of this book. There are some who became invaluable not only as sources of information and history but also as friends who lent enormous support throughout the process of interviewing hundreds of people, recording, and writing their stories. Neither role was easy for those involved, since the subject of the book was and remains complicated in the context of the ongoing history and turmoil of the Middle East. My task, as a result, was equally complicated as it concerned digesting changing facts to present them plausibly and coherently within these pages.

I am deeply grateful to Boris Hoffman for all his support, concern, and affection since the very beginning of our relationship, more than three books ago. Without him, surely, this particular book would have never become a reality. Claire Wachtel has been equally important to me throughout this past year and a half. As my editor she not only displayed a vast knowledge of the subject but also an uncanny ability to analyze events as they pertained to the people directly involved. As a friend she encouraged me with her enthusiasm and humor during the months of writing, and during our shared on-the-ground experiences throughout the Occupied Territories. My agent, Jane Gelfman, is an example of one of those rare people who takes her responsibilities beyond the limits of the classic definition of her job. I am deeply grateful to Jane for all her optimism and hard work that went into the preparation of this book.

There are others to whom I am also grateful, who either contributed to the publishing process or offered me a secure base from which to work and travel. Specifically my thanks go to Eva Koralnik, Lennart Sane, Jorge Tellerman, Ginou Richard, Christopher Jackson, Lucy Jarvis, and Ted Lee. And, as always, my love goes to Anna, Max, Stephanie, and Jonathan.

On the Israeli side of the Green Line, there were many who spent hours and days during the peace negotiations in Washington explaining facts and interpreting events as they evolved. In Israel proper, there were many who gave generously of their time, enabling me to understand the nuances of the process as well as those facts that were left unreported. Specifically I would like to thank Asher Bitan, Eitan Haber, Avi Armoni, Nomi Chazan, Danny Rothchild, Martin Himel, and Shlomo Paperblatt.

Throughout the Occupied Territories, in Ramallah, Nablus, Gaza, Jericho, and East Jerusalem, there were many Palestinians who offered, without thought to the consequences, their own stories and experiences after having lived in the middle of the conflict for their entire lives. Specifically I am grateful to Imad Iyash, Sameh Kanaan, Said Kanaan, Mamduah Aker, Mary Hass, Hana Sinora, Faisal al-Husseini, Haidar abd al-Shafi, Saeb Erekat, Salwa Ashrawi, Emil Ashrawi, and Hanan Ashrawi.

In Tunis, Amman, Cairo, Paris, New York, and Washington, many others offered both political and personal views on the situation. To those Palestinians who gave so generously of their time—Dominque Roch, Leila Shaled, Akram Hania, Nabil Shaath, and the late Abu Iyad—I am grateful. For interviews granted and time spent, I am also grateful to Prime Minister Yitzhak Rabin, former Prime Minister Yitzhak Shamir, Ambassador Itamar Rabinovitch, King Hussein, Under Secretary of State Richard Murphy, Minister Ariel Sharon, Gen. Rafael Eitan, and Ariel Mirari.

It is impossible to write the definitive book on the Middle East as borders change as rapidly as enemies become allies or a man, woman, or child becomes either a victim or a combatant. In this context many have lost their hope, youth, and ultimately their lives. It is with deep sorrow that they are remembered as the only real reason to achieve a lasting peace in the Middle East.

CAST OF CHARACTERS

Aas, Evn—Norwegian coordinator of talks at Borregard Manor

Abbas, Abu—Palestinian terrorist, behind *Achille Lauro* hijacking and other incidents

abd al-Shafi, Haidar—head of Palestinian delegation, Madrid peace talks

abd Rabbo, Yasir—adviser to Yasir Arafat

Abdullah, Sami—professor of economics; Palestinian Communist party member; member, Palestinian delegation to Madrid peace talks

Abu Jiab, Gazi Mahmud—senior Intifada activist

Adwan, Kamal—Black September deputy; killed by Israeli commandos

Agazarian, Albert—PR director, Bir Zeit University; public relations officer, Palestinian delegation to Madrid peace talks

al-'Leimi, Ziad Hassan Muhammad—captured Libyan terrorist

al-Aker, Mamduh—surgeon; member, Movement for the Liberation of Palestine; member, Palestinian delegation to Madrid peace talks

al-Alami, Wuhayr—member, Movement for the Liberation of Palestine *al-Assad, Hafez*—president of Syria

al-Hassan, Khalid—member, Movement for the Liberation of Palestine

al-Hurd, Maher—economist; Kriah aide; graduate, American University, Cairo

al-Husseini, Faisal—East Jerusalem Palestinian leader; member, steering committee, Palestinian delegation to Madrid peace talks

al-Husseini, Haj Amin—mufti of Jerusalem from the twenties through the forties

al-Malhouk, Sheikh Abdullah—Saudi ambassador to Libya

al-Najjar, Muhammad Yussef—leader of Black September who carried out Munich Olympics massacre (*nom de guerre:* Abu Yussef); killed by Israeli commando

Alul, Hamdullah—Arafat's aide

Aqedat, Muhammad Ahmad—captured Libyan terrorist

Arafat, Yasir—PLO Chairman (*nom de guerre:* Abu Ammar)

Asfour, Hassan—close Arafat aide

Ashrawi, Amal—Hanan's seventeen-year-old daughter

Ashrawi, Emil—Hanan's husband

Ashrawi, Hanan Mikhael

Ashrawi, Ibrahim—Emil's brother

Ashrawi, Nano—Emil's sister

Ashrawi, Nayfeh—Emil's grandmother

Ashrawi, Salwa—Emil's mother

Ashrawi, Sam'an—Emil's father

Ashrawi, Samir—Emil's brother

Ashrawi, Samira—Emil's sister

Ashrawi, Zeina—Hanan's thirteen-year-old daughter

Bahar, Jawad—Hamas military leader

Barak, Ehud—Israeli Chief of Staff

Barkokva, Maurice—former Israeli civil governor in Ramallah

Beilin, Yossi—Peres loyalist, Labor party; involved in secret pre-Madrid talks

Ben Aharon, Yossi—Shamir's speech writer, Madrid talks

Ben Ami, Oded—Rabin's spokesperson

Burg, Avram—Peres loyalist, Labor party; involved in secret pre-Oslo talks

Carmoun, Yigal—Rabin's former adviser on counterterrorism and Shamir's former adviser on counterterrorism

Chazan, Nomi—Knesset member

Christopher, Warren—U.S. Secretary of State

Curtzer, Dan—U.S. deputy Secretary of State for Near Eastern Affairs

Darwish, Mahmoud—Palestinian poet

Dayan, Yael—Knesset member, Labor; novelist; daughter of the late Israeli defense minister Gen. Moshe Dayan

Djerejian, Edward—Senior American official to the Middle East; former Ambassador to Syria; former Ambassador to Israel

Egeland, Jan—Norwegian deputy foreign minister

Eid, Guy—Belgian diplomat; murdered, Saudi Arabian embassy, Khartoum

Eitan, Rafael—Israeli general; former Chief of Staff, Knesset member

Erekat, Saeb—professor of political science, Najah University, Nablus; Fatah supporter; member, Palestinian delegation to Madrid peace talks

Freij, Elias—mayor of Bethlehem; member, Palestinian delegation to Madrid peace talks

Gadhafi, Muammar—Libyan leader

Gemayel, Bashir—Lebanese president, 1982 (assassinated)

Habash, George—PFLP founder, 1968

Haddad, Waddia—PFLP, George Habash's second-in-command until he broke in 1975 to create PFLP-Waddia Haddad; poisoned by Iraqi agents in 1978

Hania, Akram—PLO press representative, Tunis; liaison between Arafat and press delegation, Madrid peace talks

Hass, Mary—member, Palestinian Communist Party, Gaza

King Hassan II—king of Morocco

Hawatme, Nayef—DFLP founder

Hijazi, Mazen Ibrahim Rashid—captured Libyan terrorist

Hirschfeld, Yair—Israeli academic active in secret pre-Oslo talks

King Hussein—king of Jordan

Ishtayye, Muhammad—Arafat's aide

Iyad, Abu—Black September; assassinated, Tunis

Iyash, Imad—prominent Nablus leader

Ja'bari, Nabil—dental surgeon; chairman of the board of trustees of Hebron University; member, Palestinian delegation to Madrid peace talks

Jennings, Peter—ABC-TV newsman; former Middle East bureau chief

Jihad, Abu—Arafat's second-in-command; assassinated by Israeli commandos, Tunis

Juul, Mona—senior Norwegian diplomat; Terje Larsen's wife

Kady, Michael—founder, American-Arab Anti-Discrimination Committee

Kamel, Zahira—DFLP; Palestinian feminist teacher; member, Palestinian delegation

Kanaan, Said—prominent Nablus businessman

Kanaan, Sameh—employee, Nablus Chamber of Commerce; member, Palestinian delegation to Madrid peace talks

Kassel, Anis—DFLP member; chief editor, *Palestine Yearbook of International Law;* member, steering committee, Palestinian delegation to Madrid peace talks

Kassis, Nabil—professor of physics, Bir Zeit University; member, Palestinian delegation to Madrid peace talks

Keith, Kenton—former U.S. cultural attaché, Cairo

Khalidi, Rashid—professor of Middle East history, University of Chicago; member, steering committee, Palestinian delegation to Madrid peace talks

Khalil, Rula—jailed Palestinian murderer

Khatib, Ghassan—professor of economic development, Bir Zeit University; founder of Jerusalem Media Communications Center; member, Palestinian delegation to Madrid peace talks

Kilani, Sami—professor of physics, Najah University, Nablus; member, Palestinian delegation to Madrid peace talks

Klinghoffer, Leon—American passenger murdered on cruise ship *Achille Lauro*

Knowles, Chris—former U.S. cultural attaché, Tel Aviv

Koppel, Ted—ABC-TV newsman; host of *Nightline* program

Kriah, Ahmed Suleiman—Arafat's director of finances; member, Palestinian steering committee (*nom de guerre:* Abu Ala)

Larsen, Terje Rod—head of Norwegian Institute for Applied Social Sciences, Oslo

Malki, Riyad—Bir Zeit faculty member; West Bank PFLP spokesperson

Mansour, Camille—professor of political science, Sorbonne; member, steering committee, Palestinian delegation to Madrid peace talks

Mazen, Abu—close Arafat aide

Meddain, Fraih Abu—head of Gaza Bar Association; member, Palestinian delegation to Madrid peace talks

Miller, Aaron—Pentagon official, Mideast desk; played a role during peace negotiations

Mikhael, Abla—Hanan's sister

Mikhael, Daoud—Hanan's father; West Bank physician

Mikhael, Huda—Hanan's sister

Mikhael, Muna—Hanan's sister

Mikhael, Nadia—Hanan's sister

Mikhael, Wad'ia—Hanan's mother

Milson, Menachem—professor of Arabic literature, Hebrew University of Jerusalem; originator of Village Leagues plan

Moore, George Curtis—U.S. chargé d'affaires; murdered, Saudi Arabian embassy, Khartoum

Nabulsi, Suleiman—left-wing politician on the West Bank; head of the Socialist Party to which Daoud Mikhael belonged

Nasser, Gamal Abdel—president of Egypt, 1956–1970

Nasser, Kamel—Palestinian poet; chief PLO spokesperson, Beirut; ambushed by Israeli commandos

Natsheh, Mustafa—engineer; Fatah member; member, Palestinian delegation to Madrid peace talks

Noel, Cleo—U.S. ambassador; murdered, Saudi Arabian embassy, Khartoum

Nofel, Mahmoud—member, economic advisory committee to Palestinian delegation; PLO higher-up

Nussibeh, Sari—member, steering committee, Palestinian delegation to Madrid peace talks

Peres, Shimon—Foreign Minister of Israel (Labor)

Pickering, Thomas—former U.S. ambassador to Jordan

Pundik, Ron—Israeli academic involved in secret pre-Oslo talks

Qaddoumi, Farouq—Foreign Minister, PLO

Rabin, Yitzhak—Prime Minister of Israel; former Defense Minister (Labor)

Roch, Dominique—Palestinian journalist for Radio France

Ross, Dennis—Pentagon official, liaison to Madrid peace talks

Rubinstein, Elyakim—head of Israeli delegation, Madrid peace talks

Savir, Uri—director general, Israeli Foreign Ministry

Shaath, Nabil—Arafat adviser; current head of Palestinian delegation to peace talks

Shahal, Moshe—Israeli minister of police

Shahid, Leila—PLO representative in France

Shaked, Ronnie—journalist, *Yediot Aharanot*

Shamir, Yitzhak—former Prime Minister of Israel (Likud)

Sharon, Ariel—former Israeli Defense Minister; led Israeli invasion of Lebanon, 1982

Shek, Dany—spokesperson, Israeli embassy, Paris

Shoval, Zalman—Israeli ambassador to United States during the Madrid peace talks and member of the Israeli delegation

Shuquari, Ahmed—founding chairman of PLO, 1964

Singer, Yoel—Israeli legal expert

Sinora, Hana—Palestinian editor, *al-Fajr* newspaper

Smith, Marcus—Hanan's faculty adviser, University of Virginia

Stethem, Robert—U.S. Navy diver murdered by PLO terrorists during hijacking of TWA 847 en route to Athens

Strauss, Danny—Christopher aide

Sweidani, Ahmad—colonel, Syrian Army intelligence; headed Movement for the Liberation of Palestine

Taha, Ali Shafik Ahmed—PFLP terrorist (aka Captain Rifat) killed by Israeli commandos

Taha, Rydah—Arafat's former press secretary

Taha, Suhair—Hanan's former assistant

Tol, Abu—head of PLO secret service; murdered in Tunis

Tsemmel, Leah—Israeli lawyer in Occupied Territories who represents mostly Palestinians

Tutweiler, Margaret—State Department spokesperson, Bush administration

Vanderstuhl, Max—member, Dutch Socialist party; former Foreign Minister

Ya'ari, Ehud—journalist, Israeli television

Yassin, Adnan—arrested Mossad spy in PLO, Tunis

Yusef, Muhammad—member, Movement for the Liberation of Palestine

Zuheila, Salah—Arafat's aide

PREFACE

Until 1987 and the beginning of the Intifada, three events in the history of the Palestinian/Israeli conflict led to the Middle East peace negotiations and eventual Oslo Accord. First, in 1948 the map of the Middle East changed to make room for Israel. Given Palestinian rejection of the first partition proposed by the United Nations—which provided for an independent state side by side with Israel larger than was eventually achieved after Oslo—this was a significant date in their history. Again, in 1967, the map of the Middle East changed when the Israeli Army preempted an Arab attack to occupy the West Bank of the Jordan River and the Gaza Strip. And last, in 1982 not just geography but public opinion changed when Israeli troops slammed across the border into Lebanon. For the first time Israel was viewed as having involved itself in a conflict that went far beyond protecting its borders or strategic depth.

During those years certain Palestinian leaders who survived assassination attempts by either members of rival factions of the Palestine Liberation Organization (PLO) or Mossad, the Israeli secret service, rose in the ranks of the PLO. Among Israeli leaders—with the exception of the founding statesmen of 1948 who died of old age—military heroes went on to become political figures who emerged as the architects of peace and policy. Ironically the biggest change, from both historic and human perspectives, came with the Intifada, when Israeli soldiers armed with guns faced Palestinian civilians armed with stones. Then leaders within Israel's Labor government realized that—given the changing world order and the opprobrium heaped on their country—a Palestinian state was an inevitability. As for the Palestinians, for all the same reasons (in addition to the dismal economic situation of the PLO), a new breed of leaders, who went on to shape the course of peace in the Middle East, became visible and vocal.

My contacts as a journalist and writer go back to the beginning of the war in Lebanon, during which the countless interviews I had with leaders on both sides of the struggle provoked my ongoing interest in the area. While most of the Israeli generals and government officials remained sources throughout the years, such PLO leaders as Abu Iyad and Abu Jihad, whom I had interviewed on numerous occasions, were killed. And Arab leaders whom I had also interviewed, such as Syria's President Hafez al-Assad, King Hussein of Jordan, King Hassan of Morocco, and Muammar Gadhafi of Libya, became players in an intricate policy of realpolitik.

In 1988, in the aftermath of the downing of Pan Am 103, I was sent by Fox Broadcast News to the West Bank to interview leaders of renegade PLO factions as well as Israeli Prime Minister Yitzhak Shamir and Defense Minister Yitzhak Rabin. It was then that I heard, through my contacts both in Israel and on the West Bank, of a woman who was a fast-emerging figure in local Palestinian politics. As it turned out, she did more to change the image of the Palestinians living under Israeli occupation than any war, uprising, or terrorist attack had ever done in the past.

From 1988 until 1992, while I wrote and published three

novels, I continued to follow events in the Middle East. The emotional and political impact of the Palestinian uprising throughout the world surprised even those Palestinians who had conceived it and continued to wage its battles. What eventually became clear to even the most cynical Mideast pundits was that change, if not peace, was in the air. And, when I finally decided to tackle a book that covered not only the Intifada but the history of different waves of Palestinian leadership both inside and outside the West Bank and Gaza, I realized that it was a story that was easier to begin, to trace back to its roots, than it was to end. Nevertheless, there was no question in my mind that the one Palestinian leader who emerged as the new voice of reason, Hanan Mikhael Ashrawi, was not only crucial to any future change in the area but already representative of a change within an organization that had previously been synonymous with terror, the PLO. What was clear was that as the PLO changed its priorities and policies, Hanan communicated those changes to the world. What was unclear was if the PLO had in fact changed or had merely embraced a political pragmatism that demonstrated a transition from terror to diplomacy.

Over the fifteen months from November 1992 until February 1994, not only did I interview Hanan for hundreds of hours on tape, but I spent time with her in her home, eating lunch and dinner in her kitchen, watching her with her husband and children. On separate occasions as well, during those months, when Hanan was either in Tunis or Washington, I spent time alone with her husband, children, and mother-in-law, having quiet, reflective talks not only about the political situation but about the effect that it had on their lives. At the eighth, ninth, tenth, and eleventh rounds of the peace talks in Washington, D.C., I had the opportunity to observe Hanan in her hotel suite as she performed her duties as spokesperson for the Palestinian delegation. It was also in

Washington then that I met and interviewed two of Hanan's sisters as well as several of her friends and former professors at the University of Virginia. In that same period, starting in Madrid, where the conference opened, I spent long nights in discussion with members of both the Palestinian and Israeli delegations to the peace conference as well as meeting with them in their homes and offices upon my return to Israel and the Occupied Territories.

On the West Bank I spent weeks with Hanan's colleagues and students at Bir Zeit University; in Beirut I interviewed several of her former professors and friends at the American University. In Paris, London, and The Hague, I met with PLO representatives, some of whom had known Hanan since childhood and others who had met her as fellow students at the American University in Beirut. On the West Bank and in Israel, during my research for this book, I interviewed Israeli military and government officials as well as Palestinian prisoners, residents of refugee camps, and political leaders. Certain Israeli military officials in charge of policy on the West Bank and in Gaza permitted me to enter Tel Mond Prison in Natanya, where I listened to the stories of two Palestinian women who had been convicted of murder in the name of their cause. Through contacts with Palestinians who worked inside the refugee camps, I recorded interviews that described their experiences of life under occupation. And through friends and acquaintances I spent long hours with Israelis—either victims or families of victims—who had been attacked or killed by radical Palestinian terrorists.

It was through these interviews of people involved in the peace process—as well as those who continue to be a part of Hanan's private and professional life—that I was able to get a profound appreciation for who Hanan was and is in relation to the ongoing struggle that surrounds her. Through my personal relationships with many private Israeli and Palestinian citizens, as well as those who play an important part in negotiations, I was also able to get a sense of what peace and war really mean to those who are directly involved.

While all the material in this book is based on interviews, certain sections relied on documents obtained from Shin Bet (the Israeli internal security force), the PLO, and declassified papers from the U.S. Department of State. For other sections, specifically the personal stories of those Palestinians killed by either the Israeli Army or the Shin Bet, and for those Israelis murdered by Palestinian terrorists, I interviewed witnesses, families, and officials on both sides to reconstruct the dramatic scenes described throughout. Concerning the incident at Bir Zeit University, I recorded Hanan's version of events, quoting her directly from the tape as well as recording and quoting the Israeli commander and the students who were involved in that day's demonstration.

At the request of the families, the names that are changed within the text of this book are those victims either of Palestinian terrorists or the Israeli Shin Bet. In those instances and specifically, the names of "Dora," "Stephen Pearlman," "Raja," "Belat," and "Akram" are marked by an asterisk when they first appear.

As interviews and conversations were recorded, played, and replayed, and various experiences and anecdotes were recounted and reviewed, I developed a profound understanding of the past suffering and future expectations of both Palestinians and Israelis. Listening to the convictions and personal agendas of the fighters, soldiers, and policymakers on both sides of the struggle afforded me an indelible and vivid interpretation of the situation and enabled me to write what I hope is an evenhanded account of the Intifada and the peace process that evolved subsequently.

Throughout my every interview with those who lived through the violence of the forty-six-year struggle, I focused on Hanan Ashrawi in relation both to her family and to her people. Throughout every briefing with officials on both sides of the struggle, I concentrated not only on the present situation as it involved Hanan but also on historical precedents as they affected her family. But, more than structured interviews with Hanan and others—which provided facts, specific incidents, and dates—those numerous informal visits with her and her family allowed me to understand where she stood concerning the organization she represented. Through the eyes of Hanan, who not only lived through the violence but played an intricate role in a process that was thought to have ended in Oslo, have the hopes and fears of those who are partners in a new era of peace become clear.

A VOICE
OF REASON

CHAPTER ONE

———

SHAKING HANDS
WITH THE ENEMY

O N SEPTEMBER 13, 1993, President Bill Clinton walked
out onto the South Lawn of the White House flanked
by Israeli Prime Minister Yitzhak Rabin and PLO Chairman
Yasir Arafat. It was a surrealistic image in television history.
Two of the fiercest enemies in the world were together in
Washington to sign a peace accord, and yet the scene looked
more like a shotgun wedding than the end of decades of
hatred.

Rabin had an expression of disgust on his face that made
some spectators wonder whom, at that moment, he resented
more—his longtime enemy Yasir Arafat or the man who had
orchestrated the event, his longtime political rival Shimon
Peres. Other observers claimed that Rabin appeared restless
and condescending, indicative that he viewed his participation
in the White House ceremonies from a position of strength.
There wasn't anyone, however, who didn't notice how the
Israeli prime minister hesitated before taking the outstretched
hand of his foe, after which he turned to Foreign Minister
Peres, out of microphone range but in view of the television
cameras, to whisper, "You're next!" Later Rabin would con-
fide to close aides that "of all the hands in the world, [Arafat's]
was not the hand I wanted or even dreamed of touching."

1

He would also admit that many of those watching the ceremonies had indeed noticed him clenching his teeth.

Standing to the left of President Clinton on that fall day in Washington was Yasir Arafat. With his trademark *kaffiyeh* askew, and wearing a suit that barely buttoned across his recently acquired girth, he looked somewhat the worse for wear after a career of jetting around the Arab world in search of political approval and money. Unlike Rabin, the PLO chairman seemed in awe of his surroundings, almost disbelieving that he was a principal participant in what was only the second Israeli-Arab peace accord in the history of that war-torn region. Hardly daring to move, he gazed vaguely off into the distance until the moment came to shake Rabin's hand. Then, animated and beaming broadly, he pumped the prime minister's hand with surprising force, exuding confidence perhaps that the world had finally absolved him for the murder of thousands of innocent civilians, among them Americans.

In the audience were dignitaries and wives, who took up most of the first two rows. Tipper Gore was there, as was Hillary Clinton. The wife who was conspicuously missing was Arafat's twenty-nine-year-old bride, Suha, back in Tunis, where she was busy revamping the Palestinian health care plan, wasting no time in becoming the Hillary Clinton of the Middle East. Not missing, however, was Leah Rabin, wearing black and remembering, perhaps, other tense days in Washington years before. During an official visit to the United States by the couple, the revelation that she had an American bank account—against Israeli law—helped to end her husband's first tenure as Israeli prime minister. Back then it had been Leah who almost cost Rabin his political life. Now if Rabin's political life was on the line, he could only blame himself.

A somber-looking James Baker sat next to George Bush,

who had an expression of vague regret on his face, having lost the election and so relinquished his pivotal role in history. Another president who had failed in his quest for a second term, Jimmy Carter, was up front as well, teary eyed and visibly emotional. Gazing at the same table that had been used during the signing of the Camp David Accords, Carter was almost certainly recalling when Begin and Sadat wept and embraced for a peace that was based on mutual respect, recognition—and a profound sense of impending economic disaster. Blood and tears had become part of the package back in 1979, unlike 1993, when backroom political dealings brought enemies to the forefront of the news. In fact, rarely in the history of a peace accord had those now in the spotlight done so little to merit so much.

FOR YASIR ARAFAT that day in Washington was as much a personal as a political victory. Once again he merited the name—Teflon guerrilla—attributed to him throughout the last three decades. Back from the dead, so to speak, in a plane crash in the Libyan Desert, the PLO chairman was still the wily survivor who had outwitted countless Mossad assassination plots and Palestinian "palace coups" to finish in the spotlight of political respectability. Not that the road back had been easy for the man who consistently managed to make the wrong political decisions for his people. Most recently Arafat had been ostracized by the Gulf States for his support for Saddam Hussein during the Gulf War, costing his organization annual revenues of billions of oil dollars. Along with the monetary loss, Arafat suffered from waning popularity and diminishing power throughout the Occupied Territories. While he was clearly a victim of his own disastrous judgment, so were the Palestinians responsible for waging the financial battles of the Intifada, the Palestinian uprising in the Occupied Territories.

Salaries of Palestinians within the Occupied Territories, as well as those of PLO representatives worldwide, hadn't been paid for months, while families of fighters, residents of the refugee camps, and victims of the seven-year uprising were protesting delayed financial compensation. The realities were harsh for those West Bank and Gaza leaders who found themselves without resources. What became increasingly evident to the beleaguered PLO leader was that the only way to hold together the organization he had founded and whose international symbol he had become was to deliver something tangible to his people that would alter their lives. If not, dissenting groups outside the PLO would capture the support of his constituency, offering them hope where he had not. Or worse, other Arab nations were likely to take the first step toward peace, relegating the Palestinian agenda of self-rule once again to the back burner. There was only one alternative: Arafat had to strike a peace accord with Israel.

FROM THE OPENING DAY of the peace conference in Madrid in 1991, the tacit understanding between all the Arab participants had been that any accord with Israel would be achieved by them as a group. There was to be no repeat of Camp David. Even the most complicated issue of Jordan within the context of any comprehensive peace was to be taken on the basis of a referendum with very clear principles and objectives that would not create any internal problems within the PLO. All issues were to be dealt with bilaterally, between the Palestinians and Jordan, and not trilaterally, among Israel, the Palestinians, and Jordan. Once again the Palestinians reiterated that they would never accept the territory of Jordan as an alternative homeland. What any bilateral Palestinian-Jordanian agreement would represent, therefore, would be only a disengagement with Israel and a reengagement with Jordan, on the basis of parity, with a total redivision of the political map. As it turned out that was the least of Arafat's problems.

During that same period the Israelis had to contend with their own internal disputes and outside pressures concerning the ongoing peace negotiations. It was a gradual process that made Rabin and his advisers aware that with the collapse of the Soviet bloc, Israel was no longer viewed by the United States as the vanguard of democracy in the Middle East. Given the dismal economic situation worldwide, it seemed doubtful that Israel could expect the same amount of financial aid from Western nations to defend against a threat of Communism that no longer existed. The time was fast approaching for Israel to join the rest of the Middle East by breaking down barriers and economic blockades and cementing peace accords with enemies. And the first step on that road to trade and economic parity with Arab neighbors could only be taken after Israel put an end to its occupation of the West Bank and Gaza Strip.

Following Madrid, in 1992, long months of negotiations took place in Washington, with an absence of progress on all sides. While Israel remained steadfast in its stipulation not to include the PLO in any formal capacity, the PLO refused to give its representatives more scope to make decisions. Yet, even in less powerful forums than the Knesset (Israeli parliament), it was no secret that the PLO government-in-exile in Tunis, led by Yasir Arafat, was directing the delegates from behind the scenes. It was late fall of that same year that Prime Minister Rabin was first heard speculating that it was pointless for Israel to negotiate with a Palestinian delegation that had no authority to come to any agreement. As if to justify that political reality, Rabin began to emulate the Peace Now activists in Israel by including in his public speeches their credo, "Peace is made with enemies, not friends." It sounded almost as if the Israeli prime minister intended to keep his campaign promise, having run on a platform of making peace with the Palestinians. And what Israeli politician was better suited to make peace by relinquishing territory than the Israeli general who had led troops during the 1967 Six Day War that liberated Jerusalem for the Jews and pounded the Israeli Army far beyond its defensive borders? But, more than any political enlightenment, on-the-ground realities throughout the Occupied Territories caused both Rabin and Arafat to think along the same lines. The time had come to make peace with a situation rather than with each other. Both sides needed to defeat Hamas and the other Islamic fundamentalist groups that had become their common enemy.

Figures showed that the two main fundamentalist groups within the Occupied Territories, Hamas and the Islamic Jihad, had popular support that hovered around 35 percent. Both organizations, which defined themselves as the military wing of the Muslim Brotherhood, always had as their main objectives the liberation of Palestine from the "Jordan River to the Mediterranean Sea" and the establishment of an Islamic Palestinian state. Active in the Gaza Strip since the 1950s, Hamas' influence spread through a network of mosques and charitable and social organizations until the 1980s, when it emerged as a violent faction, challenging the influence of the PLO. What began as a rebellion against Israeli occupation turned into a cultural and existential conflict between the believers—the ultraradical fundamentalists—and the infidels—the more politicized members of the PLO— which would eventually lead to a *jihad* (holy war). Not only Jews were the targets of extremist violence, but also those Palestinians who were disposed to cement some kind of a territorial compromise with Israel. While the PLO had grudgingly learned to accept the reality of Israel, the Islamic fundamentalists remained intransigent in their belief that Palestine was a land sacred to Islam, stolen by the Jews and in part negotiated away by more moderate Arabs. For either Hamas in Gaza or Hezbollah across the border in Lebanon, Israel was a cancer in the Islamic world, put in its midst by imperialist powers and nurtured and supported by the United States. In Rabin's view Islamic fundamentalism had replaced Communism as the looming threat in the Middle East. Not unlike what had been an alliance of Western nations against the threat of Soviet expansion in Europe, Rabin's plan was to form an alliance for peace with the PLO, which was as much at risk as Israel from that spreading wave of extremism. If there was any reluctance on Rabin's part to begin an open dialogue with the PLO, it stemmed from his fear that they would be unable to deliver a majority accord. Rabin had no intention of helping to set up a fundamentalist Arab nation on Israel's doorstep.

FROM THE PLO's point of view, what had always been a tense situation between themselves and Hamas only intensified during the Gulf War. While there was almost universal support for Iraq throughout the Occupied Territories, temporarily restoring unity among the various PLO leadership groups that fueled the Intifada, Hamas expressed its solidarity with the people of Kuwait. Curiously, at the same time as Hamas fiercely criticized American intervention in the Gulf, it demanded Iraq's withdrawal along with other Western forces in Saudi Arabia. Following the Gulf War, while the PLO suffered financially for its pro-Iraq position, Hamas received increased financial support from those oil-rich Arab States as a reward for its Gulf War stand. The conditions were simple. Hamas would limit its use of the money to expand its infrastructure and grassroots base only within the Occupied Territories, far from the tenuous governments of Kuwait, Saudi Arabia, and the other Gulf States, which were constantly threatened by the rise of fundamentalism.

As a result of the sudden economic discrepancy between the PLO and Hamas, Hamas put increased pressure on Arafat when it announced, through radio broadcasts and leaflets, that it and other radical Islamic fundamentalist groups intended to overrun the Gaza Strip to become the vocal and violent majority. The unspoken warning was that not only Israeli control but also Arafat's power would be further destabilized throughout the Occupied Territories.

Following the Gulf War the sharp decline in PLO finances affected Arafat and others within the external PLO leadership in Tunis more than it did those PLO leaders within the Occupied Territories, who embodied the Palestinian national movement and who still had the support of the people. Sensing Arafat's weakening power, the internal PLO leadership suddenly demanded free elections to PLO institutions, an increase of seats within the PLO parliament, and the adoption of their own amended Israeli-Palestinian peace plan, which went far beyond the PLO's official party line then under discussion in Washington. The dissatisfaction of those Palestinian leaders living on the West Bank and in Gaza coupled with the rampant violence by Hamas presented the PLO with a battle to be waged on two fronts. It was in that atmosphere of dissension, both within the PLO itself and from outside radical Palestinian factions, that Israel made the first approach to embrace Yasir Arafat as its enemy-of-choice.

For Israel, recognizing the PLO meant acknowledging the Palestinian national identity and, as a consequence, contradicting the late Israeli Prime Minister Golda Meir, who had justified the creation of a Jewish state by proclaiming, "A land without people for a people without land." For the Palestinians, recognizing Israel meant rewriting those articles in the PLO Covenant, or Constitution, that called for a step-by-step destruction of Israel and its replacement by a Palestinian state. Yet, for all the world that watched or read, there

was still a glaring lack of progress in the ongoing peace negotiations. In fact, the crucial breakthrough in the talks occurred far from the scrutiny of the international media.

While the peace conference was going on in Washington,
behind-the-scenes meetings were taking place in Jerusalem
and London between high-ranking Israeli officials and academics and members of the PLO. It was in Oslo, however,
under the auspices of the Norwegian government, that several
close advisers to Rabin, Peres, and Arafat, over meals of
herring and during strolls near icy fjords, wrote a Document of Principle (DOP) that would serve as the basis for a
Palestinian-Israeli peace accord. Unfortunately, while the
handshakes on the White House lawn were a spectacular
media event, the DOP itself was an agreement fraught with
so many ambiguities and distortions that even one of its architects, Shimon Peres, would say, "While we have the final
chapter, what is missing is the beginning and the middle of
this complicated story." Still, no one could deny that after a
quarter century of bloodshed, the ending, incomplete though
it was, nonetheless was a monumental breakthrough. Israel
finally recognized the PLO as the legitimate voice of the Palestinian people, and the PLO finally recognized Israel's right
to exist. It was then that both leaders faced their most difficult
task.

Rabin had to prove to his supporters as well as to his
detractors that while he advocated relinquishing territory, he
would still continue to maintain security from Palestinian
terrorist attacks. After all, even as the Labor candidate running against Likud's Yitzhak Shamir, he had won the election
on the basis of his past record as the tough chief of staff of
the Israeli Defense Forces (IDF). And, as the defense minister
in a coalition government headed by Shamir, he had proved
that position when, at the beginning of the uprising, he
had given soldiers orders to quell the unrest by "breaking

Palestinian bones." But Rabin's problems, while complicated, paled against those faced by Arafat. Not only was the PLO leader obliged to enlist the support of the other Arab states, but he had also to unite his own people by satisfying the diverse factions on all sides of the struggle: the Palestinians in refugee camps who had relinquished their homes in what had become Israel proper, and those who had emerged as leaders within the Occupied Territories. Clearly Arafat faced the most difficult challenge of his career, to guide the PLO through the transition from struggle to statehood. In his favor, however, was the positive encouragement from Western observers who were willing to give Arafat and the PLO another chance.

FROM THE BEGINNING of the Intifada, and during the opening days of the peace conference in Madrid, the image of the PLO had changed sufficiently to guarantee its acceptance by the Western world as a responsible and viable peace partner for Israel. If gratitude was in order for that change, Arafat should have directed his to the woman who labored to give him and his organization a renewed political life. While Hanan Ashrawi was the one person who had made possible Arafat's presence on the South Lawn of the White House that day, she was the one public figure missing from the front row of dignitaries. Instead she found herself seated somewhere in the tenth row, craning her neck to witness the formalities of an event that she had orchestrated from its inception by setting up secret meetings in Jerusalem, London, and eventually in Oslo. But Hanan's role hadn't ended when arrangements were already made to bring in the television cameras to capture two sworn enemies shaking hands. Until the last minute there were unresolved problems that threatened to cancel the White House ceremony until she, once again, stepped in to work them out.

The drama had begun at five o'clock in the morning, when the phone rang in Hanan's hotel suite. It was Arafat himself, summoning her to solve an urgent problem: The text of the DOP had not been written according to the verbal agreement between the Americans, Israelis, and Palestinians. Arafat was threatening not to sign if the words were not changed throughout the text from "Palestinian team/delegation" to "Palestine Liberation Organization." According to Arafat the Israelis were now dealing directly with the PLO, which should have been reflected throughout the document. The discovery had actually been made several days before and dealt with on the highest level in the Pentagon, when Hanan tried to persuade her close colleague at the Pentagon, Dennis Ross, the man in charge of the Middle East peace negotiations, to make the necessary changes. For two days Ross had repeated that the Americans had no right to change what was the "official" text unless the Israelis accepted the changes as well. Now, hours before the ceremony was about to begin, Hanan was once again on the phone with the State Department's Operations Center, trying to reach Ambassador Edward Djerejian, to request the text change one last time. Otherwise Chairman Arafat would board the Moroccan aircraft lent to him by King Hassan and take off, putting an end to what was supposed to be a historic beginning.

At ten o'clock in the morning word reached the Palestinian delegation through Oded Ben Ami, Rabin's spokesman, that the Israeli prime minister had agreed to change the text. Within minutes Hanan was seated in the delegation's car, speeding without thought to traffic lights or lanes to the White House—only to find more on-the-ground complications. The guard on duty was unable to find Hanan's name on the list of invited guests and so was obliged to refuse her entry. Only by chance did ABC's Ted Koppel happen to walk by and greet Hanan, which prompted the guard suddenly to recognize her from all the times she had appeared on CNN or other American television networks. Without waiting to chat with Koppel, Hanan raced toward the area reserved for dignitaries and ducked underneath the rope, running directly toward Yoel Singer, the Israelis' legal adviser. Again nothing proved simple; both the American and Israeli legal advisers claimed they knew nothing of the changes in the text. Their only suggestion was that Abu Mazen, the PLO official signing for the Palestinians, should cross out what was wrong and, in his own handwriting, add the words "Palestine Liberation Organization" before he signed it. Hanan's response was immediate; it wasn't possible for Abu Mazen to change the text before he signed it since the official order called for the Israelis to sign first. Changing the text after Foreign Minister Peres signed would make the document illegal. The only alternative was if someone else made the changes in the DOP before the copy found its way onto the signing table, where first Peres and then Abu Mazen would sign it into history. Handing Hanan a copy of the document along with a pen, the American legal adviser suggested that Hanan simply cross out all references to the "joint Jordanian-Palestinian delegation" or "Palestinian delegation or team," and replace them by the words "Palestine Liberation Organization" or simply "PLO." Hardly hesitating, Hanan grabbed the pen and made the necessary revisions. Taking the amended draft, the two legal advisers raced toward the White House while Hanan made her way back to the area reserved for dignitaries. For several frantic minutes before the ceremonies were scheduled to begin, television cameras panned the sea of faces on the White House lawn before settling on the signing table, which was ominously bare. It was exactly 11:07 A.M., seven minutes past the official time for the ceremonies to begin. Hanan's block of seats had been appropriated by a group of teenagers from all over the world wearing green T-shirts with the words

"Seeds of Peace" written on the front. Behind her, members of the PLO delegation were desperately trying to locate the few remaining seats only to find themselves displaced. For Hanan, being excluded from the first few rows of dignitaries would prove to be the least serious of her problems after coming this far with the Palestinian struggle.

IT HAD TAKEN slightly less than three years for Hanan, an academic who held the position of dean of the Faculty of Arts at Bir Zeit University on the West Bank, and who had been appointed spokesperson for the PLO, to change the image of the PLO from that of a terrorist organization to a heartwrenching political cause. Hijacking world opinion the way her compatriots had once hijacked airplanes, Hanan in her designer scarf had replaced the Palestinian fighter in his checkered *kaffiyeh*. Countless pundits, politicians, and average citizens throughout the world watched Hanan hold her own in a succession of interviews and political debates as the peace process unfolded. The only question that arose after the talks abated and enemies shook hands was whether Arafat deserved all the glory for which she was responsible. And if he didn't, then when exactly had the clock started ticking for Hanan, who had struggled for a Palestinian homeland as a student, professor, wife, and mother and negotiated for recognition in an international arena as one of the leaders of the Palestinian cause? Where was Arafat in his tattered fighter's suit while Hanan worked eighteen-hour days, engaging in complicated discussions at the Pentagon, to convince the world that the Palestinian people had the legitimate right to self-determination? Even the speech that Hanan had written for Arafat to deliver that day in Washington had been replaced at the last minute by one written by Yasir abd Rabbo, head of the Palestinian Democratic Coalition (FIDA). At the time Arafat had indicated that Hanan's words were packed with too many emotional references and repetitive history about what the Palestinian people had suffered under occupation, including their plight as a people constantly ignored by their own Arab brothers. The consensus in Tunis was that it was counterproductive to dredge up old wounds and make recriminations against those Arab leaders whose support the PLO leader now needed to enable any conciliation with Israel. By contrast, the speech produced by Yasir abd Rabbo offered a concise acceptance of the impending accord with Israel along with a pragmatic analysis of their mutual recognition. What it did *not* offer those Palestinians living under Israeli occupation or in exile throughout the Arab world was an explanation for all the glaring political concessions incorporated in the agreement. For them there was no logical reason why so much less than what had always been the objective of a Palestinian homeland was now a signed reality. "From the beginning, not only Golda but Ben Gurion ignored and denied us," Hanan said after the fact, "before they finally discovered that while they couldn't completely erase our presence, they could and did distort us."

The distortions Hanan referred to in the DOP centered around issues that ranged from the right of return of refugees scattered throughout the Arab world to the dismantling of Israeli settlements throughout the Occupied Territories. But it was the settlements that were the most glaring defect in the agreement—those red-roofed houses on hills overlooking Arab towns and villages that carried with them the self-proclaimed right of the Israeli Army to remain, officially to protect those settlers who insisted on remaining as well. "Settlements superimpose a reality by fragmenting Palestinian territory," Hanan explains. "It is the historic settlement of Palestinian terrain which prevents the emergence of any geographically coherent Palestinian entity. And fragmentation is the principle that the Israelis apply in any negotiation of substance."

14

What remains a nonnegotiable issue with Hanan is that Palestinian occupation will never be totally solved by the return of about one-third of what is considered Palestine. What also remains is her steadfast belief that while a return to the pre-1967 borders would be acceptable to those Palestinians who are in favor of the accord, the tacit understanding is that Israel would renounce forever its plan for a "Greater Israel," or the extension of its borders into the Occupied Territories. The interpretation, however, of what constitutes control—to use the language current before, during, and after Israeli withdrawal—differs greatly on both sides.

According to most Palestinians living under occupation, if the withdrawal of both the army and the civil administration is not complete and total, including those areas around the settlements, it will be nothing more than a meaningless gesture. Indeed, what has become the most bitter complaint is that—although there has been global recognition of the PLO since the accord—there are few real changes on the ground that signal the beginning of a new era of Palestinian independence. Most residents of the Occupied Territories maintain that the situation has actually worsened, given the daily rampages by extreme-right-wing Israeli settlers. The most extreme example of that violence occurred on February 25, 1994, in Hebron when a Jewish settler named Baruch Goldstein, armed with an automatic rifle and hand grenades, gunned down dozens of Muslims on a Friday as they kneeled in prayer in a mosque. While Prime Minister Rabin described the massacre as a "loathsome criminal act," it made the situation on the ground throughout the West Bank and Gaza even more tense. What the massacre also did was to stall the peace talks until certain conditions set down by the PLO were met by the Israelis, mainly a partial withdrawal of Israeli troops from the Occupied Territories. Curiously, Hanan's comment on the massacre and her comment on the day that the agreement was signed were not dissimilar. After Arafat's disappointing speech on the South Lawn of the White House, Hanan said, "While the accord partially heals our past, Chairman Arafat's speech should have provided the people with a sign that he . . . hadn't forgotten the years of suffering and loss that had been endured until that moment." After the massacre, Hanan said, "Chairman Arafat should have considered the repercussions of the extreme right-wing Israelis before agreeing to a peace that did not include eliminating the settlements." What Hanan failed to address were those occasions when the more radical rejectionist fronts of the PLO attacked Israeli civilians.

AND OTHER QUESTIONS arose concerning Hanan's possible connection to the ongoing violence that raged on the West Bank and in Gaza as well as terrorist attacks that occurred within Israel proper. Was this articulate and cultured spokesperson an honest example of the new political change within the PLO or merely the most effective voice to convince the world that Yasir Arafat and his organization had indeed entered a new phase of the Palestinian revolution? Was Hanan Ashrawi a sincere advocate for peace, the voice of moderation, or was she a shrewd public relations ploy, gaining sympathy and respect for the Palestinian cause while the PLO remained steadfastly committed to its agenda of terror?

Months before that historic media event on the South Lawn, when a complicated set of circumstances and secret agendas presented a new chapter in an old story, Hanan had emerged as one of the architects of what would be a newly created Palestinian state. She had already convinced the world that Arafat and the PLO had taken the first step from terrorism to diplomacy. But, as the weeks and months passed after that surrealistic handshake at the White House, apprehension was already growing that any peace accord would be ill fated until all PLO factions settled into a cohesive body that could successfully govern a newly created Palestinian state. For Hanan the time had come to review the beginning of the Palestinian struggle in order to understand the obstacles that stood in the way of its ending—specifically, what accounted for the current split concerning the signing of the DOP in Washington.

Analyzing the end of occupation was a complicated task in which all the members of dissenting factions and political parties on both sides of the conflict had their own opinion of exactly when the peace process began. For some it was the onslaught of the Intifada; for others it was the opening peace conference in Madrid in 1991; and for a few it was those secret meetings in Oslo. For Hanan the peace process began with her first awareness as a Palestinian child living on the West Bank under Jordanian occupation, developed when she was a young woman living on the West Bank under Israeli occupation, and culminated in her role as a Palestinian leader fighting for independence during the most tumultuous period in Palestinian history. To understand how Hanan survived— a woman in a fundamentalist society and a Christian in a Muslim majority—means going back to the beginning of her story.

CHAPTER TWO

THE HOUSE
ON RADIO STREET

O N THE WEST BANK, about thirty miles from Jerusalem, is a predominantly Greek Orthodox Christian enclave whose name literally means "Hill of God." Ramallah, known for its temperate climate and relaxing atmosphere, was once a summer resort where rich Jordanians came to vacation. Even King Hussein was drawn to the area, so close to some of the most important Muslim holy shrines and mosques that he built a summer palace on the main road to Jerusalem. He never got to occupy it, however, as construction was completed in April 1967, just two months before the Six Day War, which ended with the Israeli Army occupying the West Bank. Although the palace has had several tenants— wealthy Palestinians with familial or political connections to Amman—it is currently unoccupied.

The approach to Ramallah is a collection of rich and poor neighborhoods that converge without any defined borders. As is the case throughout much of the West Bank, squalid refugee camps on fields of rusted appliances and carcasses of abandoned automobiles are built next to communities of opulent villas on dusty fields of stone-strewn lawns. In equal contrast are the orange and olive groves and irrigated fields of vegetables that border barren stretches of land surrounded by barbed wire. The only similar feature on so many of the houses—rich or poor—is on the roofs, where miniature Eiffel Towers bring in television signals from as far as New York (via satellite) and as near as Beirut.

By West Bank standards Ramallah is more urban and sophisticated in appearance and mentality than other local cities. One Israeli military official describes the differences by saying that people in Ramallah might have bumper stickers that read SAVE THE WHALES or NO NUKES. "Saving whales not people," the official adds cynically. "No nukes, just plenty of stones and Molotovs!" With a potential sit-in on every corner, a peace rally in every square, Ramallah is a city frozen in perpetual protest.

The streets near the city's main square are crowded with Mercedes stretch taxis, originally part of the German reparations paid to Israel after World War II and subsequently sold by them to the Palestinians. Mostly they are used commercially as jitneys, transporting Palestinians from jobs around the West Bank or back and forth across the Green Line, that visible mark where Israelis claim vegetation and irrigation begin, carrying laborers who pour into Israel on a daily basis. Given the absence of any traffic signals or lanes on the unpaved roads, regardless of the hour of the day, there is a constant cacophony of horns and near-fatal misses between cars and pedestrians. Yet there is a certain rhythm to the chaos, which allows women with baskets on their heads to stroll unharmed or men pushing wheelbarrows to appear without warning from between battered pickup trucks, all managing to cross safely to the other side. Over the past seven years, however, significant changes have turned the city into a virtual war zone. And through those changes Hanan Ashrawi has become the most visible woman in the Middle East.

From the first day of the Intifada on December 11, 1987, images flashed across television screens showing a new approach to an old story. Palestinian children armed with stones faced Israeli soldiers armed with guns. Four months later, in April 1988, Hanan was one of six people invited by Ted Koppel to appear on ABC's *Nightline*. In a town meeting broadcast from Jerusalem, three Israelis and three Palestinians discussed the problems that faced Israel on its fortieth anniversary as a state. What made that televised debate even more important was the onslaught of violence that raged throughout the Occupied Territories with no apparent end in sight. Territorial priorities became an issue even in the television studio, when Palestinians insisted that a fence be erected to separate them from the Israelis. Millions watched as Ted Koppel literally sat on the fence and moderated his six guests, proving that PLO policy was more powerful than ABC format. Despite the evening's significance as the first time that Palestinians and Israelis faced each other in a formal public dialogue, however, any real solution to the conflict was years away.

What was instantly evident to the millions throughout the United States who watched that edition of *Nightline* was how the Palestinian cause was presented as it had never been before. The audience was mesmerized by Hanan's deep, cultured voice and command of the English language. And with Hanan's sharp features; black, almond-shaped eyes; and dark hair cut close to her head, the PLO's mediagenic spokesperson was a combination of Western chic and exotic Eastern charm. Although she had defined herself on numerous occasions during lectures and interviews as an intellectual who gave little thought to her appearance, Hanan was nonetheless rarely seen without her lips painted red and her eyes outlined in blue. In fact, those who knew her back in the sixties and seventies—including her future husband and Peter Jennings, then ABC bureau chief in Beirut—remembered an attractive young woman with beautiful legs who wore only miniskirts.

But even her detractors always admitted that—beyond her physical attributes—Hanan was an imposing figure who exuded dignity and commanded respect wherever she went.

With eloquence and dignity Hanan told the Palestinian story in a language of tears. With clarity and composure she lowered the volume of disparity and dispute among the many diverse factions within the PLO. Never once did she falter in her presentation of her people's side of the struggle: injustice when it came to the Palestinians, indulgence when it came to the Israelis. Within hours Hanan became the official voice of the Palestinian people, their most effective weapon since Yasir Arafat had embraced terrorism in 1965. As far away as refugee camps in Lebanon and in cities throughout the Arab world and as near as towns and villages in the Occupied Territories, Palestinians spoke of her with pride.

What she also became was Israel's worst public relations nightmare.

IF THE UNITED STATES provided the audience that launched Hanan's star, it was Israel—albeit unintentionally—that set the stage for her debut. Had Israeli policy not forbidden Palestinians with Jerusalem identity cards from becoming delegates to the Middle East peace conference that opened in Madrid, Hanan might have faded into the background as just another member of the Palestinian negotiating team. Instead, given her marital status as a Jerusalemite, she was barred from acting in any official capacity within the delegation and ended up instead as its high-visibility spokesperson. But if she faced any criticism, it was from her own people, who perceived her as an American invention, influenced more by the Western academic world in which she had studied than by the realities occurring daily throughout the Occupied Territories.

A professor of English literature, Hanan earned her

doctorate in medieval English and textual criticism at the University of Virginia, where she picked up a political lexicon that remains with her today. An ardent feminist although she claims to reject all labels, she sounds somewhat trapped in the rhetoric of the seventies when she talks about encounter groups, consciousness-raising, and self-examination. And by substituting "Palestinian" for "female" and "feminine," she readapts expressions like "confiscation of the female voice" or "subjugation of the feminine intellect" as they pertain to the deprivation of Palestinian rights under Israeli occupation.

It takes only a trip to Ramallah, however, to realize that Hanan is indeed a Palestinian woman—by fate from the time she was born, by choice from the time she returned to the West Bank. To anyone walking around the city where she has instilled in her own children a strong connection to the land, it is clear that everyday life lacks many modern conveniences. On the most basic level, there are no supermarkets with hosed-down, neatly stacked vegetables in refrigerated cases, nor are there poultry parts packaged in plastic wrap. The stores that line the narrow sidewalks in Ramallah are filled with cans, boxes of dry groceries, crates of rice and beans spilling out of burlap sacks onto the floor, live chickens in stacked cages waiting to be sold and slaughtered, fresh vegetables in wooden stands on the sidewalks next to barrels of fruit and nuts. Plastered on almost all the shopwindows are pictures of Yasir Arafat, his smiling face shrouded in his signature black-and-white-checkered *kaffiyeh,* his hands raised high in a V-for-victory sign. Since the beginning of the Intifada, other photographs have appeared as well—images of the Palestinians who have lost their lives—rows of stilled smiling faces, captioned with names, dates of birth, and causes of death, a reminder of the toll on human life this rebellion has taken.

The last store at the end of the block has mannequins in

the window wearing the latest fashions from Amman, the dummies' heads covered in white *chadors* in deference to the increasing influence of Muslim extremists. A donkey is tied to a tree, and a Palestinian wearing a *kaffiyeh* is stuffing groceries into pouches hanging from the animal's leather saddle. Parked nearby is a dusty Subaru with yellow license plates indicating that its owner is either a Jerusalem Arab or an imprudent Israeli who has ventured into Ramallah to shop.

In this instance the Subaru is owned by Hanan's husband, Emil Ashrawi, who, between loading groceries into the trunk, pauses to inspect the side of one door, where recent dents have indeed been made by stones thrown in unknowing pro-test against his yellow plates. Except for the black-and-white *kaffiyeh* he wears around his neck or leaves on his dashboard when he remembers, he is frequently mistaken for an Israeli settler because of his heavy beard as well as the scruffy jeans and oversize work shirts that he wears almost as a uniform. Even in Ramallah, where the townspeople recognize him on sight, he is still considered an oddity in that part of the world—a man who does all the household shopping, errands, and daily chauffeuring of his two daughters to and from school. The person whom Ramallah residents don't see very often is his wife—certainly not now that she spends so much time abroad nor even before, when she taught at the university in the neighboring town of Bir Zeit. And on those rare oc-casions when she does appear—ferried from one appointment to another by an entourage of bodyguards and assistants—her presence is an event. Hounded by autograph seekers or townspeople who want to discuss recent developments in the ongoing peace conference or just touch her hand, she is the local-girl-turned-global-celebrity.

AWAY FROM THE commercial center of the city is a residential area where large stone houses are set farther back from the street. Most are surrounded by well-tended lawns and large leafy trees, unusual on the West Bank where Israeli law prohibits shrubbery or trees high enough to shield potential terrorists. One three-story house made of pink cast stone stands on Radio Street, number sixty-two, and belongs to Hanan's widowed mother. Now seventy-eight years old and in frail health, Wad'ia Mikhael spends most of her time confined to bed on the top floor of the house. Hanan, Emil, and their two daughters live downstairs.

Hanan is at home today, standing in front of her house and inspecting the rosebushes that cover the metal gate. Wearing a tailored brown coatdress with a string of pearls around her neck and a beige cardigan draped casually around her shoulders, she looks like a 1960 suburban American matron. In fact, it is easy to forget where the house is located until a glance is cast directly across the street, where a large stone structure surrounded by a barbed-wire fence takes up one square block. Several observation towers manned by soldiers holding automatic weapons are visible on its roof, while at the tallest point of the complex a blue-and-white Israeli flag waves in the wind.

The building is the headquarters for the Israeli civil governor of Ramallah and the center where Palestinians are required to apply for identity papers, tax stamps, work permits, driver's licenses, and every other bureaucratic form needed to survive under Israeli occupation. The complex also includes a jail where Palestinians are taken for interrogation before being transferred either to Jerusalem for further questioning or after trial to one of the higher-security Israeli prisons in the Negev Desert. Built originally by the British under the command of a certain Colonel Taggart and called the Taggart Fortress, the compound was taken over by the Jordanians in 1948 before it was eventually captured by the Israelis in 1967 and renamed the Civil Administration Building. Hanan says there is nothing civil about it.

24

"My family has a history with this building," she explains as she shields her eyes from the sun. "When I was a child I would watch the Jordanian soldiers exercising their horses inside the compound. Later on, after sixty-seven, I could see right into the office of the Israeli civil governor." She points to a small window, under the roof of the house, facing the street. "From my room up there, I could actually see him signing papers or talking on the phone."

AT THE AGE of forty-seven, Hanan is the youngest of five daughters of an elite Palestinian family who have managed to lose neither their possessions nor their property under Jordanian and Israeli occupations. While all the sisters are educated and accomplished in their professional lives, their personal lives have almost all been touched by sadness or complications.

Although smaller and more masculine-looking than Hanan, Huda is the sister who resembles her the most. She is also the daughter who was considered the father's favorite, the son he never had who went hunting with him and who had the distinction of owning the first motorcycle in the Occupied Territories. With affection Hanan says, "Huda was the tomboy, the daring one who loved outdoor sports and who used to drive my father's car as a kid and drive everybody crazy because she was too small to be seen over the top of the steering wheel. People used to think that the car was driving itself." A talented sculptor, Huda currently works at the Kuwaiti Embassy in Washington, but only as a means to afford the materials needed for her art supplies. Divorced at an early age, she remained bitter toward her ex-husband for many years after his death because he prevented her from taking their children from Jordan to the United States. Now grown, the children all live in the States near their mother.

Muna, Hanan's oldest sister, was widowed in her early twenties when her husband, a prominent ophthalmologist, died of a stroke. Muna, who never remarried, went on to a successful career as a high official at the World Bank in Washington. Since taking on the role of spokesperson for the Palestinian peace delegation, Hanan has grown closest with Muna. "It wasn't until I began coming to Washington that I rediscovered Muna," Hanan explains. "Before that I rarely saw her and never really knew her well."

Eight years older than Hanan, Abla, who lives in Amman, is the sister who suffered the most under occupation, when her husband's deportation by the Israelis caused the family to be dispersed and uprooted. Until the Israeli-Palestinian preliminary accord, it was difficult for Abla to get a visa to visit Hanan or her mother, who had long since been unable to make the trip across the Allenby Bridge from Jericho into Jordan.

Nadia is the sister who introduced Hanan to Emil almost twenty years ago and is the only one, other than Hanan, who still lives in Ramallah. Married to an architect, a man his late father-in-law once described as "the only Muslim in the family," Nadia is an accomplished pianist who teaches music to young Palestinians throughout the West Bank. "Nadia has the usual problems of any mixed marriage," Hanan says.

There is no separating the woman from the activist when Hanan recalls her youth, growing up on Radio Street in Ramallah under continuing occupation. Each memory is linked to the political situation since 1948, when Palestine was lost. "That was the reason why I returned to Ramallah after studying in the States," Hanan says simply. "I had a job to do here."

While she received numerous academic offers from throughout the United States, Hanan always felt that teaching Palestinian students on the West Bank was an investment in the future of any Palestinian state. Given an environment of student rebellion and often violent confrontations against the occupation in every West Bank university, there was no doubt that Hanan would find herself deeply involved. Pointing to the Civil Administration Building, she says, "When I got back from the States and was already teaching at Bir Zeit, that was where the army used to take me for interrogation after every protest march or demonstration." She smiles slightly. "Actually they didn't need an excuse. Being a Palestinian was enough to take someone in for questioning."

Maurice Barkokva, the Israeli civil governor during the late 1970s, remembers the Mikhael family very well, especially Hanan's father, with whom he shared an unusual friendship. The men would meet on Radio Street for a chat, sometimes taking time for a coffee or even lunch. According to Barkokva, Daoud Mikhael, a physician, was not only charming with a wonderful sense of humor but extremely sensitive and realistic when it came to the ongoing clashes between Palestinians and the army. Barkokva claims that it was only because of this friendship that Hanan was never formally charged or arrested for anti-Israeli activities, nor was she ever subjected to interrogation any more harsh than sitting in his office chatting informally, with an unending supply of coffee and cigarettes. "Whenever Hanan got in trouble with us for organizing demonstrations or inciting students to riot, her father would intervene and say that she was only a kid whose head was filled with ideas from America, that eventually she would settle down and learn the rhythm of our land." As it turned out, Hanan's father was wrong.

Hanan returned from the University of Virginia armed with radical techniques and left-wing slogans learned in an academic atmosphere in which most professors were anti-establishment, students were almost always engaged in violent protests, and a profound abhorrence of the Vietnam War bound the campus together regardless of all the different political agendas. Not content to remain merely an observer,

Hanan was the only white member of the Black Student Alliance, a vocal advocate for better working conditions for the Appalachian migrant farmworkers, as well as an avid participant in the women's movement. Copying the rhetoric and tactics of the Black Student Alliance, Hanan formed the American Friends for Free Palestine, University of Virginia Chapter, and later wrote for the *Virginia Weekly,* an underground newspaper committed to the rights of minorities, which she used as a vehicle to introduce the Palestinian problem.

"The black students accepted me as representative of all the Palestinians suffering under an oppressive political system," she explains. "But what was more interesting," she continues, "is that I only became aware of the Appalachian migrant farmworkers' cause because they used to come to lectures I gave in Washington on Palestinian women. From the beginning they knew more about our history than my peers at the university."

According to Hanan, what she always felt in the States was an inherent prejudice about Palestinians. She recalls a specific incident with one of her professors. After asking her name and nationality, the professor confessed that he thought all "Arabians" were called "Muhammad." Hanan recalls her response, in keeping with her feisty reputation: "I suggested that instead of calling Palestinians either 'Arabians' or 'Mohammed,' he should simply refer to them as 'Saracens.' " She smiles. "At any rate, when it came to the Palestinian problem, the academic world in America was very detached, even if most of my professors haven't quite recovered since I left Virginia."

Grounded in the classics, and with literary tastes that range from Gabriel García Márquez to Milan Kundera, from Chaucer to Ezra Pound, this is a woman who has managed to convey the moral imperative of the Palestinian struggle by putting it high up on her own intellectual agenda. Armed

with her experience of American dissident groups, Hanan
returned to the West Bank in late 1973 and set about teaching
her students at Bir Zeit the methods of protest and resistance
that she had learned in the States. Unfortunately her efforts
were less than brilliant, reflected by her failure to mobilize
public opinion with those in power in Jerusalem or to persuade Palestinian leaders on the West Bank to embrace methods she took to calling "selective passive resistance." From
the beginning her biggest error lay in her inability to differ-
entiate between the nuances of political repression in the
United States as opposed to military oppression in the Occupied Territories. What Hanan failed to realize was that
Watergate, the fall of Richard Nixon, and the Vietnam War
were issues that were in no way similar to those in the Occupied Territories, especially after the defeat of the Arabs by
the Israelis during the 1973 Yom Kippur War.

Israel had suffered tremendous losses defending itself
when Egypt attacked during the holiest of Jewish holidays—
the eve of Yom Kippur, when much of the population was
attending synagogue—while Syria and Jordan, sensing Israel's state of unpreparedness, engaged the IDF on the northern and eastern fronts. It was a combination of naïveté and
elitism that led Hanan to believe that the same tactics used
in the States to challenge the system would work on the West
Bank, where dialogue was a luxury, equality was about
women dying in equal numbers to men in the refugee camps,
and freedom of expression was punishable by up to six
months in jail. If righteousness and indignation fueled the
masses on American campuses and put those in power in
Washington on the defensive, Israeli leaders had little patience
for Palestinian discontent in the Occupied Territories. It was
in this atmosphere that Hanan mobilized her students at Bir
Zeit University in the name of the PLO to challenge the Israeli
hold on the Occupied Territories.

29

"She used to come to my office and argue that the PLO would win in the end because we had no business being in that area," Barkokva explains. "She'd predict that eventually we'd be worn down by all the protesting, rioting, and world opinion." He shakes his head sadly. "And then there were the times when she'd get offensive and violent and I'd have to call her father to calm her down." While Barkokva hastens to add that Hanan never actually involved herself in terrorist activities, he believes that her systematic incitement of students made her responsible for any loss of life during those violent clashes between soldiers and civilians. "In the Occupied Territories," Barkokva judges, "behind every terrorist is a political idea."

IT WAS DURING that same time on the West Bank, when violence between Palestinians and the Israeli Army was intensifying, that the Mikhael family suffered its own personal loss. Since 1962, for almost eleven years, Hanan's sister Abla and her husband, Alfred Tobasi, a prominent West Bank dentist, had been living in the downstairs portion of the house on Radio Street with their four children. One night Tobasi was summoned by Barkokva to a meeting at the Civil Administration Building. Without bothering to take any identity papers, Tobasi put on a jacket and walked across Radio Street. He never returned. According to Hanan, with no justification he was bound, blindfolded, thrown into a car, and driven to the East Bank of the Jordan River, where he was deposited without any explanation on the other side of the Israeli-Jordanian border. According to Barkokva, who issued the deportation order, Tobasi was expelled from Ramallah because of his membership in the National Guidance Committee, a PLO offshoot that transported weapons for terrorist activities in Israel and the Occupied Territories.

While Tobasi's family and friends remained stunned and

outraged by his deportation, Hanan's immediate reaction was to organize a march through Ramallah with the intention of continuing all the way into Jerusalem. Instructing everyone to dress in black as a symbol of mourning, she led the procession along the main road, picking up supporters in towns on the way to Jerusalem.

"When I arrived with my soldiers," Barkokva recounts, "my only concern was how to break up the protest, since it was interfering with traffic. Instead of discussing things, Hanan got into a shouting match with me, swearing and screaming and using bad language in Arabic, which since I speak fluently made me realize she wasn't a typical Oriental woman. I told her that if she hadn't gotten her education in America, she never would have behaved like that." Looking incredulous still, Barkokva asks, "Do you know what she answered?"

Now, more than twenty years later, as Hanan stands in front of that same house, facing Barkokva's old office, she seems almost amused by the memory. "I simply asked Maurice why he was so upset since I was just expressing my ideas," Hanan says. "After all, it was always the Israelis who claimed we were living in the only democracy in the Middle East."

A memory that doesn't amuse Hanan is how Tobasi's deportation almost destroyed an entire family. For a while Abla remained in the house on Radio Street and commuted to Amman every few weeks to visit her husband, vowing not to let it disrupt the children's routine and schooling. Eventually, however, she couldn't take the separation anymore and left permanently to live in Jordan with her husband. When Hanan talks about what happened to her brother-in-law, she adds that there are hundreds of similar cases of what she calls "invisible deportations"—Palestinians who are simply rounded up and thrown out of their homes.

Drawing on a literary comparison, Hanan cites a short

story by Vladimir Nabokov, *A Visit to a Museum,* in which a man has managed to escape Soviet Russia and immigrate to the West. One day he enters a museum in his new home-town and becomes hopelessly lost in a maze of rooms and corridors. Wandering through the museum, in and out of a series of doors, he finally exits to find himself back on the streets of Soviet Russia. But despite the surrealistic quality of the Nabokov story to which Hanan compares life under oc-cupation, she cites the one crucial difference: For Hanan there is nothing comparable between Palestinians and the world's other "émigrés," including those Russians who lost their homes and land to an invading power. In that context it is necessary that she define the meaning of the words *exile* and *diaspora.*

"Frankly speaking," Hanan begins, "diaspora is a Jewish experience and within itself has romantic yearnings of people living outside all their lives yet still having an attachment to a certain land and identity. Diaspora doesn't mean a complete exile as we [Palestinians] know it, where people had concrete lands and homes they were kicked out of. Exile is concrete, while diaspora is abstract, so when people talk about the Palestinian diaspora after 1948, they really don't understand how painful and artificial the separation was, like tearing apart something organic."

It is precisely Hanan's style of explaining current events by veering off on a literary tangent that creates the impression among her own people that she is removed from the life-and-death realities that occur every day in the West Bank and Gaza.

Imad Iyash is a Palestinian from a prominent family in Nablus who served twelve years in an Israeli prison for setting explosives in Ben Gurion Airport. A critic of Hanan, his main objection is that she has never suffered in jail or in a refugee camp and has fewer credentials, in his opinion, to represent the Palestinian cause than does his own mother. "My mother didn't sleep for the twelve years that I was in prison," he says. "She could explain our suffering to the world better than Hanan, only my mother doesn't speak English." Iyash is resolute when he adds that Hanan is not in any way typical of the Palestinian woman living under occupation. "Not only doesn't Hanan resemble any other Palestinian woman intellectually, but she sets herself apart even physically." Making reference to her mannish haircut (which is featured as the "Hanan cut" in beauty salons across the Jordan River in Amman), he concludes, "What Hanan does is to supply the American politicians with the image they need to sell us to their constituency."

Another Palestinian, Sameh Kanaan, a member of the original Palestinian delegation who, along with Iyash, served ten years in that same Israeli jail for setting explosives in Israel, shares similar opinions about Hanan.

Kanaan is a walking contradiction—a man who has always aligned himself with the PLO even though in the eyes of the Israelis he is a Jew. As a young girl his mother fell in love with Kanaan's father, a Muslim who was her next-door neighbor. Before their wedding she converted and raised all her children in her husband's religion. Kanaan is a chubby man with a cherubic face and an infectious smile who breaks into laughter at the slightest provocation. While Kanaan agrees with Iyash that Hanan's main credential for leadership is her knowledge of English, he considers her pride in never having learned Hebrew to be one of her biggest flaws: "If she refuses to stay at home to care for her family the way other Palestinian women do, then what she should be doing instead of traveling all over the world is learn[ing] the language of our enemy. That way she could watch Israeli television and read the Israeli press to understand their mentality. It doesn't help our cause that she is an expert in foreign literature."

Hanan possesses a self-assurance typical of someone from a privileged and educated background. In her own defense she insists that it was precisely education and privilege that allowed her to come of age as a woman in the United States in the seventies during the feminist revolution. It was an experience, she claims, that taught her how to fight for the rights of women and other minorities in a male-dominated, oppressive society. In response to both Iyash's and Kanaan's criticisms, Hanan says that from literature as from history, lessons are to be learned that can change future outcomes.

What is certain for Hanan as well as for every other Palestinian living under occupation is that there isn't anyone—regardless of his or her intellect, job, or social or political position—who hasn't been affected. Not a single Palestinian living in the Occupied Territories lacks a neighbor, friend, or relative who has been wounded, killed, deported, imprisoned, interrogated, or humiliated; who has lost a job, house, or identity card; or who has suffered any combination of the foregoing. And while not every Palestinian has been damaged in physical extremes, all have been affected by a collective absorption of other people's pain. Hanan calmly describes how occupation has affected her life.

"The power of the army is a renewable shock every day," she begins. "The fact that you have no right to your own humanity or privacy while they give themselves rights that nobody anywhere dares to take. And it can be expressed in little ways that aren't so dramatic or tragic, like getting into your car to drive to the university and not knowing if you're going to get there or be stopped at a roadblock by soldiers who decide to question you just because you're a Palestinian."

When it comes to claims by other Palestinians that Hanan lives a protected life and consequently has never experienced any physical abuse firsthand, she defends herself. "While it's true that I've been interrogated many times without being beaten," she says, "I've sat in a room and listened to the screams of my students being beaten in the next room." She pauses. "I'm not sure which is worse, to be beaten or to know that you're completely powerless to help others."

One particular incident remains with Hanan—when she was detained briefly in the Russian Compound, the central Israeli police station in Jerusalem. "While my interrogator never touched me," she admits, "he was vulgar and extremely harsh verbally, swearing at me and calling me names. But what struck me as surrealistic was how he would calmly leave me to walk across the hall and beat my students. At the time I remember thinking how average and normal he looked in his jeans with 'Lee' written on the waistband, and how his hands were chubby and covered with hair. I imagined that with those same hands . . . he would go home at night and hug his wife or carry his child. Later on I learned that people called him the 'genital man' because of his particular expertise."

More than just suffering through the physical abuse of her students, Hanan claims to have been personally involved in demonstrations in which, while not singled out, she was attacked by the army. "I've been shot at and teargassed for throwing stones," she says. "Oh, yes, I have, and I even remember four years ago coming home and not being able to breathe, having terrible stomach pains because the gas the Israelis use is so highly concentrated that I really thought I was finished. My children were terrified when they saw me doubled over in pain. But the most frightening experience was the dogs, the way they're trained to jump over stones and fences, frothing at the mouth as the soldiers encourage them to attack us during a peace march. It brought back all those horrible memories of segregation in the South when I studied in the States."

Pausing, she examines her rosebushes briefly before

turning around to add, "We [the Palestinians] have always paid a very serious price for the tragedy of the Jews, which is why they of all people shouldn't re-create another Holocaust here."

If she angers other Palestinians with her intellectual rhetoric, she outrages most Israelis with her constant comparison of the bloodshed in the Occupied Territories and the slaughter of six million Jews in Europe. "Just comparing us to the Nazis," one high-ranking Israeli military official says, "proves that Hanan Ashrawi has no idea what Jews consider sacred. After all, do we call the Palestinians pigs or dogs—names that are the most insulting to them?"

"As a matter of fact," Hanan answers sharply, "the Israelis have used those very words, while Shamir actually called us grasshoppers and General Eitan, the Israeli Chief of Staff during the Lebanon War in 1982, once called us two-legged vermin."

There is still no resolution to the story of Alfred Tobasi's deportation. Although there have been several Israeli civil governors since 1973, when Barkokva was in command, and a series of policy changes throughout the West Bank, Tobasi's repeated petitions to return to Ramallah have been all denied on the grounds that he is still an active member of the PLO, specifically of the Palestine National Council. Recently, after the signing of the DOP, Alfred Tobasi was given permission by the Israeli authorities to return for the first time to Ramallah, spending several days visiting Hanan and her family and his mother-in-law in the house on Radio Street.

As for Maurice Barkokva, the last time he saw Hanan was in 1988, long after he had retired and she had gone on to begin a second career and to become world famous. "She was browsing in a jewelry shop in Jerusalem when I bumped into her," Barkokva says. "I asked about her father because I'd heard that he was very ill." He smiles sadly. "It was the only time she ever spoke to me in a civil tone. I guess she was grateful that I cared."

Hanan remembers, too, for her expression suddenly softens. "How Maurice loved my father," she says quietly. "How they used to sit for hours and talk about everything."

Turning to cast a final glance across the street toward the Civil Administration Building, Hanan turns to head slowly toward the house and through a set of double doors made of beveled glass. Walking down several steps into a large, airless room that is cluttered with old furniture, a rusty standing fan, and a plastic plant, she pushes through another set of double doors to enter the downstairs main living room of the Ashrawi home. An ancient hookah leans against a modern bookcase filled with books, papers, and CDs.

THERE IS A FEELING of intellectual clutter throughout the house on Radio Street. The room where Hanan chooses to sit is off the main living area and is filled with antiques and paintings that look as if they were acquired less for value than for sentiment. An upright piano is pushed against the stone wall in one corner, classical music piled on top, some yellowed with age and others marked up with notes and numbers. Amal, Hanan's seventeen-year-old daughter, studies classical piano and plays so well that from the other side of a closed door, the music sounds as if it has been recorded by a concert pianist. In the center of the room is a large coffee table on which are more books in English and Arabic, CDs, newspapers, a small brass pot filled with tattered beaded flowers, and piles of official-looking faxes, some with government seals, others marked SECRET. Four couches are grouped around the table, three framed in wood and the fourth a contemporary sofa upholstered in white muslin. All are on an Oriental rug that looks slightly frayed around its edges. Hanan sits in a brown velour BarcaLounger; near her right hand is a small table on which is an ashtray overflowing with cigarettes smoked down to their filters, her ever-present pack of Salem Lights, and a disposable lighter.

The casement windows that run along two of the walls are covered with heavy green velvet draperies. Regardless of the weather—and today happens to be cold and windy—Saja, the family dog, is tied up outside. A sweet brown-eyed mutt with long blond hair and a bushy tail, who incongruously resembles Lady from *Lady and the Tramp,* Saja barks incessantly. Hanan explains that she doesn't allow animals inside the house. While it is not unusual for animals to be kept outside in most Arab cultures, it is unusual for an Arab family to keep a dog as a pet unless it's for protection. When the question of Saja is presented to Hanan as another example of her cultural ambiguity, she dismisses the notion by saying, "If anything, Saja is another example of how the Ashrawi home functions as a democracy." Zeina, Hanan's thirteen-year-old daughter, constantly asks if Saja can come inside for a visit, while Amal agrees with her mother that the dog should remain outside. As the democratic tiebreaker, however, Emil Ashrawi doesn't consider the issue important enough to vote on, proving that Saja is the victim of one partner's apathy and another's dogma. "Saja is perfectly happy outside," Hanan says. "The neighborhood shepherds visit her every day and bring her food."

(Six months later Saja is dead, poisoned by food that one of those neighborhood shepherds brought her to eat. According to Emil, the poisoned food had been left around intentionally by the army to rid Ramallah of stray dogs. According to Hanan, Saja was just another casualty of the Intifada.)

On this particular day Saja's barking, according to Hanan, doesn't interfere with other neighborhood sounds that can be heard along Radio Street. "We hear everything that goes

on across the street," Hanan claims, "all the screams of prisoners being beaten or tortured and we can see the children
sitting on the roof with knapsacks on their backs, detained
sometimes for twelve and fourteen hours at a time on suspicion of throwing stones."*

RADIO STREET HAS always been a well-known landmark in
Ramallah, but since Hanan's rise to fame it has become as
familiar to foreign journalists and visiting dignitaries as the
Knesset in Jerusalem. Yet, long before the West Bank fell
under Israeli rule, there was a time when Radio Street was
known as the address where the best-loved doctor in all the
West Bank lived and worked.

People on both sides of the struggle loved Hanan's father.
A warm and generous man who was dedicated to his patients
and committed to saving human life, Daoud Mikhael began
his medical career working for the British Army during the
Mandate, in what was then Palestine. Because of that job,
which meant moving every two years to a different city on
the West Bank, Hanan was born in Nablus (on October 8,
1946); Nadia, the next in line, and Abla, after her, were also
born in Nablus; Muna was born in Jerusalem, and Huda in
Hebron.

Daoud Mikhael made no distinction between his personal
and professional life, approaching both in consistently unor-
thodox ways. Although a devoted husband and father, he
was absent much of the time; his interest in his patients was

---

*When I informed several Israeli military officials in charge of the West Bank of the
above statement made by Hanan, they conducted a test in front of me where a radio
was blasted in one of the interrogation rooms. Standing on the street *outside* the
Ashrawi house, I was unable to hear the radio. As for detaining children on the roof
of the Civil Administration Building, a spokesman for the Israeli Army admitted
that only when there are incidents of throwing stones either at soldiers or civilians,
the army's policy is to round up minors and hold them until their parents come to
claim them.

all-consuming, transcending the professional as he traveled from one town to the next, lingering after examinations to share a meal or philosophizing long into the night about the plight of his people. Hanan remembers her father as a simple man who often eschewed conventional medical procedures but rather responded to those with incurable diseases with humor and optimism and to those with minor ailments by prescribing herbal teas and plants and other natural medicines. Many of his patients and friends claim that Daoud was the first holistic doctor in the region. As a businessman, however, Daoud was admittedly a disaster. "But he didn't care," Hanan says, laughing. "His family owned a lot of land, and he would buy and sell houses and hectares and always end up with less than what he started out with." She shakes her head. "He was a peasant in the true sense of the word—a man of the earth who didn't care at all about money."

While Daoud Mikhael's own family roots were in Ramallah for generations, like most wealthy West Bankers, he was educated in Beirut, where he finished medical school at the American University (later Hanan's alma mater as well). In those days the Arab world was small and closely contained, with three or four major areas where people traveled easily back and forth across common borders. For those who could afford it there were vacations in Lebanon or business transactions in Syria. Beginning right after he graduated from medical school and until 1975, when civil war broke out in Lebanon, Daoud would return regularly to Beirut to visit professors, old friends, and colleagues. It was through one of these that he found a young Lebanese woman to replace one of his scrub nurses, who was leaving to get married.

When a male assistant brought the replacement back from the train station in Jerusalem on a donkey, Daoud asked what she was like. "She has eyes like a white cow," was the response—a compliment in that part of the world, where white cows were known for their beautiful brown eyes. It took only weeks for Daoud to break his engagement to a Ramallah woman and ask Wad'ia's father for her hand in marriage. But while Wad'ia had fallen in love with the dashing doctor, her father—a wealthy Lebanese businessman—was less than enchanted with his daughter's choice of husband. Wad'ia was richer, better educated, and older by at least five years than Daoud. "My mother would never tell us how many years' difference there was between her and my father," Hanan says. "She always refused to discuss her age."

In the end Daoud and Wad'ia prevailed, and her father gave the couple his blessing to marry in Jerusalem. If Hanan were forced to sum up the most fundamental difference between her parents, she could do it in one sentence: "One grandmother wore Victorian clothes," she explains, "while the other wore Palestinian peasant gowns. They were from entirely different backgrounds and cultures, each having country and city values and priorities."

It was her maternal grandmother who wore the Victorian clothes and who came to live with the Mikhaels when Hanan was a small child. A former missionary, this deeply religious woman tried to instill the fear of God in her grandchildren. "My grandmother was certain that I would burn in hell because I spent all my pocket money on lollipops," Hanan remembers.

Another of Hanan's memories illustrating her grandmother's faith was born one morning when she wandered into her mother's room where both women were sewing. Restless and lonely because all her sisters were off at school, Hanan delivered an ultimatum that either she should be allowed to join them or her mother would have to give her a baby brother to keep her company. Her grandmother's response to the three-year-old was immediate: Though she was too young to go to school, a baby brother was possible but only if she prayed very hard. "I remember getting down on my knees right there in the bedroom and praying and even before I got up, asking my mother where my baby brother was." Again her grandmother answered, explaining that God didn't work that fast, and baby brothers could take at least nine months, which prompted Hanan to revert to her alternative ultimatum of joining her older sisters at school.

From that day on Abla was charged with the responsibility of teaching Hanan to read and write. The sisters would sit on a living room windowsill, with Abla teaching her baby sister words and letters from a big picture book that she had brought home from school. When Hanan was not quite four, she entered what was the equivalent of kindergarten and, thanks to Abla, could already read and write in both English and Arabic.

While Hanan claims in another conversation never to have known a Jew or an Israeli until after the Six Day War, when she was studying at the American University in Beirut, her sister Huda remembers having many Jewish friends when they were small children and the family lived in Tiberias. "Most of the neighborhood children were sons and daughters of Russian immigrants who came to Tiberias in the twenties and thirties, fleeing the pogroms," Huda says.

It was in that house overlooking the Lake of Tiberias (the Sea of Galilee) that Daoud and Wad'ia first settled after they married. The family remained in Tiberias until 1948 when Hanan was two years old, shortly before Israel became a state. It was then that Daoud became deeply involved in the Arab resistance against the British. Fearing for their safety, he sent his wife and daughters to live in Amman until the British left and Palestine would once again be independent and in Arab hands. But when the situation showed no signs of improving, Daoud—having no intention of allowing a family separation that might have lasted for years—brought his family back

from Amman to settle in Ramallah. The decision Hanan's
father took was in keeping with a reality that was spreading
among West Bank Palestinians. It was felt that Britain's sudden position regarding a Jewish homeland was only a continuation of its pro-Jewish policy of allowing large-scale
Jewish immigration into the region after World War I. And
that began with the Balfour Declaration in 1921, when British
Foreign Secretary Lord Balfour made a formal commitment
to create a Jewish homeland in Palestine.

On May 14, 1948, David Ben Gurion officially proclaimed
the establishment of the State of Israel, appealing to the Arab
population to stay and "play their part in the development
of the state, with full and equal citizenship." Certain of victory, within weeks of Ben Gurion's proclamation the armies
of Egypt, Lebanon, Syria, Iraq, Transjordan (later Jordan),
and Saudi Arabia invaded Israel. It was to be the beginning
of a political agenda in which the Arab states would unite
against Israel supposedly to liberate Palestine for the Palestinians. That political justification continued for decades, as
the Palestinians served as a convenient front-line force in the
Arabs' covert war against Israel, avoiding the risk of humil-
iating defeats such as were eventually suffered in overt battle
during the Six Day and Yom Kippur Wars. Tragically, while
that agenda suited the Arabs, allowing them to pursue either
their own territorial ambitions or the destruction of Israel, it
would also cost the lives of thousands of innocent civilians
who fell victim to random terrorist attacks. And what remains
equally tragic is that never did the Arab world take into
consideration the legitimate goals of the Palestinian people.

When the cease-fire was finally called, with the Arab armies defeated by the Israelis, the opportunity presented itself
to create a Palestinian state from those lands that had not
fallen under Israeli control. For the second time the offer of
creating a Palestinian state alongside Israel would be rejected

by the Arabs (the first being the original partition plan offered by the United Nations in 1947). Instead Syria annexed the small town of al-Hamma in the north of Galilee, and Egypt took over the Gaza Strip, while the British gave Jordan's King Abdullah a stretch of land now known as the West Bank, that territory comprising both the East and West Banks of the Jordan River, including the Old City of Jerusalem.

It didn't take long for the Jordanian king to demonstrate his dissatisfaction with the size of the territory, however, announcing his intention of expanding it to include Greater Syria and all of Palestine. Not only did the Israelis oppose Abdullah's plan, but also those Palestinians who were followers of Haj Amin al-Husseini, the mufti of Jerusalem. Husseini's reasons were clearly less altruistic than they were expansionist when he expressed his intention of establishing an independent Palestinian state with himself as its leader. Once again David Ben Gurion, believing that he could come to some kind of conciliation with his Arab neighbors, approached King Abdullah with a proposal. In exchange for not including the State of Israel in any plan he had to expand the borders of Jordan, Ben Gurion guaranteed him Israeli support in his quest for control over the rest of the West Bank. It was to be a short-lived alliance. When Husseini found out that Abdullah had entered into a mutually advantageous agreement with Israel, he accused Abdullah of having sold out to the Jews. Predictably—and without any warning— Husseini declared an independent Palestinian government in the area known as Gaza, with plans to take over the rest of Palestine that was currently under Abdullah's control. In response Abdullah banned the use of the word "Palestine" and forbade the people living throughout the West Bank to refer to themselves as Palestinians. In April 1950 King Abdullah formally annexed the territory. And on July 21, 1951, as he entered the al-Aqsa Mosque in Jerusalem to pray, he was assassinated by those loyal to Haj Amin al-Husseini. It was in this atmosphere of unrest that Daoud settled his brood in a modest house in the middle of the town of Ramallah, about six miles north of Jerusalem, where he also set up a medical practice. From then until his death in 1988, Hanan's father remained deeply involved in the quest for Palestinian independence.

Even after the death of King Abdullah, it was not prudent to espouse nationalism as it pertained to the Palestinian cause. Abdullah's nephew and heir, Hussein, the young king of Jordan, also believed that the only way to achieve Jordanian national unity was to forbid his West Bank subjects to refer to themselves as Palestinians. Hanan remembers the effect the law had on her family, specifically on herself as a young girl.

"I've always felt Palestinian because it was something my father conveyed to us and insisted on—that while we should believe in Arab nationalism, we were Palestinians despite the fact that the West Bank was part of Jordan. After King Hussein banned us from even saying we were Palestinian, it became something precious that we took out and examined on our own in secret, something we cherished for ourselves. And of course what happened was that the more we were denied our identity, the more adamant we became about preserving it."

In October 1956, Jordanians on the West Bank were in chaos over an Israeli reprisal attack on the West Bank town of Qalqilya. In an appeasement tactic, King Hussein decided to hold democratic elections on the West Bank within the framework of his constitutional monarchy. Unexpectedly the winners were left-wing West Bankers with allegiance to both Egypt's Gen. Gamal Abdel Nasser and to Syrian leaders already closely connected with what would become their benefactor state until its collapse: the Soviet Union. Two of the biggest political winners in that group were Daoud Mikhael and Suleiman Nabulsi.

It didn't take long for King Hussein to realize, as his uncle had before him, that a bigger threat to his kingdom than the one from the Israelis came from the West Bank Palestinians who sought independence from Jordan. King Hussein invalidated the elections and dismissed Nabulsi's newly elected cabinet, announcing as justification that he had uncovered a Syrian-Egyptian plot to overthrow his throne. At the end of 1956 the National Socialist party was officially outlawed, and Daoud Mikhael was arrested and charged with agitating for a Palestinian state on the West Bank. Convicted, he was sentenced to six years in prison.

If asked to remember the most painful memory of her childhood, Hanan will immediately answer that it was falling off a balcony of the Ramallah house. While those wounds have healed, the ones she suffered from her most real and distressing memory is still at times too painful to discuss. Even after so many years, Hanan finds it no less difficult when she talks about her father's imprisonment.

What she remembers from that bleak time in her life are sporadic incidents not in any sequential order. A vivid image is that of an uncle as he rushed into her father's office adjacent to the house to destroy papers and documents before the Jordanian soldiers arrived. Another is Jordanian soldiers arriving on horseback and shooting randomly in all directions. "Apparently they were trying to shoot down the sign hanging from my father's clinic, which was the symbol of the National Socialist party," Hanan explains, "and after they'd shot it down they began trampling on it as if the sign itself were something dangerous and alive. I guess that was my first introduction to the importance of political symbols."

While she has blocked out the image of the Jordanian soldiers actually coming to the house on Radio Street to take her father away, she does recall being consciously aware of his presence across the street. For Hanan and her sisters, he was so near and yet so far since for the first few weeks of his incarceration the family was forbidden to visit him. Finally, after many petitions and the intervention of family friends who were close to King Hussein, permission was granted for the Mikhaels to visit their husband and father. Hanan was ten years old when she and her sisters were dressed in their Sunday best with ribbons tied in their hair. Carrying a picnic basket and handmade gifts, Wad'ia led her brood across Radio Street and into the Taggart Fortress, where Daoud was being held. For Hanan the experience was both shocking and troublesome. Jail held only negative connotations for the child; her father languishing in prison was a disgrace. It wasn't until her civics teacher, Mrs. Faris, at the Quaker Friends School in Ramallah, explained that going to jail for the reasons her father had was a sign of integrity and principle—that only good people were punished for their political ideas and values. "In a way that was the beginning of my political awareness," Hanan says. "It was Mrs. Faris who made me aware of the price we paid for being Palestinian. It was also the first time I understood commitment to a political belief."

Again, family connections accounted for Daoud's release from prison two years before the end of his six-year sentence. In 1957, when King Hussein began construction of his summer palace in Ramallah, he would stay at the only villa nearby that had enough grounds to land his helicopter. As fate would have it, the villa belonged to Muna, who had recently married a wealthy Palestinian eye surgeon from Jaffa. Four years later, in 1961, Daoud was still in prison on Radio Street. Whether out of insensitivity or ignorance or merely for convenience, King Hussein, accompanied by his second wife, the English-woman Antoinette Gardner, and children, were frequent guests at yet another Mikhael residence, this one in Aqaba. Huda recalls, "Toni would be running around the beach with little Abdullah and Faisal while my father still sat in jail."

Finally, after unrelenting efforts to persuade Hussein to com-
mute Daoud's prison term, the king relented. Citing Dr. Mikhael's failing health, Hussein arranged for Daoud's transfer
to a hospital in Ramallah, where he was placed under constant surveillance until he was released a month later in August 1961.

Any efforts Daoud made on behalf of the Palestinian cause
only escalated after his release from prison. Less concerned
with any Israeli victory on the West Bank, he concentrated
on resisting Jordanian expansion by working underground
with Nabulsi and the National Socialist party. While some
Israelis claim that Daoud Mikhael was one of the founders
of Fatah, Arafat's faction of the PLO, he was, in fact, one of
the organizers of the PLO itself, which grew out of Nabulsi's
party during the time when Arafat was still an engineering
student at Cairo University.

In January 1964, the first Arab Summit in Cairo was
convened by Nasser in an attempt to unite the Arab world
under the theme of the loss of Palestine in 1948. Clearly it
was a more popular idea—and one that garnered more widespread support for the Egyptian president—than his previous
one of taking over Syria and Yemen in order to realize his
goal of leading a greater Arab world. It was during that same
summit in Cairo that Nasser proposed the creation of the
PLO, a movement whose goal would be a Palestinian state
and whose methods would include armed resistance to any
persons or power that stood in its way. To head the organization that became known as the PLO, Nasser chose an
unassuming lawyer named Ahmed Shuquari, whose family
came from the Acre region of Palestine and whose father had
played an important role in resisting the creation of the Israeli
state in 1948. Curiously, while Shuquari's father, Assad, was
one of the most vocal opponents of selling Arab land to the
Jews during that crucial period, Assad personally sold nearly
all of his own acreage to his Jewish neighbors.

Between January and May of that same year, Shuquari toured the Middle East recruiting representatives from each Palestinian community. According to records kept during those early days, Shuquari explained his formula of representation in the following manner: "Preparatory committees and subcommittees will be set up by [Shuquari] and will be entrusted with the task of nominating and preparing the final list of members."

When the Palestine National Council (PNC) met in May 1964, its members were mainly Palestinian notables, usually elected Palestinian public officials and middle-class professionals and businessmen including members of the Jordanian parliament from the Gaza Strip, mayors and presidents of urban and rural councils, and professionals from categories as varied as clergymen, pharmacists, professors, lawyers, doctors, engineers, businessmen, bankers, and industrialists. To further round out the council, farmers, labor leaders, and representatives of refugee camps and women's and student's groups were included, bringing the total to 422 members. As a physician, Daoud Mikhael was one of those chosen from Ramallah as a representative.

The opening session of the council was held in Jerusalem during May and June 1964, with Shuquari proclaiming that Jerusalem would forever be the permanent headquarters for the PLO. It was there in the Holy City that the now-infamous Palestinian National Charter or PLO Covenant was written by Shuquari and the other members of the council, embodying the three fundamental principles of the PLO that remain in practice today. First, the charter declared that Palestine was an Arab homeland, and that Arab unity and the liberation of Palestine were its joint and complementary aims, two points on which there was no wavering and that went back to the time of King Abdullah's reign. Second, as it concerned Palestine as a Palestinian homeland, armed struggle was deemed the only way to liberate the land from the Jews. And

last, the charter went on to condemn Zionism as racist, imperialist, and fascist, points that the UN adopted as Resolution 3379 on November 10, 1975, revoked in December
1991. While Hanan was aware from the time she was a child
of her father's involvement in the early days of the PLO, she
claims now that his activities were limited to surveying potential members from various West Bank youth organizations.

After her father was released from prison in 1961, Hanan
developed an even greater awareness of the Palestinian problem. Again, it was during one of Mrs. Faris's civics classes at
the Friends School in Ramallah that two questions arose that
for her were integral to any eventual solution to the question
of Palestinian independence: "What is more important, the
United States or the United Nations?" and "Why can't we
say that we are Palestinians?" Given the influence of the
United States as it affected global opinion about Israel, for
Hanan the UN was clearly secondary in its attempt to implement several resolutions dealing with the problem. And,
having lived under laws set down by Jordan, Hanan knew
that any expression of Palestinian nationalism was also secondary to any laws promulgated by an occupying power. The
political awakening of Hanan Mikhael had already begun
when she was fifteen. But it wasn't until years later, in 1967,
when she was preparing to leave Ramallah for Beirut, where
she would be attending the American University, that she
became painfully aware of imminent realities that would forever affect her life.

A moment transpired between father and daughter in January 1964, as they stood together on the balcony of the house
on Radio Street and Daoud made an ominous prediction.
Pointing out Tel Aviv and Jaffa (Yafo) on the coast—close
in actual kilometers but a world away as they were Israeli
cities and technically in another country, he warned his

daughter that the death of Palestine and the birth of Israel
were only the beginning of what would be an eventual Israeli
occupation of the entire West Bank of the Jordan River. "I
remember thinking then that it could never happen," she
continues. "The whole idea was outrageous to me. After all,
how could one country just walk in and take over another?
There was something called international law; there were
rules to this game." She pauses. "You see," she continues,
"before I went to Beirut I had never seen a Jew or met an
Israeli, that's how sheltered and naive I was." Judging from
the events that were about to unfold, Hanan Mikhael was
even more sheltered and naive than she imagined.

CHAPTER THREE

IN EXILE

IT WAS IN 1964, after she arrived at the American University in Beirut, that Hanan first went into the refugee camps to meet Palestinians. Leila Shahid, the current PLO representative in France, a descendant of the grand mufti of Jerusalem, and a cousin of Faisal al-Husseini, a prominent Palestinian leader from East Jerusalem, became close friends with Hanan back then.

An emotional woman, Shahid suffers from asthma, a condition she attributes to the tragedies in Palestinian history. Shahid's way of coping after finishing her studies at the American University with what became a profound sadness about the fate of her people was to run away to Morocco to live a quiet academic life. The man she eventually married is a prominent writer and professor of English literature. "I used Morocco as a rest cure until it drove me crazy that I was so removed from our struggle," Shahid explains. "Until Chairman Arafat asked me to serve as the PLO representative, first in The Hague and then in Paris. I jumped at the chance because I knew I had to do something tangible to stop my people's pain."

During the sixties, when Leila and Hanan were together in Beirut, they were part of a community of exiled Palestinians. But while Leila became depressed, Hanan went into the refugee camps to distribute food, clothing, and hope. "She was one of those people," Shahid says about Hanan, "who rose to every occasion. But then, she was more used to hardship than I was since she had grown up under occupation."

It was also during those years in Beirut that Hanan cemented a friendship with the ABC television bureau chief, Peter Jennings. It was a relationship that some say was a love affair and others claim was just a mutually convenient friendship between a war correspondent caught up in the turmoil of the Middle East and an outspoken feminist anxious to further her people's cause as well as her own personal liberation. Whatever the basis of the relationship, there was no doubt that Hanan, given her intellectual and physical attributes, stood out from most of the other foreign students studying at the American University. Fluent in English, articulate, and full of self-confidence, Hanan Mikhael in her habitual miniskirt was the ideal source the dashing correspondent used as his expert on Palestinian affairs. Hanan says of Jennings, "We were both unencumbered adults so there was nothing clandestine about our relationship, and even now Peter and I remain good friends."

During the years when Hanan was in Beirut, making contacts that would endure throughout the years and learning firsthand about the suffering of the Palestinian refugee, the PLO began emerging as an important factor in the struggle. Even in the beginning there were divisions, with factions that were loyal to different Arab countries: some under the auspices of Nasser and Egyptian influence, others linked to Syria who supported a rival group of *fedayeen,* Palestinian guerrillas led by one of the heads of Syrian Army intelligence, Col. Ahmad Sweidani. Coincidentally, it was in Beirut that an agent for Sweidani was approached by a group of men who had formed a movement of their own, which they called the Movement for the Liberation of Palestine. These new leaders had all been expelled from their homes in Jaffa, Haifa, and Jerusalem. Their names were Yasir Arafat, Salah Khalaf, Khalil al-Wazir, Khalid al-Hassan, Farouq Qaddoumi, Wuhayr al-Alami, Kamal Adwan, and Muhammad Yusef. While the original concept of the movement was a collective leadership, before many months passed Yasir Arafat emerged as their leader.

As rumblings of war approached, Hanan and her sister Nadia, also studying in Beirut, were recruited by the Lebanese Army to make camouflage nets. "I remember making those nets and one day looking at my sister who was always making the nets and laughing. This was our contribution to the war effort on behalf of the Palestinian people—making camouflage nets for the Lebanese Army!"

When war finally broke out, Hanan, along with her sister and other foreign students, spent the six days in the basement of the Student Center at the American University. Listening to Radio Egypt, Radio Jordan, and Radio Syria, the group heard only reports of the glorious victory of the Arab armies as they defeated the Israelis. According to the broadcasts it was just a matter of days before all of Palestine would be liberated. "The audacity of such a tremendous lie!" Hanan says twenty-six years later. "In a sense, it diminished my idea of the whole system of government, raising people's hopes and then dashing them like that. After it was all over, I didn't know what to be more angry about, the defeat or the lies." It was only when a fellow student, an American, came down to the basement where everybody had been hiding that Hanan learned the truth. "He told us not to believe anything we heard on the radio because the war was already over. In fact, the war had been over from the first day, when the Israelis completely finished off the Egyptian Air Force."

The reaction among the foreign students in the basement

was at first disbelief and then despair, with the exception of one student, a Lebanese Phalangist (member of the Lebanese Christian centrist party headed by the Gemayel family). "I'll never forget the way he looked at me," Hanan recalls, "and said that now that the Palestinians couldn't go home, it solved the problem of finding domestic help in Lebanon. At least for his mother a big problem was solved." Hanan's memory of what happened next is unclear except that a Syrian student, Adnan, suddenly picked up a sugar bowl to throw at the Phalangist. "He hit him with the sugar bowl," Hanan continues. "I was shocked, but I remember sugar flying all over the place; all my images of that time, every disappointment, were all over that room in the form of sticky, crunchy sugar."

Worse than the insult was the fear that back home in Ramallah, the Mikhael family had not survived those six days of war. Apparently both Hanan and Nadia had heard that the family house had been destroyed and everybody in it killed. "We couldn't talk about the possibility of what had happened in Ramallah," Hanan says. "It was just too painful to address. Each of us had heard the same story and neither of us wanted to talk about it with the other. We couldn't get in touch with people; we couldn't call because the telephone lines were all down. Eventually we were able to call Huda, who was in the States, but she didn't know anything either. We stood in line at the Red Cross because obviously everybody wanted news of their family. Finally we sent a message through my uncle's wife, who was in America, who got a message back to us through the American Counsel that while our house in Ramallah had been shelled, nobody had been injured and the house hadn't collapsed." Hanan pauses. "Six days can be a lifetime if you don't know if your family is dead or alive."

Hanan's reaction to the events that took place after the 1967 war was not uncommon among the more elite and educated second-generation Palestinians growing up on the West Bank under Jordanian rule. Between 1967 and 1970, there was a movement in the refugee camps in Lebanon that the people called an Intifada, which, literally translated from the Arabic, was a "shaking off" or an "awakening." Contrary to the definition that denotes a more cerebral process, in both instances, the Intifada was a physical rejection of occupation or subjugation. Suddenly there were half a million Palestinians who had always accepted their status as second-class citizens or permanent guests throughout the Arab world, with no authority over their own lives. It was only after the defeat of the Arabs by the Israelis that attitudes changed.

THE END OF the Six Day War in 1967 also marked the end of the dream of a united Arab world, which included the total destruction of the State of Israel. But as the rest of the Arab world seemed resigned to defeat, a group of young Palestinian intellectuals, in an effort to revitalize the movement, joined the ranks of the PLO. While these young revolutionaries were ideologically bound to the PLO and prepared to die for the cause of liberating Palestine, they also rebelled against oppressive Arab societies. It was because of the inherent weakness in Lebanon, with its many fragmented ruling parties and family rivalries, that Beirut became the center for these left-wing fighters. Not unlike the left-wing radicals who emerged in the United States during the sixties, Palestinian intellectuals came to use Beirut as the center for free expression. It was during that period in Beirut that Hanan came to believe that all Palestinians—whether they were in exile, in universities, or in refugee camps—were held together by a series of tragedies that translated into a collective fate. "The only way we survived as a people," she says, "was to suffer our plight as a nation, which meant that it made no difference if I came from a rich family or a refugee camp. A Palestinian is a

Palestinian." Just as Yasir Arafat came along at the right time, when Palestinians were refugees waiting for a handout of beans and rice from the United Nations, and transformed them into revolutionaries willing to die for their cause, Hanan came along at the right time to change the image of those revolutionaries or terrorists into a people prepared to negotiate for their cause. "We were denied for so long," Hanan says, "not only our land but our identity, that the blood of those innocent victims who died during our acts of revolution are on the hands of the Jews and other Western nations, not solely on ours. And because all Palestinians are equal, an academic such as myself has as much importance as any of our martyrs who committed those revolutionary acts."

During those years, while Hanan was still at the American University, her early affiliations with the PLO were with the Democratic Front for the Liberation of Palestine (DFLP), a pro-Soviet, pro-Socialist faction with Marxist-Leninist ideology. Established in 1969 by Nayef Hawatme as a result of a split with George Habash's Popular Front for the Liberation of Palestine (PFLP), the DFLP advocated violence as a means of achieving a Palestinian state. In its history the DFLP has committed major terrorist attacks on civilians, the most infamous being at Ma'alot in Israel in 1974, in which twenty-five Israeli schoolchildren were killed and sixty-six injured. What is significant is that as recently as 1988, when Hanan was making her media debut on ABC's *Nightline,* Nayef Hawatme coordinated nine separate terrorist attacks on civilians in Israel.*

On April 21, 1989, Hawatme made a statement to Reuters

---

*On February 23 a three-man DFLP squad was intercepted by the Israelis as they made their way toward a Tel Aviv beach; on March 2 five DFLP members made their way to Zarit, a civilian farming community in the Galilee; and on June 4 a three-man DFLP team headed toward Kibbutz Misgav Am armed with Kalashnikov assault rifles, LAW rockets, grenades, and other explosives.

in Damascus that PLO leaders, meeting in Tunis, had agreed to coordinate future raids against Israel. "This agreement was endorsed by the presence of all factions of the PLO including Yasir Arafat's Fatah," Hawatme claimed. Speaking in Abu Dhabi one month later, on May 21, Hawatme again declared, "We have recently launched a series of attacks against Israel and we will launch more. Such attacks are a sacred right for our people." Following her appearance on *Nightline* and in her capacity as spokesperson for the PLO, Hanan responded to those attacks committed by Hawatme and the DFLP by stating, "While I am against terrorism and the harming of innocent civilians, actions taken in the Occupied Territories for the purpose of liberating Palestine fall under a different heading. You have to realize that Palestinians are like children; when they are ignored, they will do anything to get attention, even negative attention."

In 1969 a grassroots movement began where Palestinians wanted to go "home," back to Palestine, a sentiment that evoked tremendous support throughout the Arab world. In a show of solidarity with the residents of fifteen different refugee camps throughout Lebanon, Hanan took to the streets of Beirut in a peaceful demonstration. "We wanted to get out from under the Lebanese authorities," she explains. "We wanted to run our own lives and make our own committees, organize courses for people, exactly what happened during the Intifada in the Occupied Territories. Suddenly we had a sense of self-determination through those grassroots committees." Predictably, the Lebanese—as the Jordanians did in 1970—resisted the Palestinians' taking charge of their own political destiny. "The first thing that happens when there's a collective political assertion," Hanan states, "is a confrontation with the local authorities within the state itself. In that case it was the Lebanese authorities."

It was in the fall of 1969, during the first conference of

the General Union of Palestinian Students (GUPS), held in Amman, that Hanan Mikhael first met Yasir Arafat. Later, she would claim that he impressed her as the "first real leader the Palestinians ever had." Chosen as the spokesperson for a Lebanese chapter of GUPS, Hanan was the only woman present during that conference. While it was her initial experience as a spokesperson for the Palestinian cause, it was also the first time that a woman had represented the PLO; the event was a harbinger of things to come. With many conflicting factions and other militant and diverse groups emerging within the PLO, Hanan had her first taste of debating under conditions of extreme pressure.

After graduating from the American University in 1969, Hanan jumped at the opportunity to study at the University of Virginia. "The irony is that, had it not been for the sixty-seven war when I couldn't go back home and was forced to continue studying in America," Hanan says, "I probably would have become a doctor and not an English major." While her father would take her on rounds with him to different towns throughout the West Bank, he was the first person to discourage her from becoming a doctor. Drawing on his own experiences, he would always warn that medicine was a profession that consumed twenty-four hours of every day, a life that would permit little time for friends and family. Given Hanan's life now and limited personal time, her father's words seem almost prophetic of what would be her fate regardless of which profession she chose. "I listened to my father and became an academic and still spend twenty-four hours a day consumed by my work," she says with a small smile before adding, "but my interest in Chaucer and Beowulf came gradually, since I kept hanging on to this thing about alleviating pain." It was actually Daoud who nurtured his daughter in her passion for literature and her talent for writing, encouraging her to keep a notebook to record her thoughts and impressions derived from all the books she constantly read. "It was like that old Victorian habit of keeping a commonplace book," Hanan explains, "and writing down everything read or experienced. My father always showed a special interest in everything I wrote."

Still, Hanan majored in physics at the American University in Beirut and won many academic prizes not only in science but also in language. "And then suddenly," she says, "while I was still in Beirut, I decided that science was too abstract and too detached, while in the English Department, I had all these brilliant professors who made everything so human. I loved English literature, and it was so easy for me to write papers, both in English and Arabic. I loved language, expression, playing with words, creating words, living through books. It gave me a different perspective on life."

Despite Hanan's appreciation for English literature, her scholarship in Virginia was in the Science Department. Arriving in Virginia from Beirut, she began taking a variety of science courses until several months later, her undergraduate adviser, Marcus Smith, wondered what she was doing studying science given her excellent verbal and written skills. It was Smith who encouraged Hanan to switch her major to English. "I did something very pedantic," Hanan confesses, "because I have these two streaks, creative and imaginative, abstract and human. But I began dating manuscripts, folios, and quartos, cutting sheets, folding them, looking closely at texts. And through that," she continues, "I discovered a whole new world and new language, Old English. What I loved most about it was the sense of exploration of yet another unknown. It was almost scientific to be able to research something by following one clue after another to get to a certain conclusion." In 1973 Hanan was awarded a Ph.D. in Textural Criticism. All that was left was to return home.

From the end of the 1967 war, it took Hanan seven years

to get permission from the Israelis to come back to Ramallah. "What I found most ironic was that I needed permission from the people who were illegally occupying my land to return home." Eventually, when Hanan did manage to return, it was under a law that the Israelis called "family reunion," bringing back those Palestinians who had been stranded out of the country when the war broke out and who were finally able to apply for a visa to be reunited with their families. "In a sense, getting home was a quest," Hanan explains, "even though people in the States would constantly ask me why I didn't accept any of the teaching positions that were offered to me. My response was always the same, that I needed and wanted to go home." And home was always Ramallah. "Not that I didn't want to get something out of my studies," she continues, "because obviously I did, but my ultimate goal was to go back. It was a right that I had no intention of relinquishing."

When Hanan finally did go back, she found her father as vehemently against Israeli occupation as he had been against Jordanian. Daoud Mikhael was no different from most Palestinians born before 1948 who were old enough to remember the Arab rejection of the First Partition, which provided for a Palestinian state alongside what had been declared Israel. These were the same Palestinians who had lived through the defeat in 1967—when Israel preempted an Arab attack and went on to take over the West Bank and Gaza Strip—many of whom currently comprise what is called the "rejectionist front," those who still remain opposed to any two-state solution. Despite Hanan's ready admission that she learned everything about the history of Israeli occupation from her father, she nonetheless takes credit for changing Daoud's views when it came to the practicality of a two-state solution. According to Hanan, she spent long hours convincing her father that there was no other viable option than Israel and

Palestine existing side by side on that small, disputed piece of land. Hanan insists that, at the end of his life, her father finally accepted the reality of Israel when he came to believe that sharing the land was better than having none at all. At least that way the incentive was for his children and grandchildren, who deserved more than a legacy of anger and deprivation to be handed down from generation to generation. "It became clear that the only people who could stop that cycle of revenge and retribution were us, the victims," Hanan says carefully, "and in the end, when my father was still lucid, he understood."

What Hanan considers a sign of maturity and courage is that not only her father but a majority of the members of the PNC voted in 1988 to accept a two-state solution, which amounts to another way of finally accepting the existence of the State of Israel. In fact, several months after her father's death, Hanan wrote an article for an underground newspaper on the West Bank, in which she addressed the issue of what she called the "bottom line."

"What I wrote was that conditions for a Palestinian state are considerably less than what was offered and rejected in 1947. Of course in retrospect we made a big mistake, and one that we tried and failed to rectify over the years, which is probably why certain people consider that my father was a hard-liner, because he never gave up the dream until he realized he was perpetuating a nightmare."

There are some Israelis who claim that Daoud Mikhael remained a hard-liner until his death. Hanan disagrees adamantly. "My father *is* against violence, just like I'm against violence," she says and stops. "Funny, how I always refer to him in the present even though he's dead, but maybe that's because he's always with me." She begins again. "My father *was* against violence," she corrects, "even though he *was* also committed to Palestine." Other Israelis go even further, insisting that underneath Hanan's own moderate facade and intellectual exterior lurks a hard-liner as well. The argument remains that despite all the words and rhetoric, she represents a terrorist organization that has changed neither its covenant nor its leader, a man identified with countless terrorist attacks.

Before Arafat became Rabin's partner in peace, Hanan consistently defended his continuing leadership of the Palestinian people. Ever the academic, Hanan was careful to admit that no one really knew the extent of alienation between those Palestinians living under occupation and those living in exile throughout the world. Ever the spokesperson, she talked about the PLO as a united entity always with Arafat as its leader. And ever the diplomat, she described the democratic process from within the structure that allowed Arafat to remain in power and his policies to remain in practice by the will of the people. Specifically, when the United States and Israel insisted that the PLO, given its history of terrorism, not be represented at the negotiating table, Hanan claimed that their involvement was a sovereign right of the Palestinian people, not to be tampered with by outside entities. Battling to include the PLO at the conference table, Hanan made an emotional plea:

> It is not Yasir Arafat who is forcing himself on his people, it is the people who want the PLO involved. Abu Ammar [Arafat's *nom de guerre*] is perfectly prepared to step aside should the people judge him to be an impediment to the peace process. But those making decisions are the Zionists and certain Americans under the influence of the Jewish lobby in Washington. Abu Ammar said something very important at the last PNC about how his main concern wasn't to protect or guarantee the future of the PLO but rather the well-being of the Palestinian people who, in the final analysis,

are the decision makers. What is critical is that Abu Ammar knows that the PLO was created by the Palestinian people out of a need at the time, which means if a new phase emerges which produces a different need, a new PLO will emerge.

It would be difficult to imagine a more articulate spokesperson than Hanan when it comes to offering a new perspective on the Palestinian struggle. Again, before the signing of the peace accord between Israel and the PLO, Hanan spoke mostly in abstractions. "People think in images," she began:

I left this food on this table; I set this table and went out for a walk; I left the electricity on because I thought we would only be gone for the day; I left a message for my child that the key was under such and such a stone. People think in concrete images—a stone in a wall, a specific dish on the table or a tree on their land, how they left, where they went—because it's very hard to be kicked out of your own house and off your own land. But now the Palestinian commitment has changed, where it's one of national identity and not an identity with a house or a key. And that is precisely what the PLO and Arafat have done for the Palestinian people, replaced the dish on the table by offering them a sense of belonging and a feeling of dignity. It's because of Abu Ammar that we aren't scattered and lost, because of him that there's a unifying sense of nationalism of belonging to a nation instead of a house, which all gets back to our changing image.

Yasir Arafat couldn't have come up with a better person to project that changing image than Hanan. Yet, there are others within the hierarchy of the PLO who dispute the notion of any premeditated plan.

Nabil Shaath is a charming and brilliant man who is a close adviser to Yasir Arafat and who currently heads the Palestinian delegation to the peace conference. A successful businessman who runs a consulting firm in Cairo, he began his career as a professor of business management at the University of Pennsylvania's Wharton School. On the subject of "image," Shaath smiles when he insists that the PLO didn't write a job description for a spokesperson. "Wanted," he says in mock seriousness. "Woman, Christian, articulate, to change the image of a group of freedom fighters into intellectuals to satisfy the Occidental world." Shaath maintains it was less a question of changing an image than it was of readapting to a new world order and an increasingly intransigent Israeli position. According to Shaath, Hanan is not a new "discovery" but rather someone who has been in the political fray for her entire career, both as a lecturer who represented Palestinians at international peace conferences and as a feminist who represented Palestinian women at international seminars. "After years of making the wrong choices," Shaath says, "let's just say we got lucky this time when we found someone with Hanan's talent." And, on the subject of Hanan's Christianity, Shaath admits that it is unquestionably easier for a Christian woman to travel around the world than for a Muslim one. "Granted," Shaath says, "there's a chemistry between Hanan and the American people, where the typical white Anglo-Saxon Christian from Middle America can identify better with her than with a woman in *chador*."

By her own admission, more than luck, experience, talent, or religion, the most important factor in Hanan's success is her marriage to a man who made it possible for her to concentrate on her career and make a contribution to the Palestinian cause.

CHAPTER FOUR

EMIL

THEY WERE MARRIED at Saint George's Church in East Jerusalem on August 8, 1975. Nobody bothered to send out the traditional invitations or wedding cards, as is the custom in any Christian ceremony throughout the world. Instead they just called up a few close friends at the last minute and invited them to witness the event. The bride wore beige, as did the groom—she in an ankle-length beige dress with a matching floppy hat; he in beige corduroys, workshirt, and rumpled beige jacket. To their surprise, 650 people showed up. The bride said the crowd came because they didn't believe they would actually go through with the wedding; the groom claimed everybody came because they did believe it and wanted to demonstrate their solidarity and support. Both were correct, since it was no secret that bride and groom were fundamentally against the institution of marriage itself: The whole concept was ridiculous to them. While the marriage of Hanan Mikhael and Emil Ashrawi was the wedding of the year in the Middle East, the bride went on to become the woman of the decade, the next two decades. But back on that summer Friday morning in East Jerusalem, it was beyond the realm of anybody's imagination that the slim, dark-haired, twenty-nine-year-old woman would someday cross the Allenby Bridge from Jericho to Amman to be transported to Madrid and onto the world stage of legitimate causes.

After the wedding ceremony there was a family lunch at the Ashrawi house, a white stone structure inside Saint George's Greek Orthodox Convent in the Old City of Jerusalem, where Emil and his siblings grew up. After lunch the couple left to finish painting the dingy apartment they had rented near the center of Ramallah and discovered to their dismay that it was infested by an army of cockroaches. Their wedding night was spent battling the bugs until finally, early the following morning, they departed for Gaza, where they had decided to spend an abbreviated honeymoon on the beach, away from family, phones, and responsibilities. Hanan's uncle, her father's brother, a prominent dentist in Ramallah, had reserved the honeymoon suite for them in a modest beachfront hotel. Neither Hanan nor Emil owned a car, and neither earned enough money back then to rent one. Adamant about spending only what they could afford, they declined Daoud's offer to borrow his luxury sedan for the drive to Gaza. Instead, they took a *sharoot,* one of those stretch Mercedes taxis that picked up ten or twelve people and made as many stops along the way.

When Hanan and Emil finally arrived, they were not only exhausted from the trip but were wearing the same dirty work clothes they had worn all night. While the clerk at the hotel indeed had a reservation in the name of Ashrawi, he had trouble believing that the two scruffy people who stood before him were that couple.

FROM THE BEGINNING of their marriage, there was a conscious decision on both Hanan's and Emil's parts not to play the traditional roles of husband and wife, dominant and passive. "Gender doesn't determine role," Hanan says nineteen years later, "except for the sex act and giving birth." She always insisted that her husband wouldn't have a traditional male ego or care about who earned more money. That was fortunate, since when they married, Hanan, as dean of the Faculty of Arts at Bir Zeit University, earned far more than Emil, who had only started his job as a photographer for the UN several months earlier, on February 19. The couple's approach to marriage was an anathema on the West Bank, as was the fact that Emil was five years younger, from a less prestigious family, and far less educated.

Given the hard financial times throughout the Occupied Territories, Emil never had the opportunity to finish his university studies but rather left after two years, earning only an associate degree in business administration. This qualified him for a job as a clerk at the Barclay's Bank in East Jerusalem, where he remained for five unhappy years, from 1969 until 1973, when he quit. "I couldn't see myself working in a bank, it was too stifling." Through a friend Emil applied for a job with the UN Truce Supervision Organization. "When I got there, they told me that unfortunately they had nothing in an office, only an opening in the photography section." It was exactly what Emil wanted, the freedom to travel around the country and take photographs, even if they were official rather than creative. "Life doesn't scare my husband," Hanan explains, "which is why I married him. Actually, I was convinced that I would remain single because it was so difficult to find a liberated man in that part of the world and I was determined to work—there was so much I had to do here. When I met Emil I knew that he was not only a wonderful person but someone with enough self-confidence to make it work. He's secure enough to live with an aggressive woman, which makes ours the perfect relationship."

There were many people, however, who were shocked by the couple's unconventional way of life. "We knew people viewed us as odd, but for us the important thing was that

Emil was never jealous of my professional activities," Hanan continues, "because he always had his own friends and interests." She smiles slightly. "You know, at the time I met Emil, his mother wanted him to marry an eighteen-year-old who would have no other occupation except to care for the house and have lots of children. When he married me, I would say that he picked the extreme opposite."

Emil describes his mother as having many traits commonly attributed to a typical Jewish mother: spending her entire life working for her family, expressing her pride in them, worrying about them, and telling them constantly how much she loved and admired them. An attractive woman who looks younger than her sixty-seven years, Salwa Ashrawi has dark reddish hair, carefully coiffed and colored, beautiful deep-set green eyes, and a lively sense of humor. If Salwa resents anything during her life, it was less the many wars and losses that she has endured than her own family making her leave school in what was the equivalent of seventh grade. Having taught herself English, when her son first married Hanan she used to question her daughter-in-law about the meaning of certain words. While Salwa is extremely intelligent, Emil has always maintained that the reason the relationship between his wife and mother has never been particularly close is the vast cultural differences between the two women.

Salwa Ashrawi's house is modest even by Old City standards. It sits in a courtyard crammed near several other houses, and separated from them by alleys leading to porticos that open onto vast courtyards. (Reconstruction of the ancient monastery has been in progress for several years, with artisans working to restore the stone walls and clay tiles.) The front door opens into a narrow hallway leading to two small bedrooms, and another door leads to the kitchen, which is next to a living room. Two brown-plaid-upholstered sofas line both sides of the room. The only window is built high on the wall and faces the back of the house of an Orthodox Jewish family. While there is little natural sunlight on even the brightest of days, when her neighbors block the window with a *sukkah* (branch-roofed hut or arbor erected for Sukkoth, the Jewish holiday that corresponds with the fall harvest) the only light comes from a dim ceiling fixture. And when those same neighbors refuse to move their chicken coops away from Salwa's window, there is little relief from either the smell or the noise.

Affixed to a living room wall are images of Jesus Christ surrounding an embroidery that says in Arabic, "I have seen times changing where neither happiness nor sadness lasts." On several shelves in a corner of the room is a collection of family photographs, including one of Emil on his wedding day, standing next to his bride. What is interesting is that among the collection of photographs of Salwa's sons and daughters and their families, the daughter-in-law who now meets with kings, presidents, and other dignitaries is not given any more prominence than the others. Having personally suffered as a Palestinian from the disastrous political decisions made by those kings, presidents, and other dignitaries, perhaps Salwa Ashrawi is simply not impressed.

In 1947 and 1948, during the two years of armed conflict between Jews and Arabs, Salwa lived with her husband, mother-in-law, and newborn baby, Sondra, in a small house in Jerusalem in front of Saint George's Cathedral near the Damascus Gate and the Russian Compound. One day, at noon, a mortar crashed down on the house over the kitchen, and Salwa took her baby, grabbing only some diapers, to escape with her husband and mother-in-law to the Old City. A friend arranged for the family to take refuge inside the Armenian Convent, in a room in the London Jewish Society School, which at the time belonged to the Christs Church.

Israeli soldiers shooting tear-gas canisters at students at Bir Zeit University. *(Courtesy Zoom)*

Albert Agazarian with soldiers at the entrance to Bir Zeit University, July 1983. *(Courtesy Zoom)*

Hanan Ashrawi and
Albert Agazarian
at Bir Zeit
University, 1986.
(Courtesy Zoom)

The Ashrawi family. *Left to right:* Emil, Zeina, Hanan, and Amal.
(Courtesy Zoom)

A student protest at Bir Zeit University. *(Courtesy Zoom)*

Students in a makeshift campus on the grounds after the closure of
Bir Zeit University. *(Courtesy Zoom)*

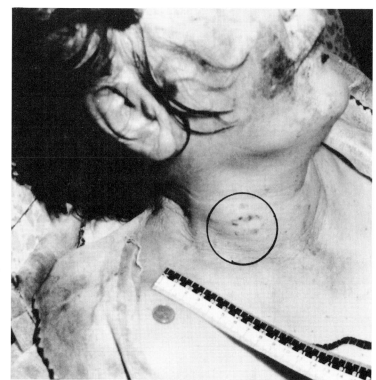

A police photograph of Dora Lempick,* murdered in her kitchen near Gaza. *(Courtesy Shin Bet)*

Downtown Ramallah. *(Barbara Victor)*

The Civil Administration Building in Ramallah,
viewed from Ashrawi's house. *(Barbara Victor)*

The music room in Ashrawi's house on Radio Street in Ramallah.
(Barbara Victor)

Bethlehem under curfew, 1992. *(Barbara Victor)*

Children in Gaza, January 1993. *(Courtesy Zoom)*

Israeli and Palestinian Women for Peace on Women's Day, 1991.
Left to right: Ashrawi, Nomi Chazan (minister, Knesset, Meretz Party),
Shulamit Aloni (minister, Knesset, Meretz Party). *(Courtesy Zoom)*

The Friends School, Ramallah. *(Barbara Victor)*

A Fatah protest, October 1992. *(Courtesy Zoom)*

Israeli settlers throwing stones in Ramallah. *(Courtesy Zoom)*

"After we were there a few days," Salwa remembers, "a man came to ask me if I wanted a cupboard for my things." She shakes her head. "I told him that it wasn't necessary since I had nothing, I owned nothing, I had no clothes."

Emil and his two brothers, Ibrahim and Samir, were born in that tiny room in Christs Church, while two more daughters, Nano and Samira, were born after the war when the family managed to rent the house where Salwa still lives, within the walls of Saint George's Greek Convent. Only after 1967 did Salwa go back to visit her original home, which she had left along with everything that the family owned. "My heart cried at that moment," she says, "because all our possessions were just left for strangers who found it ready to occupy." While Salwa didn't dare to ring the bell, she peeked inside the glass-enclosed entrance and noticed that the house had been divided to accommodate four separate Jewish families. "I will never forget what happened in forty-eight," she says, "which is why I refused during the Six Day War in sixty-seven to leave my home again. I insisted on staying in the house regardless of what would happen. I just refused to start again from zero."

On June 6, 1967, when the Six Day War broke out, Salwa remained in her house, refusing to leave even when Israeli soldiers came to the door for entry to the roof, which they used as a lookout. But while Salwa stayed at home with her husband, mother-in-law, and four of her children, Samir—her oldest son—happened to be visiting relatives in Ramallah. As bombs exploded and armies exchanged gunfire, all Salwa could think about was how to get Samir back home. "I ran out into the street, and the police stopped me, asking if I was crazy to go outside in the middle of a war. They made me take cover in a flower shop, where I waited from eleven in the morning until three in the afternoon. Finally I just left. It made no difference to me if I died in the flower shop or in the street. I wanted to go home, and, more, I wanted my son there too."

When Salwa returned to the house that afternoon, she found that Samir was still in Ramallah, obviously unable to make it back to Jerusalem on foot. As Emil and his brother Ibrahim watched their mother grow increasingly upset, suffering for her missing son and unable to eat, finally, without telling anyone, they decided that Ibrahim would set out on foot for Ramallah to bring Samir back home. "Can you imagine?!" Salwa asks now. "Not one son out of the house but two. When Emil told me what Ibrahim had done, that he was walking all the way to Ramallah in the middle of a war to bring his brother home, I fainted. I just couldn't take it." The following day both brothers appeared, having walked all the way back from Ramallah. "I was so angry," Salwa remembers. "How could they dare do that to me?" Emil remembers the scene very well. "Mother waited only long enough to yell at them before she ran to the Greek Orthodox Church across from our home to kneel at the door in prayer."

Emil claims not to remember the parts of his childhood that are connected with political events throughout the Occupied Territories. Those memories that he has been unable to forget, however, he claims are the reasons why he embraces pacifism almost as a religion. His most vivid recollection is walking from town to town in the aftermath of the Six Day War and seeing bodies strewn along the roads. Yet, despite the enormous losses suffered on all sides after the swift Israeli victory in 1967, for Emil life changed throughout the Occupied Territories, producing very mixed emotions. "Even at the beginning," he says, "there was a social and intellectual aspect of Israeli occupation that I sensed would be positive. For some reason I had the feeling that those expressions I had always dreamed about that had to do with music, social relationships, even architecture, would finally change for the better."

A child of the sixties, Emil was a believer in Gandhi and

flower power, a fan of John Lennon. Consumed by the arts, Emil had always had his heart set on a career as an actor, singer, musician, or photographer. While he always managed to take photographs, he was also forced to work at odd jobs while going to night school to supplement the family income. There were ten people to feed in the Ashrawi family, including his grandmother, who remained with the family until she died in 1972 at the age of ninety-three. All Palestinians have at least one family story or legacy concerning their experiences living under the many different occupying forces. For Emil his grandmother's experiences epitomize the Ashrawi family's suffering.

Nayfeh Ashrawi lost her entire family—with the exception of Emil's father—during a ten-year span. Her husband, Emil's grandfather, was hanged by the Turks, while one daughter succumbed to the plague, another died in a drowning accident, and finally one son committed suicide. Emil's father, Sam'an, Nayfeh's only surviving child, was separated from his mother and lost during one of the sieges of Jerusalem. While Sam'an ended up in a British-run orphanage, where he lived for fifteen years, Nayfeh went to work as a cook for a British officer in Jerusalem. In the course of a conversation with her employer, she mentioned that although she had lost her husband and three children, she had been searching for another son whom she believed was still alive. After several months of inquiries, the boy was finally found and reunited with his mother. Sam'an Ashrawi—educated in a vocational school, where he studied business administration—eventually went to work as a clerk for the United Nations Relief and Works Agency (UNRWA), which, among its other activities, remains responsible for the refugee camps within the Occupied Territories.

IN 1969 Emil begged his father for permission to leave Jerusalem for a while to travel around the Arab world. It would be his last chance before settling down with his own family responsibilities. It might also be the last chance before another war broke out. With a knapsack on his back, a guitar slung over one shoulder, and sporting a heavy beard, Emil set off for Lebanon, Jordan, and Egypt to investigate theater in other cities. In Egypt, however, his travels ended. "I was picked up, detained for nine hours at the airport, and then summarily thrown out of the country," Emil recalls. "I'll probably never know why, since all I had with me were some letters from actors inviting me to visit their theaters in Cairo, my guitar, and some shirts and underwear in my suitcase." Returning to Jerusalem via Beirut, Emil took the first job he found, in Barclay's Bank, and spent unhappy days dreaming about his missed opportunities in the arts. Emil's only outlet back then was music, and it was his fierce need to do something creative that gave him the idea to form a rock group with his brothers, equally dissatisfied with their jobs. They named the group the Blooms—a literal translation from the Arabic, Emil explains, having to do with flowers blooming. Playing lead guitar, mostly Beatles and Rolling Stones tunes or straight Western rock-and-roll, the Blooms performed at weddings and parties all over the West Bank. It was in 1970, however, that the Blooms changed their repertoire to play protest songs in Arabic, words and music patterned after Joan Baez. The political climate throughout the Occupied Territories was increasingly tense, a situation that made life difficult not only for the Palestinians living under Israeli occupation but also for Palestinians in Jordan. Before long it became evident that a confrontation between them and King Hussein was about to take place. Neither protest songs nor outside political intervention could change the climate of war that was spreading from the East Bank of the Jordan River to the West Bank, under Israeli control.

Yasir Arafat's faction of the PLO, al-Fatah, had set up a

state-within-a-state on the southern portion of land between the East and West Banks of the Jordan River, an area that became known as "Fatahland." Many Palestinians, including Emil's future father-in-law, Daoud Mikhael, believed that King Hussein would rather have abdicated than incur the wrath of what amounted to 60 percent of his population— those Palestinians living within his Hashemite kingdom—by moving against the PLO, which was camping on the banks of the Jordan River.

A complicated series of political events and cross-alliances came into play, involving the United States, Egypt, Iraq, and Jordan, culminating in a proposal aimed at persuading the Israelis to relinquish control of the West Bank to Jordan. The outcome of that particular political maneuver, however, was merely a contributing factor to what would become a bloody September 1970 for the PLO, a month known forever as "Black September," when King Hussein finally made his move against the organization.

If any one group was to blame for incurring the king's wrath, it was a radical faction of the PLO that embarked on a campaign of terror in the name of the Palestinian cause. In the years that followed George Habash's creation of PFLP in 1968, the group gained notoriety for their bloody attacks on Israeli and Western aircraft. The first operation was the hijacking of a TWA aircraft en route from Rome to Tel Aviv on July 22, 1968. After takeoff from Rome, the plane was forced to fly to Algiers and land there, bringing the Palestinian struggle into the international spotlight for the first time. A year later another hijacking occurred, a Lufthansa 747 en route from New Delhi to Athens. Coincidentally, among the passengers on that flight was Joseph Kennedy, Jr., the son of Robert Kennedy, which only made the hijacking that much more newsworthy. The most spectacular terrorist attack implemented by the PFLP, however, occurred on September 6,

1970, and served as the last straw for the Jordanian High Command, whose patience was already strained by the un-invited Palestinian guests on their soil.

Three planes were hijacked simultaneously and destroyed after their passengers had been allowed to disembark. A Pan Am jumbo jet was blown up at Beirut Airport, while a TWA aircraft and one belonging to Swissair were both forced down at Dawson's Field, a deserted airstrip in the Jordanian Desert. There waiting on Jordanian soil, according to plan, were more PFLP terrorists. At the end of a day's work, a total of three very expensive aircraft and about 600 hostages were in PFLP hands. That was the final chapter in the story, days before the massacre that was Black September began. The beginning, while not as visually spectacular, was just as dangerous.

Several months before the triple hijacking, on July 23, 1970, U.S. Secretary of State William Rogers, presented a plan to the United Nations known as the Rogers Plan. What Secretary Rogers's principles summarized was that Israel should withdraw from the West Bank, handing the territory to Jordan, which would insure the security of Israel's western border from attacks by Palestinian terrorists. Further, on Is-rael's agreement to turn over the West Bank, Egypt and Jor-dan would begin to formalize an agreement between the three countries, with Swedish diplomat Gunnar Jarring acting as UN mediator, that would be the beginning of a peace agree-ment. Surprisingly Egypt's President Nasser, while historically backing the PLO, reacted favorably to any plan that would relieve Israel of the West Bank even if the land would, once again, bypass the Palestinians for Jordan. In response to Nas-ser's position, Arafat spoke for the entire PLO, conveying to the world that the Palestinians, rather than accept any transfer of the West Bank to Jordan, would continue with their armed struggle until all of Palestine was liberated from foreign con-trol. The triple hijacking that occurred a mere two months later was apparently proof that Arafat intended to keep his promise of armed struggle. But even before that, within days of the announcement of the Rogers Plan, Nasser's agreement, and Arafat's response, Palestinian leftists took to the streets in Amman with slogans and banners condemning Nasser as a "traitor" and an "agent of American imperialism," thereby condemning themselves to the wrath of both Nasser and King Hussein.

In what turned out to be another example of Arafat's consistently faulty political judgment, the PLO leader gathered his executive committee to announce that in the event of any Jordanian offensive against the PLO, he had been assured by Iraq that seventeen thousand Iraqi troops would come to his aid. What he neglected to take into consideration, however, was that relations between Baghdad and Cairo were especially tense at that time, which meant that Nasser would have even more reason to be infuriated with Arafat for seeking Iraqi support in any clash between the PLO and Jordan. Nasser's response was swift: He sent word to King Hussein that he would not object if the king launched an offensive against Arafat's *fedayeen* positioned in Fatahland.

In early August 1970, one month before the aircraft were blown up on Dawson's Field, King Hussein began to deploy forces across the border from Israel, including all strategic areas around Amman and other Jordanian cities. Without much analysis it became clear to many Fatah officers that the main Jordanian target was not Israel but rather those Palestinians camped on the banks of the Jordan River. Preparing for battle, the Jordanians prevented the Iraqi defense minister from coming to the aid of the PLO by giving him a large cash bribe to stay out of the fighting. In response many Palestinians who were bona fide citizens of Jordan and serving in the King's army defected to the PLO after the fighting began, prompting a law that stated that any Jordanian officer or civilian on the West Bank who joined the PLO would be hanged. But despite the support of the defecting Jordanian fighters and West Bank Palestinian leaders—including Daoud Mikhael—who were in favor of launching a preemptive attack against Jordan, Arafat's confidence was waning. The PLO leader had already been warned by Nasser that any further provocation to Hussein's army would carry a high price, and without solid Iraqi support, he was loath to take on the Jordanians alone. In the end it was the Jordanian Army that attacked the PLO in Fatahland, so that by the end of September 1970, weeks after the triple hijacking, there were no more PLO bases left in Jordan.

One month after Black September ended, the Americans once again put themselves in the middle of the fray as the key to any negotiation and subsequent settlement of the problem. Drawing on the Rogers Plan again, King Hussein announced to his generals that the Americans had promised that the Jordanians could reclaim the West Bank if the fighting between them and the PLO was definitely over. According to Hussein, the Americans had further assured him that they would put sufficient pressure on the Israelis to force them to withdraw from the West Bank in return for a guarantee of security and absence of PLO terrorist attacks. In essence Jordan would get the land in return for acting as its watchman.

To the more pragmatic PLO leaders, such as Yasir Arafat, as opposed to the more radical such as George Habash, given the demographics of the Hashemite kingdom, any return of the West Bank to Jordan would ultimately mean that the territory occupied by Israel would end up in Palestinian hands. For a brief moment Arafat was prepared to salute King Hussein and his efforts to accept the Rogers Plan if a behind-the-scenes agreement could be reached whereby the West Bank would indeed be turned over to the Palestinians as the first stage of an eventual Palestinian state. Unfortu-

nately, by 1971 any influence that Secretary Rogers had enjoyed in the Middle East was over with the arrival of the
Nixon administration and Henry Kissinger. The new secretary of state wasn't interested in any Middle East peace plan.
In fact, Secretary Kissinger's only interest in the Middle East
was getting the Soviets out of Egypt. What became increasingly clear to the PLO, King Hussein, and Israel was that
Kissinger had successfully defeated any influence from William Rogers and had no intention of overseeing the return of
the West Bank to either the Jordanians or the Palestinians.

Through the entire two months of political maneuvering,
Emil Ashrawi sang protest songs, optimistic that passive resistance would force the Israelis and the Jordanians to hear
the Palestinian voice, convinced that his lyrics would give his
own people hope.

SHORTLY AFTER HANAN RETURNED from Virginia at the end
of 1972, she, along with dozens of other professors and students from Bir Zeit University, was arrested by the Israelis
for participating in a demonstration against the occupation.
Scheduled to surrender herself to the Civil Administration in
Ramallah on Christmas Day to stand trial, Hanan stayed at
home on Radio Street on Christmas Eve, receiving friends
and family who came by to offer their solidarity and support.

Hanan's sister Nadia happened to be a friend of one of
the musicians from the Blooms. Along with Samir Ashrawi,
Nadia suggested to Emil that they all go over to see Hanan
before she faced a possible jail sentence for what the authorities cited as "public disorder." (As it turned out, Hanan
never actually served time in prison but received a suspended
sentence and a fine, which the university paid.)

It wasn't love at first sight for either Hanan or Emil. In
retrospect, however, Emil admits how taken he was with her
the first time they met. "She was very beautiful," he says,

"thin and vibrant, exciting, definitely someone you couldn't ignore, especially in a miniskirt with her short hair. She looked great!" While Emil was already involved with an eighteen-year-old girlfriend, Hanan was far too consumed with politics and protests at Bir Zeit to think about her personal life. Several weeks later on New Year's Eve, once again over her protestations of having too much work, Nadia convinced Hanan to accompany her to a concert by the Blooms, succeeding only when she told her that the group would be singing protest songs. But it wasn't until after the concert, when the group went back to a friend's house for a party, that the relationship between Hanan and Emil began. "My brother convinced me to come to this New Year's Eve party as well," Emil remembers, "because, frankly, I was depressed over a fight I had had with my girlfriend. But since I had nothing else to do, I went, and ended up spending most of the evening sitting by myself in the kitchen."

The pretty young woman in a miniskirt with a cigarette in her hand wandered in for a drink of water and saw Emil sitting dejectedly at the table. "What's wrong?" she asked, pulling up a chair. "I had a fight with my girlfriend," Emil replied. They talked about politics, music, mutual friends, his problems with his girlfriend, her problems at the university, until, at midnight, they got up to dance. "We've been dancing ever since," Emil concludes.

After two years of keeping steady company, in which Emil would often spend the night in a guest room at Hanan's house on Radio Street after a date, if marriage wasn't on their minds, it was certainly on everyone else's. When the words were actually spoken, however, it was during an afternoon on which Emil came to visit Hanan, who was sick in bed with a bad cold and fever. He can't really remember what prompted the question, but he suddenly heard himself asking her if she would consider marrying him. To his surprise she jumped out of bed, threw her arms around his neck, and accepted. Even now Hanan seems amused by the memory. "It wasn't even a question of having babies," she admits, "since I never thought about it until one of my sisters had children. It just seemed like the right time to get married." What both remember is that there was a kind of mutual acceptance of an inevitability that prompted Emil to ask and Hanan to accept. "What inspired the change was simple," Emil agrees. "We loved each other and wanted to live together and in that society, we couldn't without being legally bound."

Marriage didn't change anything affecting Hanan's status with the Israeli authorities. She was still on their list of "intellectual inciters," unaware though they were that she no longer lived in her father's house on Radio Street. Even after the couple had moved into their own apartment in Ramallah, the army continued to show up at Daoud's house with summonses and subpoenas for Hanan on charges that ranged from demonstrating on campus to organizing marches throughout the West Bank. "Whenever the authorities took what they called 'preventative measures,' they would round up the same group, and I had a long record," Hanan recalls.

Daoud Mikhael was deeply concerned when it came to his daughter's ongoing battles with the Israeli authorities. "Only Nadia and I were living in Ramallah at the time," Hanan explains. "Muna, Abla, and Huda were either in America, Jordan, or Kuwait and since Nadia never gave my father anything to worry about, I was the only one who didn't make life very peaceful for him." But as the years passed, Daoud Mikhael was not the only member of Hanan's family who suffered the consequences of her involvement with the Israeli authorities. And Emil learned quickly that when it came to his wife, nothing was ever boring or predictable.

CHAPTER FIVE

A FAMILY AFFAIR

FORTUNATELY Emil Ashrawi is a tolerant man with a good sense of humor. Not only has he lost his sweaters when Hanan emptied out his drawers to distribute them to prisoners across the street but he has also witnessed his house turned into a commune. Many times during the height of the Intifada, fifty to sixty people were sleeping on couches, chairs, or in sleeping bags on the floor—released prisoners or families of prisoners waiting for them to be released. "The Israelis tend to let people go after midnight when there's a curfew in effect," Emil explains, "so if they try to make it back to their villages, the chances are that they'll be rearrested for breaking curfew." According to both Emil and Hanan, it actually reached a point at the height of the Intifada several years ago where the army would release people and automatically direct them to the Ashrawi house, recommending that they wait there until dawn. According to a spokesman for the Civil Administration in Ramallah, if prisoners were ever released at night, it was because of an overcrowding in the jail after a specific march or demonstration. Any prisoners released after curfew, according to this Israeli, were provided with a *laissez-passer* that would protect them from rearrest by the authorities. In addition, the Israelis maintain that most prisoners held in the Civil Administration Prison in Ramallah did not have a long way to go home. "I like to think of this house as a haven," Hanan continues, "not just for people coming out of jail but also for Palestinians who come to discuss their problems living under occupation."

Hanan has become a familiar figure at the gate leading to the Civil Administration Building on Radio Street, begging the soldiers on duty to allow her to pass along food and warm clothing for the Palestinians who are detained inside. Most times she is sent away, although occasionally a soldier will relent, less out of human kindness, she claims, than because she has worn him down with her persistence. Those on duty have come to realize that whenever she makes the trip across Radio Street, she is prepared to become a one-woman sit-in for as long as it takes until she gets what she wants. In the end the soldier on duty usually summons one of his commanders, with whom Hanan will begin low-level negotiations that could take all day. If the commander on duty refuses her requests, however, she has been known to demand to see everyone from the civil governor to the commanding general of the Occupied Territories.

When Hanan describes her efforts in organizing friends and neighbors on behalf of Palestinians who have been arrested, or when she talks about how her house has been transformed into a commune, her eyes light up and she glows with excitement. This is a woman born to protest, happiest when she is fighting for a cause or rallying others to join in. It is fortuitous that she lives on the West Bank, an area frozen in time in perpetual protest.

While Hanan has neither the authority nor the means to distribute money to those who have suffered the financial brunt of the Intifada, there are people, mostly women, who find her easier to approach than some of the local male leaders, who are more concerned with the military aspects of the uprising. "I've had women come here whose sons were arrested or deported or killed and who find themselves with no visible means of support," Hanan explains, "and I've had entire families come here because a neighbor's house was demolished by the army and the neighbor's family has simply moved in with them." Hanan admits that while she can't always find a solution, she tries to direct the women to the proper Palestinian agencies or at least individuals who can either mediate the problem or arrange for temporary support for those who are destitute.

Mary Hass is a Lauren Bacall–type tough and sexy woman who has survived sixty-seven years of war and occupation in the Occupied Territories. Hass always dresses in olive-drab army fatigues and sensible shoes, with a red-and-white checked *kaffiyeh* draped around her neck, the symbol of the Palestinian Communist party. Curiously, the only glaring contradiction to her "worker's" appearance are her long, tapered, blood-red fingernails. There is something glamorous about Hass, with her heavily lined face devoid of any makeup, her spectacular bone structure, black eyes, and hair pulled back in an unstylish ponytail.

Born in 1927 in Haifa, Hass, like Hanan, is an Anglican Christian, although that is where all similarity between the two women ends. Unlike Hanan, she is married to a Muslim. Her husband, Muhammad, was arrested in 1947 in Gaza by the Egyptians and brought to Tel Aviv where he was handed over to the British. Two years later he was released and left to settle in Haifa where Mary still had family. In 1967, when the West Bank fell into Israeli hands, the Hass family left Israel and went to live in Gaza. Although they had Israeli citizenship as Israeli Arabs, the entire family renounced it in 1970 in protest to the continuing Israeli occupation. Currently Hass remains an active and vocal member of the Palestinian Communist party as well as running an early-childhood-education program in Gaza connected to the

United Nations and sponsored by Norway and the American Quaker Organization. She doesn't mince words about Hanan's involvement with Palestinian women.

"Hanan was never involved in any feminist cause," Hass says simply, "unless she directly benefited from it." Her tone is vaguely sarcastic when she adds, "Oh, yes, all those photographs of Lady Hanan and Israeli feminists like Yael Dayan [Moshe Dayan's daughter and a Labor party member of the Knesset] holding hands and singing peace songs make very good television. But tell me, when did Hanan ever dirty those hands helping a hungry child or a battered woman or treating the wounded in the refugee camps?"

There is a general strike in Gaza on the day that Hass is discussing Hanan, called by local Hamas leaders. The streets are deserted except for a few official vehicles with emergency passes pasted on their windshields. Hass drives one of them. Accelerating around a large mud slide in what was once a residential neighborhood, where a group of children now splash barefoot through the icy puddles, Hass comments, "This is the reality of occupation, and not those fancy leaders who talk on television or who sit on the Riviera and discuss peace accords." As she drives Hass compares Hanan to the idle rich women who tend to charitable causes more to fill their own egos or days than to better the lives of others. "The first of those Lady Bountifuls were the women who came here during the British Mandate," she says, "and gave tea parties for the poor, another version of the let-them-eat-cake ladies who pretended to care because they thought it would keep the natives quiet." Her black eyes glitter. "This business about liberating our land along with our women is bullshit," she announces. "It's shameful when an upper-class woman like Hanan takes over the role of the faithful in our refugee camps. For me it's an honor to represent the real Palestinian women, and Hanan is not counted among them."

Hass goes on to describe Hanan as an American creation:

a Christian Palestinian woman in a vocal position who gives the impression that she has the sanction of the majority, as if she speaks for everyone in what remains a male-dominated, Muslim society. Or as if she is an example of how women live and are treated in that culture. "The other day an old man in one of the camps murdered his own daughter because she was raped," Hass begins, "and while he suffers, a young girl is dead."

Although several Western feminists have traveled to the Occupied Territories to interview Palestinian women on their changing role in society since the Intifada, their contacts were mostly within the confines of academia and the more educated and culturally elite, making their conclusions far from the reality. Contrary to what these women have written or reported, Hass and other Palestinians who work in the refugee camps maintain that the Intifada has not liberated the average woman to new heights of economic and sexual freedom. Given the spread of Islamic fundamentalism throughout the West Bank and Gaza, more women are wearing long gowns and covering their heads with *chadors* or scarves. If there has been a change for women since the eruption of the Intifada, it is that more women are forced to take on the responsibility of the family in those cases in which the men are either imprisoned or dead. But those men who are free and able are not in the kitchen while women are out in the streets throwing stones. And if Palestinian women are outside confronting the Israeli Army, they are home in time to make dinner. Once again Hanan is the exception.

Across Radio Street in front of the Civil Administration Building, several Palestinians sit on the ground waiting while several more linger in front of the gate holding papers that might be as innocuous as an application for a driver's license or as serious as a summons that could mean the confiscation of a work permit. In the next room Zeina sings a melodic folk song in Arabic, her soprano voice pure and clear, while Emil accompanies her on his guitar. A maid knocks and enters, carrying a tray of Turkish coffee and home-baked cookies. Without being asked, Hanan announces that she never watches her weight, has a particular weakness for chocolates, and does no exercise except to cough regularly from all the cigarettes she smokes every day. She also volunteers that—having few homemaking skills—she wasn't the one who baked the cakes. "The purest definition of slavery is a woman who works outside the house and also as a housewife." She takes a cake. "When I married Emil," she begins, "he understood from the beginning that I had no intention of being the typical housewife."

When it comes to Hanan's life as it relates to her house, she seems like a visitor, a woman who has never been properly introduced to her appliances. The only exception is in the kitchen, where she is extremely adept at using her microwave oven, usually heating up a typical lamb dish on rice pilaf. It is not unusual to find her sitting in that spacious kitchen with the radio blasting an all-news station in Arabic, more than likely reporting on her latest statements concerning the peace conference, while she carries on a conversation with a daughter about curfew, or pauses to take a call from the U.S. secretary of state, or receives a journalist who is there for an interview. Occasionally the focus of action will move from the kitchen into the bedroom, which is usually in a state of total chaos with clothes strewn everywhere, either going into or coming out of a suitcase. Even in the adjoining bathroom there is a political message: A map of Palestine is printed on the pink plastic shower curtain.

ZAHIRA KAMEL, a leading Palestinian feminist, teacher, and former member of the Palestinian delegation to the peace talks, also regularly makes the rounds of the refugee camps

to instruct women on birth control and infant care. She believes that Hanan owes much of her freedom to Emil. "While
Hanan could have married someone more educated and richer
than Emil Ashrawi," Zahira begins, "having a husband like
him who isn't high-powered or macho makes it easier for her
to function. And while it's true that some people criticize him
for putting up with her traveling around the world, I respect
them both for living as they please in such a closed society
as the West Bank."

What is unusual about the Ashrawis as a couple is that
each has created a style that is in total conflict with the atmosphere in which they live. A certain weariness creeps into
her tone as Hanan attempts to explain her marriage, as if she
has defended against the same criticism countless times, which
she has, and has been met with complete misunderstanding,
which she has. "We always say there are three lives going on
in this house: his, mine, and ours." Emil is a self-proclaimed
pacifist in a society where people flash the peace sign on their
way to prison for bombing a kindergarten or wear T-shirts
on which is written PEACE after stabbing to death a nature
hiker. But while Emil professes to be uninvolved in politics,
he finds that to be almost impossible given his surroundings.
"All these PLO and other factions are nothing more than
glorified tribes, and I abhor that," he says. "I don't believe
in nationalism either; it's always been the downfall of a
people. And tribalism is nothing more than reducing nationalism to a situation where every tribe feels entitled to have
their own state." He smiles. "But that's part of my own
existential problem; on one hand I understand why people
are fighting for their nation, but on the other hand, I don't
see the point, which is probably why I somehow got stuck
in the mentality of the sixties."

If Hanan—with her all-consuming involvement in feminism and equal rights—never made it out of the seventies,

Emil never left the sixties and all of its unstructured idealism. Each seems somehow stranded in another time. A soft-spoken man, Emil has a keen sense of humor and a passion for his family, spending, as he puts it, "quality time" with them, in which he plays board games or watches teen variety shows on television with his daughters. Emil spent fifteen years taking passport pictures, recording meetings, conferences, projects, spare parts, or documenting car accidents for the UN; he currently works in the inventory section for the same organization. But despite his work all those years taking official pictures, his real talent for photography had little to do with his job.

Before the outbreak of the Intifada, Emil used to wander the West Bank in the company of his daughters, mostly when they were on one of their frequent hikes or picnics, shooting pictures of interesting faces or landscapes that captured the beauty of the area. For the past several years, however, Emil claims that he hasn't touched his camera for pleasure and has lost any motivation to find interesting scenes to capture on film—a "reactive depression," given the situation around the West Bank. Although he may have lost interest in other activities, he still plays his guitar, usually to accompany his daughters in song or just to strum quietly on his own while his wife gives interviews or debates the fate of the Palestinian people in a corner of the living room. According to Emil, he has taken up a new art form—mothering. "I gave up most of my interest in the arts to concentrate on raising my children," he says. At only forty-two Emil readily admits that he sometimes feels ancient. "Occupation is physically reflective," he explains. "People are in a constant state of worry whether there will be a strike or a shooting or a roadblock. There's always a choice to be made about which road to take going to work, school, or the market."

On the subject of his wife, Emil scores points with the

feminists when he says, "I've always preferred older women because they're intellectually and sexually more stimulating, and because whenever I've been with a younger woman, I've always felt as if I were corrupting her." Talking as well about his feelings during Hanan's two pregnancies, he seems oblivious to the fact that once again he is portraying himself as an anomaly in that part of the world. He freely admits that he suffered more symptoms than she did. "I've done everything for a baby except breast-feed," he announces.

When Hanan became pregnant both times, she worked right until the last month. When she went into labor, once again the couple was considered avant-garde and shocking when they insisted on Emil's staying with Hanan in the delivery room. "The doctor couldn't believe it. We had to tell him several times that this was absolutely what we wanted, since it just wasn't acceptable practice to have a man in the delivery room." After each baby was born, Emil continued to be involved, once again becoming a trendsetter on the West Bank. He requested and received three months off from work to take care of his children because, in his words, "I wanted to share the experience and take an active part in their upbringing from the beginning."

While Hanan and Emil read all the appropriate books, including Dr. Spock's and Dr. Brazelton's, they finally decided to act on instinct rather than rule. If the baby cried, there was a reason, even if she only needed to be cuddled. "Hanan stayed with each child for the first two months, since both girls were born in July, which meant she was off until she resumed teaching again in October." But even after she resumed her teaching schedule at Bir Zeit, she would race home to breast-feed her baby during the day.

Yet, in other areas of his life, Emil, like Hanan, is a series of contradictions. While he claims to be against all possessions and societally imposed legal shackles, he nonetheless married into one of the most prominent Palestinian families on the West Bank and lives in what is considered one of the most imposing houses in the area. Also, claiming to make a practice of never listening to the news, he is the one person in the house who speaks and understands Hebrew, translating the TV news for his wife as it concerns misstatements made about her or the PLO. For Emil, his studied apoliticism is as precious as any political cause, causing him to choose the most "politically correct" words and phrases to avoid, as he puts it, "any political implication or sexist connotation that would demonstrate that I wasn't for either human or women's rights." Even when he refers to the Palestinian men who guard the family, he makes a point of calling them *shabab*, meaning "youth," instead of *shabiba*, implying membership in Fatah, Arafat's faction of the PLO.

Emil approaches the changes that have occurred in the family with a combination of resignation and a deep sense of responsibility not only to his wife's limited time at home but also to her increased importance to others. While Hanan has taken on the role of spokesperson and political activist for her people, Emil functions as the caretaker for his family.

In the next room an outburst of what sounds like the Ashrawi sisters bickering suddenly erupts before the door bursts open and Zeina enters, followed by Amal. Both girls speak English fluently, Zeina in a husky voice and Amal with a British accent picked up in a year at school in England. It is interesting that despite Hanan's hectic schedule and frequent visitors, her children feel secure enough to interrupt if they need their mother. Heading directly for Hanan's lap, Zeina cuddles up to whisper in Arabic her side of the dispute. Amal stands, calmly interrupting from time to time to interject or correct. After a brief exchange with Hanan, also in Arabic, Emil reverts to English when he addresses his daughters. "This goes against our agreement," he says.

Amal, a serene and beautiful girl, is tall and slim, while Zeina is all limbs and pudgy fingers, not unlike a large puppy that hasn't quite grown into its paws. An adorable child, Zeina has her mother's beautiful legs and skin, a mischievous gleam in her soft brown eyes, and a prepubescent awkwardness that marks the approach of adolescence. The argument between them, once again, is about the use of the telephone.

On Radio Street, where the infrastructure is less than adequate, Hanan has managed to have "call waiting" put on the telephone line that serves for both fax and phone. Amal, like any typical teenager with a busy social life, has been known to ignore the beep that signals another call to continue her own conversation. Whether the caller is President Clinton or Egypt's President Hosni Mubarak, they are occasionally forced to endure hours of empty ringing on Hanan's line during which neither a human voice nor an answering machine picks up. While Hanan seems unfazed by the interruption, Emil is apparently disturbed that the girls have broken an agreement they made with him.

"I don't think any other family in the world ever experienced a kind of electronic reunion that we did," Emil says, with a loving gaze at each daughter. "Zeina and I were in the home base in Ramallah when Amal called from England while Hanan was in Washington on CNN. It was fantastic! I put the telephone next to the television for Amal to hear her mother, while Zeina and I watched her from our living room." He pauses. "Which gets back to our agreement. You see, in the beginning, when Hanan was so busy here, Zeina or Amal would come crying with problems that weren't important, or when Hanan went away for a long time and would call home, Zeina more than Amal would cry even more. One day Zeina and I had a talk, and I told her that we were here, in our home with our things and our family and friends, while Amal was studying in England all alone and Hanan was alone somewhere else even if she was surrounded by a lot of people. So when Hanan called home it was because she needed a charge, and since she couldn't always call Amal, she'd call Zeina not only to say, 'Hello, Zeina, how are you?' but for Zeina to give her that charge. If Zeina cried, she couldn't give it to her. I tried to explain to both Zeina and Amal that they could cry with me but never on the phone with Hanan. 'Let's agree on one thing,' I said. 'You're power base number one when Mama calls to get a charge.' " Emil smiles thoughtfully. "Zeina apparently liked the idea of being the power base until it occurred to her that perhaps she might need a charge, too. What we decided was that we would be power base number one on Radio Street while Hanan and Amal were away, and I would also be power base number two for Zeina, which meant that she could always come to me." Emil touches Amal's cheek. "And of course Amal is the oldest, so she should be more considerate and understand the pressure we're all under." A truce goes into effect as Zeina slips off her mother's lap and heads out the door, followed by Amal, who assures her parents that she will leave the phone free. It seems that Hanan is expecting a call at any time from Yasir Arafat.

After the children leave, with Emil seated near her, Hanan describes the mechanics of her relationships with her daughters and how different they are from the relationship she had with her own mother. According to Hanan, a certain formality was always observed with her mother, which she claims is not present with her own children. With Amal and Zeina, Hanan can talk about everything. "Perhaps I couldn't talk to my mother because it was another time, when parents and children didn't discuss certain subjects," she says. "With my girls, it's different. I share their lives because they're part of mine."

Hanan identifies with what she describes as Zeina's tough and aggressive facade that hides a sensitive interior. "I'm very

soft and get hurt very easily," Hanan confesses, "and sometimes I see Zeina's reactions and recognize them as mine."
Hanan admits that while Zeina resembles her more emotionally, Amal has inherited her love for literature, especially
poetry, as well as her deep introspection about life and her
future role in the world. Referring to Amal, Hanan explains,
"She's still young even though she looks like a woman, and
she sometimes wants to know if it was as tough for me when
I was a teenager. All I can do is assure her that it was and
try to tell her that I felt as if nobody understood me—how
I felt so all alone. I think it comforts Amal to know that she
isn't the only one to go through these doubts, especially when
I manage to convince her that every single one of her friends
undoubtedly has those same feelings, although they probably
just don't express them."

While Hanan was certainly closer in many ways to her
father than to her mother, Emil enjoyed a relationship with
Daoud that surpassed any biological ties. Hanan finds it ironic
that there are so many similarities between her father and
her husband. "And not just because he's also five years
younger, the way my father was than my mother . . ."

"Or that I come from a less educated and elite background," Emil interrupts.

"In all fairness," Hanan continues, "it was more Emil's
family who objected to our marriage than mine. My father
adored him. They were closer than any of us were to him."

The relationship between Emil and Daoud Mikhael was
so close that when Hanan sent Emil to ask her father for
permission to marry her, the two men ended up talking about
everything else except the reason for Emil's visit. "My father
and Emil had their own private language where they communicated without words," Hanan adds.

"It was right in this room where I came to ask for Hanan's
hand," Emil says quietly.

"In the end, when we announced we were getting married," Hanan remembers, "my father wondered if we were asking him or telling him, although it didn't make any difference since he was just so happy we were getting married."

That close relationship between Emil and his father-in-law lasted until the end of Daoud's life, with the special language between them eventually becoming the only way for the older man to communicate.

Daoud had suffered a heart attack in the late seventies, and in keeping with his stubborn and independent character, refused to go to the hospital. Sitting up in bed and tended by a colleague from a neighboring town, Daoud announced to his wife and family that he had no intention of either dying or staying in bed. In fact, he informed the priest Wad'ia had summoned that he had a brother who had converted to Southern Baptist, another brother who was a Catholic, a son-in-law who was a Muslim, and a wife who was an Anglican Christian, which meant that all religious bases were covered. Welcoming the priest into his house, Daoud made it clear that he was receiving him as a friend and a guest but forbade him to pray for his soul, which was and would remain for the foreseeable future very much a part of his body. The next day, against doctor's orders, Daoud was digging in his garden, and by the following week he had resumed his regular hours and was driving all over the West Bank visiting patients. Five years later, however, his physical decline began when he suffered the first of a series of small, debilitating strokes.

At first the family noticed little things, like Daoud's holding up his shoes and wondering what he was meant to do with them. Then his behavior became increasingly bizarre, and he would put on his wife's clothes. As is the tragedy in most cases of dementia or Alzheimer's disease in their early stages, Daoud was cognizant enough to realize that his actions were strange but not sufficiently in control to stop himself. But through it all he retained his humor, making self-deprecating jokes while his friends and family watched in despair as he lost his power of reason.

The family's biggest fear was always that one day Daoud would wander off. "He wanted out all the time," Emil says. "He never wanted to stay indoors, and I couldn't be there all the time because I worked."

It was imperative that someone be there all the time to watch him, and usually someone was—except for one evening, two days before Christmas 1988, barely a year after the Intifada erupted in the Occupied Territories. The Mikhael family had returned from a holiday visit with friends. With Emil at the wheel of the car, Hanan next to him, and Daoud and Wad'ia in the backseat, the family arrived at the house on Radio Street a little before eight o'clock in the evening. While Emil pulled the car into the garage next to the house, Hanan went inside with her parents, watching as they climbed the stairs to their apartment.

No one will ever know who (nor does anyone at this point really want to find out), but someone forgot to lock the front door. After everyone else had retired, Emil—unable to sleep—went upstairs on a hunch to check on his father-in-law. To his horror he found that Daoud's bed was empty. Apparently Daoud had gotten up, tiptoed downstairs, found the door unlocked, and simply slipped out, taking off into the night while the rest of the family slept.

During those beginning months and years of the Intifada, the only positive aspect throughout the West Bank was committees set up by local Ramallah residents by which everybody, regardless of their political alliances or financial circumstances, made themselves available to help other Palestinians who were in trouble. Also during the first few years of the uprising a constant curfew was in effect, whereby Palestinians weren't allowed out past eight o'clock at night. After

Emil woke the rest of the family to announce that Daoud had
wandered off, it was decided that Hanan would remain with
her mother while Emil defied the curfew and went out to
search for his father-in-law.

Bad news travels fast on the West Bank. By midnight at
least one hundred men and boys were organized, with maps
and flashlights, looking for Daoud. The weather was un-
usually bad that December, heavy fog making it difficult to
see more than a few feet, and rain mixed with snow and hail
making it dangerous to drive. Emil decided that the house
on Radio Street would be the base with the *shabab* going out
in shifts, some drying themselves off while others would be
just starting out, each group canvassing different areas of
Ramallah.

It took three days of dogged search before most of Ramallah and the surrounding towns and village had been covered, to no avail. Daoud Mikhael was still missing. There
was finally no choice but to go to the Israeli authorities, if
for nothing else than to inform them that the doctor was
missing and a group of their own people were currently comb-
ing the area looking for him.

"We crossed the road and went to the Civil Administration, where the response was predictable," Hanan says bit-
terly. "They told us they had their hands full with *our* uprising
and weren't available to look for missing people, especially
a senile old man who didn't present a security threat."

Emil adds, "Under ordinary circumstances we could never
get the police to come if there was a robbery."

"Or a fire," Hanan interrupts. "The best way to get an
instant response from either the police or the fire department
was to tell them that a Palestinian had been spotted with a
weapon. Then they'd appear before you could even hang up
the phone."

Hanan continues. "We told the authorities that we

weren't asking for help. All we wanted was to let them know that a person was missing, so if they happened to find him, whatever condition he was in, they would know whom to contact since obviously my father hadn't wandered off with identification."

"We told them that he was confused, and we just wanted them not to frighten him if they found him," Emil adds.

On the night of the third day, the family tried to get permission to use a megaphone when they made the rounds of the towns and villages where Daoud used to travel to see his patients. At first the authorities refused, but after persistent pleading, they finally compromised and agreed to allow announcements in the newspapers and on radio and television, giving Daoud's description and medical condition. After another day the authorities also agreed to let Emil and the others pass out leaflets, provided that the family paid to have them printed.

They never needed to distribute the leaflets. The call came on the afternoon Emil went to pick them up at a local printing company. Hanan was at home with her mother, two daughters, and sister Nadia. In the wadi where he used to go hunting as a young man, the *shabab* had found Daoud Mikhael. He had apparently died of exposure.

Accompanied by several of the *shabab,* Emil went to the wadi and found his father-in-law lying on his back under an olive tree, where a pool of water created by the heavy rain surrounded him. "He must have been very cold," Emil continues, "because his hands were clenched on his chest, but otherwise he looked so peaceful, so comfortable." Emil and the others just stood there for several minutes in silence until a light snow began to fall, which suddenly covered Daoud with a fine sheet of white powder. "We missed finding him alive only by a few hours," Emil says softly. "But can you imagine how beautiful that was, seeing him lying there so peacefully, all covered with that fine layer of white snow? It was a very sad moment but at the same time it was very beautiful."

Later, with the help of Nadia's husband and several of the *shabab,* the men carried Daoud to the hospital in Ramallah. "I cleaned him and dressed him," Emil says simply, "tied his tie, and sat with him for a long time. There was still so much to say."

While her father's death was an enormous personal loss for Hanan, it happened during one of the most anguished periods in the history of the Palestinian-Israeli conflict. On a daily basis throughout the West Bank and in Israel, friends, students, and neighbors suffered their own losses on both sides of a conflict without front lines. Almost exactly one year before the Intifada began, and two years before Daoud Mikhael's death, Hanan found herself confronted with a situation that was to mark the beginning of a tragedy that has yet to end.

CHAPTER SIX

GRENDEL
AND OTHER MONSTERS

PROFESSOR ASHRAWI was in the middle of a lecture on Beowulf when the Israeli Army stormed Bir Zeit University on a December day in 1986. A student who had managed to slip away in those first few moments of confusion burst into her class to announce that the Israeli Army was already rounding up demonstrators. In a show of solidarity with Palestinian prisoners who had gone on a hunger strike, a group of students and some residents of Bir Zeit were protesting for better conditions in Israeli prisons. As head of the human rights committee at the university, Hanan had been aware of the demonstration since its planning stages several weeks before. She was also aware that those intending to march would be out there as much for themselves as for those already in jail, since all had been or would be arrested at least once during the school year and would undoubtedly be jailed again. If anything surprised her it was that the army hadn't appeared before the demonstration began, as—given their stable of informers and taps into certain telephone lines—they knew everything that happened in the West Bank and Gaza.

Hanan had just finished that section of the text in which Beowulf dives down into the lake behind the castle to rescue King Hrothgar and slay the monster, Grendel. She put down

the book and listened as the student described the situation.
Soldiers were already standing at five-foot intervals around
the complex and on rooftops, some armed with conventional
rifles and machine guns, others carrying weapons fitted with
tear-gas canisters. Along the main roads of the town itself,
jeeps, trucks, and several tanks were in combat-ready positions. As was the style throughout Israel and the West Bank,
private houses were built almost to the edge of the sidewalks.
Bir Zeit had been a private residence (donated to the university by a wealthy West Bank family named Nasser), which
made it possible for the army to surround the campus even
if the gates were closed.

Subtle changes had been taking place throughout the Occupied Territories lately: Rather than avoid confrontation
with the army, people seemed more willing to risk curfew
and casualties. It wasn't surprising, therefore, that once again
the university was under siege. Followed by her students,
Hanan walked to a window that faced the street.

It was obvious that the town of Bir Zeit had already been
put under curfew. What was usually a neighborhood bustling
with noisy activity, people crowding on dusty sidewalks, animals roaming freely through the streets, was now deserted
except for the military. Planks of wood with protruding spikes
had been placed in the middle of the roads, preventing cars
from either leaving or entering. At the far end of the street
were two unmarked white vans, typical of the vehicles used
by the Shin Bet.

Hanan's first concern was the students under guard, sitting on the side of the road with their hands clasped behind
their heads. She was about to say something about going
down to the front gate to begin negotiations for their release
when she noticed the jeep. Apparently everyone else noticed
it, too, as a hushed silence fell over the group. Passing directly
in front of the window, the vehicle continued to the end of

101

the street, where it turned the corner and disappeared. Two soldiers sat in the front while a hooded, handcuffed man, flanked by two civilians, sat in the back. Everyone waited for the jeep to reappear. Within minutes it did, driving slowly beneath the window and continuing toward the end of the street where once again it turned the corner and disappeared.

Hanan moved away from the window and walked slowly back to her desk. Standing in front of her class, Hanan tried a small smile before remarking, "I guess Grendel will just have to wait while we deal with those other monsters." There were a few nervous laughs.

Hanan began by pointing out that at least the army never varied its routine. At the first sign of any demonstration, soldiers appeared on campus and used tear gas to disperse the crowd. In response the students threw stones, ran into the surrounding fields, or fled back within the University compound. In those instances when students threw Molotov cocktails or used weapons, the army responded with live ammunition until the violence quickly escalated to critical levels where there was no retreating into negotiation, until many on both sides of the lines had been injured or killed. Still, what disturbed her more immediately was the jeep that kept making lazy circles around the perimeter of the building. She made an instant decision. She would find Albert Agazarian, the director of public relations and a member of the university's Human Rights Committee, which she chaired. Together, once again they would begin a dialogue with the Israeli commander in charge in an effort to stop any confrontation from escalating.

Albert likes to say that his job then had less to do with changing the image of the university or garnering publicity to increase enrollment than it did with basic survival. Half the day was spent badgering various international human rights organizations for news of students who were being held without being charged or who had died under mysterious circumstances in Israeli jails. The other half was spent negotiating solutions to disputes between different factions of the PLO and the radical Islamic groups within the structure of the University. With the emergence of such fundamentalist groups as Hamas, the Islamic Jihad, and the Red Panthers, there was increasing conflict between them and al-Fatah. During the last internecine dispute on campus, members of Hamas took several faculty members hostage, and it wasn't until Albert was able to negotiate a satisfactory compromise that they were released. The mosque under construction in the center of the campus was the result of Albert's concessions to those Islamic factions.

A Palestinian of Armenian origin, Albert has deep roots in Jerusalem—six generations on both sides of his family—which makes him one of the most recognizable and colorful figures around the cafés in the Old City. With his penchant for British clothes—tweed jackets with leather patches on the elbows and a Sherlock Holmes–style hat in the winter, khakis and blue blazers in the summer, his trademark rosewood-bowl pipe in his hand in all seasons—and an English peppered with American colloquialisms, he looks and sounds more Western than indicated by his Levantine ancestry. Stocky and of medium height, with dark, expressive eyes, a sculptured beard, and a stubborn lock of hair that flops constantly over his forehead, Albert is attractive in a disheveled way. Part of his charm is his use of New York Jewish humor, picked up during years of dealing with the American television media.

Even Israelis have been known to find him amusing during tense moments of debate, except when he reminisces about the 1970s, when American Jewish girls came to Israel to visit and ended up on the West Bank with Palestinian boyfriends. While his own experience in that area is reputed to be extensive, it was his brother who married the daughter of a well-to-do Jewish dress manufacturer in New York. After fifteen years and three children, that marriage ended in divorce while Albert lived with his wife and their three children inside the Greek Orthodox convent in the Old City. His cheery nature notwithstanding, Albert was known as a hardliner when it came to the occupation.

Despite their different backgrounds Hanan and Albert complemented each other. With her eloquent command of language, Hanan tended to focus on the human side of any dispute, with just enough legal nuance thrown in to give her emotional appeal credibility. And while both spoke English and Arabic, Albert was also fluent in Hebrew. They made a good team.

Hanan was almost in the middle of the courtyard when she spotted Albert in the near distance. Catching up with him, she listened as he briefed her on their way to the front gate. From what Albert had already learned, the man in the jeep that Hanan had seen from the window was the father of one of the students. The army had in custody not only the father but also the student's cousin, who was being held for murder at Moscabiya, the Israeli Central Police Station inside the Russian Compound in Jerusalem. The story that Albert had gotten so far was that the cousin had implicated the student as his accomplice. As they neared the front gate, Hanan's only question was if the army had proof of either boy's guilt, and if so, why they hadn't gone directly to the boy's house in Gaza or at least notified the faculty before putting the entire student body at risk. Albert stopped to take Hanan firmly by the shoulders. "Apparently the army *did* go to the student's house, because that's where they arrested the cousin and the father," he reminded her.

The Israeli commander in charge of the operation held the rank of colonel and was fluent both in English and Arabic. He was a soft-spoken, pleasant-looking man under forty, clean-shaven and prematurely gray-haired, with thick, clear-framed glasses that accentuated his light eyes. With his long legs stretched out toward the ground he sat in the passenger side of the jeep holding a walkie-talkie and what appeared to be two photographs. He got right to the point: Surrender the killer so he could be taken into custody, interrogated, charged, and sent for trial. The faster the faculty complied with the army's demands, the sooner the students under guard would be released, along with the father of the suspect in question. He gestured to the side of the road several meters away, where a group of students still sat with their hands clasped behind their heads. Furthermore, if the faculty co-operated without incident he would personally advise the military governor not to issue an order to close Bir Zeit for disciplinary reasons relating to the demonstration that morning. "Classes would resume," he added quite cheerfully. "All military personnel would retreat, and life could go back to normal."

Hanan almost laughed out loud. "This *is* normal, colonel," she replied. "These ludicrous accusations, demands, and conditions for turning over a student whom you decide is guilty of murder without offering us any proof, witnesses, or a warrant for his arrest. That's normal behavior around here."

Instinctively Albert moved closer to Hanan as the colonel placed his walkie-talkie on the seat next to him. Without a word he held out the two photographs. Hanan took them. One was a picture of an elderly woman, obviously dead, with stab wounds over her neck and upper body. The other was a close-up of the same woman from the shoulders up, where a set of teeth marks were visible on the left side of her neck. After studying the pictures for several moments, Hanan handed them back.

In a voice devoid of emotion, the colonel explained that

the woman was a Holocaust survivor who had moved to Israel from New York as a haven away from crime and violence. "We're very sensitive about our failure to protect our citizens," the colonel said quietly, "especially survivors of the Holocaust."

Hanan's immediate inclination was to cite the ironic coincidence that Palestinian leaders were equally sensitive about their failure to protect their own from the inhumanities of the Israeli Army. Instead she concentrated on the issue at hand. "These pictures only show me the result of a murder; they don't offer any proof that my student committed the crime."

The colonel shrugged. If Dr. Ashrawi persisted in taking an unreasonable position, he would be forced to order a lineup in the courtyard where all students would be checked against their IDs until they found the one they were looking for. "The problem with that, Dr. Ashrawi, is that in addition to taking a very long time, there's no telling what we'll find in the process."

"Release the old man," Hanan replied coldly. "He's got nothing to do with anything that happened to that woman."

"If he suffers a heart attack and dies," Albert added, "you'll be as guilty of murder as the person who stabbed that woman."

The colonel dismissed the notion with a wave of his hand. "That woman was an innocent victim," he said.

"What about that man?" Hanan asked.

"He's the father of a terrorist," the Colonel replied matter-of-factly.

"Suspect," Hanan corrected.

Albert's tone was sarcastic when he interrupted, addressing only Hanan. "Aren't you aware that the army justifies shooting Palestinian children by claiming they all grow up to become terrorists?"

Ignoring the comment, the colonel went on to point out that a lineup was only the beginning, since what would follow would be a room-to-room search of every single building on campus. "Time is running out," he warned as he checked his watch.

Barely able to control her anger, Hanan demanded to know where was the proof—details like witnesses, murder weapons, and warrants.

The colonel replied quite calmly that witnesses and murder weapons would be presented in due course during the trial—if the suspect ever *made* it to trial given Dr. Ashrawi's reluctance to insure his safety by turning him over to the army before things got out of hand. As for warrants, he was only too happy to provide her with a paper signed by him to the effect that the army was authorized to search Bir Zeit to apprehend a terrorist.

Suppose the student wasn't on campus?

He was.

Suppose he was innocent?

He wasn't.

In response, as if to prove guilt or justify the army's presence, the colonel again held out the two photographs. Hanan ignored him. Shrugging, the colonel put them back in his pocket and checked his watch once more before informing her that she had exactly five minutes to make up her mind.

"Thirty," she countered instantly.

"Fifteen," he retorted.

"I refuse to comply with your terror tactics," she said with surprising calm. "I've got to reach our lawyer." She thought for a moment, her mind focusing on Leah Tsemmel, an Israeli lawyer who represents mostly Palestinians. "What I *can* promise you is that regardless of how long that takes, I'll be back here at the gate in no more than thirty minutes." That said, and without waiting for a reply, she turned to head back to her office in the Fine Arts Building. The first round of negotiations had begun.

When she was halfway across the courtyard, Hanan heard the blast. An enormous crash followed, and then several successive shots, followed by repeated rounds of gunfire. Whirling around, she saw soldiers pouring inside the compound while students rushed out of the men's dormitory. From one second to the next, doors were down, windows were smashed, and there was chaos everywhere as smoke filled the air from the continuous artillery rounds. As was usually the case in any confrontation between students and soldiers, the identity of the source of the violence depended on which side was recounting the event. In this case the official report from the army claimed that soldiers had only responded in self-defense to shooting coming from the men's dormitory.

Albert had already caught up with Hanan, to stare in disbelief as several soldiers dragged two students, one barely awake, the other half naked and dripping wet, out the front door. Both boys were already covered with blood and welts from blows received from the butt of a rifle. According to students who witnessed the incident, one of the boys had been dragged out of a sickbed while the other had been pulled from under a shower.

Without even thinking Hanan and Albert rushed forward, he physically trying to free the students from the soldiers' grasp while she pleaded for their release, at least until they could get dried and dressed. It was useless. Neither of them could do a thing as the soldiers dragged the boys over to a flatbed truck and handcuffed them to the metal loop hanging from one side. Albert didn't wait around to argue, racing back to the door of the dorm, where more soldiers were trying to drag out another group of students. Hanan realized the futility of trying to match muscles or attempt to reason with the army. As far as she was concerned, her only alternative was to try and make it back to her office to call Leah. Holding her shawl over her mouth and nose against the fumes from a tear-gas canister that had been set off somewhere near the mosque, she inched her way along the side of the building in the direction of her office.

The bullet that whizzed past her face came without warning, lodging in a stone barely three meters from where she stood. Instinct rather than the impact of the shot caused her to slam back against the wall. Looking up, she saw a soldier standing directly above her on a low roof, his rifle aimed at her head. Almost immediately a second shot rang out, this bullet missing her by mere centimeters and hitting the ground near her left foot. Closing her eyes, Hanan made a dash for the wall under the roof where the soldier stood and collapsed against it. While Hanan always claimed to have participated in countless peace marches and demonstrations in which she had been shot at with rubber bullets as well as live ammunition, and to have kicked many a tear-gas canister in her career, she had never before been targeted by a soldier. It was something new to add to her list of credentials.

Her head ached and her heart pounded as she tried to figure out her next move. Daring to peek out from underneath the roof, she noticed that the soldier was no longer there. But any relief she might have felt was short-lived when she turned to see him, flanked by two others, advancing toward her on the ground. Trapped where she stood, she was barely able to struggle as one soldier held her arms while the other slammed her against the wall and another screamed insults. Later she would remember the gesture and recall the words—an index finger slicing across a throat and threats to the effect that all Arabs should be slaughtered like animals. It was only the clattering of gunfire erupting in the distance that caused the soldiers to release her. Without considering the risk, Hanan followed the trio as they ran toward the noise, only to be caught up in the middle of a crowd of students and faculty members who were heading for the dining hall. Through bits of disjointed sentences, Hanan managed to understand that the army was trying to break down the doors to the dining room, where two hundred students had taken refuge—a potential massacre if they were successful or if the students weren't given a chance to surrender. According to several faculty members, seventeen wounded were already in the infirmary while another fifteen were being treated at first-aid stations set up around campus. More crucial than calling Leah right then was returning to the front gate to work something out with the colonel, or casualties would be the highest they had ever been. Time was running out. It would be too late to wait until the army decided whether or not to allow an ambulance through. The injured had to be transported to the hospital immediately or they would die.

By the time she reached the front gate she was beyond any self-control. Rushing up to the colonel she launched into a tirade. "This is a university," she began emotionally, "not a battlefield, and I'm in charge around here, not you!"

With his voice infuriatingly calm, the colonel asked, "What about that lineup, Dr. Ashrawi?"

Through clenched teeth, she continued. "You've got your blood price, for God's sake! At least thirty students are injured, some critically, so consider it a victory, call off your men, and let the ambulances through. Call off your soldiers from the dining room before there's a massacre." And when he didn't reply, she could stop neither the words nor the tears. "Please, colonel, think of these kids like your own," she pleaded. "Think about how you've put everything into them, all your hopes and dreams, and imagine how you'd feel if suddenly everything was lost!"

He surprised her. "All right, Dr. Ashrawi," the colonel said quietly. "I'll allow one ambulance through and I'll call

off my men from around the dining hall on one condition."
He paused. "Turn over the terrorist."

It was that simple. But even as Hanan weighed the alter-
natives, she knew it was impossible. Never in her career had
she handed over a single student to the army and she had no
intention of starting now. Sensing her reluctance, the colonel
pressed. "Don't be foolish, Dr. Ashrawi. What I'm offering
you is quite a compromise, only one student and it's all over."

As she shook her head slowly from side to side the word
"no" was clearly visible in her eyes before she actually uttered
it. "No," she said, just above a whisper, and then again in a
normal tone. "No."

The colonel remained calm. "I'll instruct my men to put
down their weapons and retreat from around the dining hall,
Dr. Ashrawi," he repeated, "and two hundred students can
come out unharmed."

She said nothing.

"After one ambulance has left with the first batch of
wounded," he continued, "I'll consider allowing another one
through. Don't be foolish, Dr. Ashrawi. Only one student,
isn't that worth hundreds of lives?"

Before Hanan had a chance to respond, she was suddenly
startled by the sound of screeching tires. It took only seconds
for her to realize that the vehicle coming into view from
around the left side of the men's dormitory was being driven
by one of her colleagues. After that, everything happened too
fast for her to react when the jeep suddenly reappeared, carrying the student's father—the old man no longer hooded or
handcuffed and with tears streaming down his cheeks—and
two Shin Bet operatives. Swerving out of the way of the other
car, the jeep slammed to a stop only meters from where she
and the colonel stood. Picking up speed the car continued
toward the gate as shots rang out from the top of one of the
roofs, a barrage of bullets hitting its tires and causing it to

plow into a tree. Another round of gunfire erupted as soldiers surrounded the vehicle. At the same time the Shin Bet men jumped out of the jeep and rushed toward the driver of the car. One restrained him while the other wrestled keys out of his hand. Apparently the old man understood what was happening before anyone else. With his hands clasped together in prayer, he cried out to Hanan in Arabic, "My son is innocent! Tell them he's not here! I put him on a bus for Amman! He wasn't even in Gaza when that Jew was killed!"

Hanan could barely believe her eyes when one of the Shin Bet operatives flung open the trunk of the car to pull out a man who had been hiding inside. A scuffle ensued, and Hanan would remember seeing the glint of a large knife as the fugitive lunged in the colonel's direction before he fell under the weight of one of the Shin Bet. The old man continued screaming. Hanan suddenly understood that he had finally found his son—a reunion that was to be all too brief. While one Shin Bet officer continued to struggle with the suspect, the other clutched his gun in both hands and aimed, firing three consecutive shots into the suspect's neck and chest.

As if a hidden camera had slowed all motion while an unseen hand had switched off the sound, the boy crumpled soundlessly to the ground. Crying with outstretched arms, Hanan rushed forward before sinking to her knees next to the injured boy. Somewhere far away in the distance she could hear the colonel shouting orders through a megaphone for his men to cease fire. Seconds more elapsed before she became aware of an eerie silence throughout the compound— suddenly quiet except for the wrenching sound of an old man's sobs.

The boy was bleeding profusely from his chest and neck. With tears streaming down her cheeks, Hanan gathered him in her arms, waiting for the medics in the Red Crescent ambulance to maneuver their way through the roadblocks and around the planks of wood with protruding spikes to reach the campus. She would say later that as she rocked him back and forth, the image of Kent State flashed through her head—the unforgettable picture of grief and despair that had been etched in her memory when other soldiers opened fire on other civilians who fell on another campus so far away and long ago.

The boy's breathing was getting shallow and his color turning pale and gray as life seeped out of his body faster than the ambulance could make its way through the gates. Pressing her shawl against his wounds to stanch the flow of blood, she willed him to live. A chill ran through her as she saw his eyes suddenly flutter open to search her face in a look of sheer panic, his body twitching once in her arms before he lay perfectly still. He was dead.

A long and pitiful wail came from deep within the old man, piercing the crashing silence surrounding everyone who was there that day to witness the boy's death. Nothing was left to do or say, no more words to plead for an ambulance or a lawyer. With the boy still cradled in her arms, Hanan was vaguely aware of the small group of people who had gathered around her, Albert and the colonel among them. She could barely contain her tears as she looked up to ask, in a voice filled with grief, "Tell me, colonel, is this the job of an academic—to cradle the head of a dying student?"

Dora

THE STUDENT who was shot and killed at Bir Zeit University on that brisk December day in 1986 lived in the Gaza Strip. His death set off demonstrations that started in his hometown before spreading to the refugee camps and schools in the surrounding areas. In reaction to the increasing violence and protests, the Israeli Army arrested dozens of boys and men who were known agitators and who had been arrested in the past for violent anti-Israeli activities. All were confined to a Gaza police station. By the middle of the month so many Palestinians were in custody that the Israelis were forced to convert an army camp at the edge of Gaza City into a prison to accommodate the growing number of prisoners. By the end of the month authorities had detained more than 250 people of all ages in a four-room cell within the army camp. The Palestinians in Gaza named the camp Ansar II after Ansar I, the prison camp that Israel had set up in Southern Lebanon during the Lebanon War of 1982. For Palestinians throughout the Occupied Territories, Gaza became a symbol of everything that was intolerable under Israeli occupation.

A year after that incident at Bir Zeit University, in which a student was shot and killed by the Shin Bet, on December 6, 1987, a Jewish businessman named Shlomo Takal was murdered. That incident provoked Defense Minister Rabin to issue the following statement: "This terrorist attack has been carried out against a terrorist national background, perhaps even a nationalist religious one." What Rabin intended to acknowledge was the strength of the Islamic forces in the Gaza Strip—particularly the Islamic Jihad, which had been responsible for the recent deaths of a number of Israelis. Two days later, on December 8, 1987, an Israeli truck accidentally hit two vans, killing four Palestinians who were residents of Jabaliya, the largest refugee camp in Gaza. Rumors began spreading that the driver of the truck was a relative of Shlomo Takal's, and that the accident had been an intentional act of violence in retribution for his death. Over the next few days more violence erupted throughout the Gaza Strip, spreading into Ramallah, the Qalandriya refugee camp north of Jerusalem, and the Balata camp near Nablus and other camps in the area before reaching the city of Nablus itself. During the month of December, the Occupied Territories were engulfed in an unprecedented wave of spontaneous street violence that was the beginning of what was to become known as the Intifada. One particular woman, however, never lived to witness any of it.

At the beginning of December 1986, Dora Lempick* had been living in Israel for only three years. What had been an arduous fifteen-year struggle to convince her to leave her apartment in Washington Heights in Upper Manhattan had finally succeeded. David, Dora's son, had been pleading with his mother to leave New York and move with his family to a small agricultural village in the Gaza Strip ever since his father, Isador, had died and the neighborhood had become increasingly dangerous. David never wavered in his belief that moving to Israel was the fulfillment of every Jew's dream. Even after the Lebanon War that ravaged Israel in 1982, David believed that the problems were political and not something that would put his mother at constant risk. Every day in the newspapers in New York, there were reports of random street violence. David used to say that he never knew when he went out for a newspaper if he would return to find the area roped off with yellow tape that indicated a crime zone. On several occasions he had actually come back from work or medical school to find police cars blocking the street, a chalk outline of a body, and a froth of soap and water as the only remaining traces of what had once been a human being.

David's father, Isador, had been a rabbi in a small Conservative synagogue on Fort Washington Avenue, not far from the shabby apartment where the Lempick family lived. Survivors of Auschwitz, they had their only son, David, late in life.

As a kid David had especially hated the summers in New York, when his parents and their friends sat on folding chairs in front of the building, the tattooed numbers from the concentration camps visible on their arms in the glaring sun.

David also hated summers in New York because only the black kids were allowed to run through the spray from the open fire hydrants to cool off. Jewish boys could get germs or, worse, fall and break their hands. And if that happened, what was the point of his parents' having survived the Holocaust if their only son wouldn't be able to operate when he grew up?

Dora would continue the discussion back in her kitchen, beginning with the story about David's paternal grandfather, according to her, the most respected rabbi in Berlin and how he was murdered protecting the Talmud when the Nazis stormed his synagogue in 1938. Two generations of rabbis, Dora would say proudly, and now David, the third generation, would be a doctor. What always fascinated David was how his mother could create a direct link between his grandfather's murder at the hands of the Nazis and his running through an open fire hydrant on a sweltering summer day in Washington Heights. But that was Dora with her infuriating logic.

David would never get over his guilt for dating a Catholic girl during his last year of high school. It was his only rebellion, David tried to tell himself—the only time he asserted his independence—although perhaps if Dora had allowed him to run through the water from those open hydrants he wouldn't have taken up with Mary Beth.

On the subject of his father's death, however, David grew cynical, for him the only way to deal with his inconsolable grief. God had obviously gotten around to the old-business in-box when he reached down into the pile stacked six million high and found David's case. Mary Beth, that sweet Catholic girl, had a brother who belonged to a street gang that broke into the synagogue one Friday night after Sabbath services and stabbed Rabbi Isador Lempick to death. The police said the gang probably figured to find a collection plate filled with money. What the gang didn't understand was that even in the rich downtown synagogues in Manhattan, Jews gave checks and bonds, rarely cash. What the police didn't understand was that the members of Rabbi Lempick's congregation could barely feed themselves.

Fifteen years after her husband's senseless death, Dora had finally agreed to close up her apartment and move to that quiet agricultural village near Gaza.

DAVID WAS IN THE OPERATING ROOM, his wife was teaching at a nearby elementary school, and his two sons were in class when Dora heard the knock on the door. Opening it, she recognized the two Palestinians as local boys who did odd jobs around the village. One of them, she remembered, had just completed some construction work for a family of new immigrants next door. The boys said they were thirsty, and Dora didn't hesitate to invite them in for some water. After all, this was Israel; it wasn't Nazi Germany or even Washington Heights.

When she turned toward the sink to get the glasses from the drainboard one of the boys grabbed her from behind. Dora Lempick—survivor of Auschwitz; daughter-in-law of Solomon Lempick, murdered by the Nazis; widow of Isador Lempick, murdered by a street gang; mother of David Lempick, who begged her to leave the violence of New York for the safety of Israel—was stabbed sixteen times in the face, neck, and upper body and left slumped over her kitchen table. According to the autopsy report it took approximately twelve minutes for Dora to exsanguinate, after which one of her assailants bit her. A set of teeth marks was found on the left side of her neck.

Three days later the Israeli Army apprehended a suspect who confessed to the murder. The boy also implicated his cousin, whom he swore was the one who had left the teeth marks in the victim's neck. Several weeks later during a surprise search for the suspect on the campus of Bir Zeit University, the army captured him as he tried to escape in the trunk of a professor's car.

The suspect who had confessed to the murder of Dora Lempick was tried, convicted, and sentenced to the maximum penalty under Israeli law of twenty-five years in prison without parole. The other suspect died in the arms of his English professor, Hanan Ashrawi.

CHAPTER SEVEN

THE RUMOR MILL

EVERYONE CALLS HER HANAN. Her supporters say it is a mark of prominence, while her detractors claim it is a sign of disrespect. And so begins a series of rumors that weave back and forth across the Green Line, that imaginary border separating Israel from the Occupied Territories. Hanan, as she is called by everyone—whether out of prominence or disrespect—is the most visible woman in the Middle East. As a consequence her every action or utterance has become grist for a rumor mill that, in that part of the world, carries gossip faster than a satellite dish spreads news across international wire services. Notwithstanding all her efforts "to carry the PLO on my shoulders," as she put it, "throughout the entire peace process while I was the spokesperson," she still faced her toughest critics within her own community on the West Bank. She has been called everything from the Golda Meir of the Palestinian people to the Marie Antoinette of the Occupied Territories. The more moderate among her people consider her a savior who has given dignity and hope to their cause, while the more radical brand her a traitor for even considering less than all the land of Israel as a Palestinian state. By those Palestinians who have gone to her for help in finding relatives and friends in Israeli prisons, she is consid-

ered "Mother Palestine." By those who have been relegated
to the political sidelines since her rise to fame, she is called
"Lady Hanan" and rumored to be ambitious and cold. In the
six years that she has acted as spokesperson for the Palestinian
delegation to the Middle East peace talks, she has caused
almost as much controversy and evoked almost as much reaction as there are opinions on the Palestinian-Israeli conflict.
There is hardly anyone who doesn't have an opinion.

Cradling dying students, organizing peace marches, or
winning debates on American television does not necessarily
give an unknown academic sufficient credentials to represent
an organization that has been synonymous with terror. For
a while, however, the relationship between the quintessential
terrorist and the cultured English professor was based on
mutual need, to change Arafat's image throughout the world
and to give Hanan credibility throughout the Occupied Territories. It was a symbiotic relationship in which Arafat wel-
comed news stories of Hanan trekking to Tunis for advice
and consultation and Hanan needed to be seen enveloped in
Arafat's approving embrace.

High-ranking officials in the Pentagon, who were in
charge of the peace negotiations during the Bush administration, sought to win press and public support for an eventual
accord between Israel and the Palestinians. Hanan was the
most viable image to represent the new, legitimate voice of
the PLO, far removed from the bloody past of the organization's old guard. Yet Arafat, with all his defects, was a
known quantity to his people, a man who paid the price for
his faulty political decisions even if he caused others to pay
it as well. And Hanan, despite all her political activism and
Western media exposure, was still seen by her own people as
part of an elite minority within the context of West Bank
academia. This was always the main criticism by Hanan's
compatriots—that she had no constituency or on-the-ground

support, that the rhythm of the Intifada eluded her. While Hanan's popularity soared in the United States, it did little to ingratiate her with her fellow Palestinians.

At Bir Zeit University, where Hanan gained most of her negotiating experience by dealing with the Israeli Army on a daily basis, and where her students generally respected and even revered her, certain of her colleagues downplayed her popularity and denigrated her influence. Riyad Malki is one of them.

An attractive man of forty-two, tall and slim, with dark curly hair and an Omar Sharif mustache, Malki met Hanan years ago when he first joined the Engineering Department at Bir Zeit University. Educated in the United States, Malki earned a Ph.D. in engineering at the University of California, although he seems as proud of a love affair and near-brush with matrimony with a Jewish girl whom he met in Los Angeles as he is of his academic career. In near-perfect English he explains, "Her family disapproved of me because they believed in that stereotypical image that all Palestinians are terrorists. For my family there was no problem, except as that typical Zionist racism would affect my happiness." What Malki neglects to mention is that the year of his love affair happened to be 1982, when a series of hijackings and bombings in the name of the Palestinian cause caused global fear, injury, and death, doing little to dispel that stereotypical image of the Palestinian.

Currently, in addition to his official job of teaching engineering at Bir Zeit, Malki is the spokesperson on the West Bank for the PFLP, a faction of the PLO that is part of the "rejectionist front," which is against any negotiation with Israel that doesn't begin with the establishment of a separate Palestinian state. Ironically, it was also the PFLP that perpetrated most of the terrorist attacks back in the 1980s, when Malki was studying in California.

El Quds University in East Jerusalem is a small, ivy-covered, white walk-up whose glass entrance door is smashed and whose intercom system is a tangled mess of wires spilling from a hole in the wall. It is there, in a borrowed office, that Malki disputes what Hanan claims were her activities at Bir Zeit before she left to act as spokesperson for the Palestinian delegation.

"When it came to protesting against the army," Malki begins, "it's unlikely that Hanan was involved in any negotiation on behalf of students since students and teachers had separate activities. Unless we made specific arrangements to join forces, the teachers followed their own union policy, which was that the Public Relations Department at Bir Zeit was in charge of all contact with the army." Malki goes on: "Concerning any human rights committee at Bir Zeit, to the best of my memory there was nothing that resembled anything like that until long after the Intifada began and the Red Cross and other international organizations got involved."

Malki remains adamant that even if there was a human rights committee, it would have been impossible for Hanan to have had the time to track down students under its auspices and still carry her full teaching load. "In my opinion," he suggests, "this is just another case of Hanan creating a past for herself that justified her role in the peace negotiations." And on the subject of "roles," Malki has a dissenting view as well concerning Hanan's vocal opposition to Israeli occupation even during the early eighties before the uprising began. "Back then, Hanan and myself were only simple teachers with no clear political vision," Malki continues. "It was only after the Intifada broke out in 1987 that we finally took a political stand—which, by the way, was far from the campus since it was during that period that the army closed down the university for four years." Malki says simply, "There was no activity on campus because there was no campus."

While Hanan has grown almost inured to criticism of her abilities to speak for the PLO in the political arena, she reacts emotionally when it comes to being challenged on her activities at Bir Zeit University. "After all these years I thought Riyad and I were in this thing together with a common goal to fight a common enemy. It makes no sense that he would turn on me, since the whole point was always to end the occupation. Obviously Riyad's priorities are confused if it's more important for him to negate my credentials than to push me to the top for the sake of our collective cause."

In response Malki acknowledges that during the first four years of the Intifada, when Bir Zeit was closed, classes were held in the homes of various professors throughout the West Bank. "Obviously, holding illegal gatherings in private houses led to confrontations between the faculty, students, and the army," he admits, "but never ever on campus and certainly not in that context. Palestinians who gathered in large numbers or even informal groups of more than three people were always at risk of arrest because it was against the law. We still have to get special permits from the Israelis for weddings or graduation parties, so holding private classes away from the campus was absolutely forbidden. Maybe there were incidents like that where she tried to protect her students from getting arrested." His voice grows agitated: "But if Hanan tells you that she was the only one who opened her house or did something daring for her students, she's lying to improve her image so she can rewrite history and justify her participation now."

Malki contends that rather than any political credentials or special leadership qualities, it was Hanan's superb command of English that accounted for her success. "And her special relationships with certain highly placed American officials," he adds, "not to mention her popularity with the international media."

To prove her involvement in the creation of that human rights committee as well as substantiate her credentials as a Palestinian who has suffered under occupation, Hanan suggests that Albert Agazarian knows the truth. "At least I'm sure of Albert's loyalty," she says quietly. "I know that we both have a high regard for one another without any risk of competition or pettiness coming between us. Ask Albert," she adds. "He knows that I have no personal agenda and that my only interest in this fight is to achieve self-determination for my people."

SITTING IN THE Café St. Michel, a small coffeehouse in the Old City of Jerusalem, Albert Agazarian is constantly interrupted by someone either congratulating him for a job well done in Madrid or asking him to intervene with the authorities. Agazarian, who began his career as the director of public relations for Bir Zeit University, also directed all press relations for the Palestinian delegation at the opening peace conference in Madrid. He has since returned to Bir Zeit to continue in the same capacity.

Albert is a man with vast connections throughout all the different religious and political communities in Jerusalem—with contacts so broad and with such a reputation for getting things done that if elections were held for mayor of East Jerusalem, Albert would surely be the uncontested winner. When it comes to Riyad Malki's allegations, Albert's defense of Hanan is unconditional. According to Agazarian, not only was there a human rights committee on Bir Zeit's campus but Hanan was indeed its founder and eventual chairperson. "There wasn't one time when Hanan wasn't involved on campus negotiating with the army," he says without hesitation. "Not a single incident when she wasn't right there in the middle of things, and I should know because as head of the PR Department I was called in every time there was trouble." Yet he is equally definite when he discusses the reasons that Hanan is criticized by her peers.

"Hanan's credentials were never the problem," Albert adds thoughtfully. "The problem was that she never made up her mind who she was or what image she wanted to project to her own people. She always vacillated between the images of feminist, academic, politician, wife, and mother. And if *she* didn't know who she was, then how was anybody else supposed to know in order to accept her in any clear role?"

Agazarian believes that one of the basic problems that Malki or other critics have with Hanan is that she adjusts her views to any situation as it best benefits her own image in the Western media. "In my opinion," Albert continues, "one perfect example of her identity conflict is her so-called feminism. After she married Emil Ashrawi she continued to use her maiden name, Mikhael, which is an obviously Christian name, until she began having problems with some of the more radical Muslim groups at Bir Zeit. When she found her position as dean of the Faculty of Arts challenged by Muslim groups who wanted to replace her with one of their own, she began using her husband's name, which isn't as obviously Christian as her own. Now she has taken to using both names, perhaps because it's in vogue for professional women to use both their maiden and married names, like Hillary Rodham Clinton, for instance." It is this characteristic that provokes Albert's opinion that perhaps Hanan's most serious flaw is that she has no idea of her effect on people.

WHEN ONE MEETS HANAN for the first time, she announces almost instantly that she is an academic and not a politician. Ask her to define her role of spokesperson for the Palestinian delegation and she claims that she was merely expressing the hopes and dreams of all Palestinians rather than calculating to change any political agenda or image. Ever mindful of the tarnished image of the PLO, Hanan made a point of defining her job as limited to the human aspect of the tragedy and not the politics of the dilemma.

With the beginning of the Intifada the world became aware of every burning, beating, curfew, and closure that transpired between Israeli and Palestinian, with the former losing media support and the latter gaining it. It was during this media phase of the Palestinian revolution that Hanan offered a new slant on the issue of Palestinian independence. Her prowess in debate and her command of language indicated to the world that the PLO had indeed entered the diplomatic phase in its thirty-year struggle. But while liberal Israelis, devoted Palestinians, and hopeful Americans considered Hanan representative of the new peace-through-negotiation agenda of the PLO, they also were aware of the stigma connected to the organization. It was on those occasions when Hanan tried too hard to distance herself from PLO internal politics that she created problems for herself with the Palestinian leadership in Tunis.

Sameh Kanaan recalls an incident that occurred during the negotiations in Washington. It was an especially tense moment when the Syrian negotiating team threatened not to attend the next round of talks, given Israel's refusal to agree to relinquish the Golan Heights. "When Hanan was asked by a group of journalists if the Palestinians would attend the next round of talks even if the Syrians walked out," Kanaan recounts, "her immediate response was affirmative—that we would attend regardless of the Syrian position."

Hanan's response was damaging both because she didn't first consult the leadership in Tunis to understand the current situation and because of the timing. As it happened, Arafat was on his way to Damascus to meet with Syrian President Hafez al-Assad, for the first time in years, to repair what had been a ruptured relationship. "It was a stupid answer," Kanaan continues, "because it could have ended a PLO-Syrian reconciliation before it began. But while most of us were disappointed with her, we also understand her personal motivation. After all, if there was no Palestinian participation in the conference, there would be no more limelight for Hanan Ashrawi."

With the exception of that plane crash in the Libyan Desert four years ago, in which Arafat was feared missing and presumed dead and Hanan buried the PLO chairman too fast by calling for democratic elections, she has always tried to interject him into her speeches. Ever the academic, Hanan was careful to admit that no one really knew the extent of alienation between those Palestinians living under occupation and those living in exile throughout the world. Ever the spokesperson, she consistently talked about the PLO as a united entity with Arafat as its leader. Ever the diplomat, she scrupulously described the democratic process from within the PLO structure that allowed Arafat to remain in power and his policies to remain in practice by the "will of the people." Predictably, when she took that position there were those who challenged her commitment to peace.

Certain of her critics claimed that behind Hanan's cultured voice and moderate facade lurked a woman who was unwilling to compromise on any issue or nuance that dredged up past actions of the PLO or that gave Israel the slightest negotiating edge. Even one of her most vocal advocates, former Secretary of State James Baker, recalled that when he once described the negotiations as the "carrot-and-stick" approach to peace, Hanan snapped, "Why do the Israelis always get the carrot while the Palestinians always get the stick?" Yet, regardless of her reaction, those same critics agreed that with her killer smile—which conveyed in equally brilliant flashes entitlement, patience, ruthlessness, and sunlight—her razor-sharp responses captured world opinion each time she faced a camera. Off camera there were other problems.

One of Hanan's fundamental flaws is that she gives the

impression of being a walking aptitude test, asking leading questions and appraising answers before filing people away in mental categories of friend, enemy, potential friend, or eventual enemy of the Palestinian people. While she judges herself to be more intelligent than most, she also prides herself on an ability to strike a compatible level of dialogue with anyone regardless of his or her social or intellectual credentials—a technique that occasionally creates a sense that she is talking down to people. By her own admission she has no patience for stupidity and even less for ignorance. Another of Hanan's fundamental flaws is that she gives so many interviews, makes so many speeches, and answers so many questions that she has a tendency to forget what she says and ends up contradicting herself. One top Israeli military official, who keeps a file on every interview and statement that she has made, calls her a chameleon. Citing articles from the American, European, Arabic, and Israeli press, he contends that Hanan changes her position to fit the publication, tailors her response to satisfy the politics and nationality of the audience. Responding to such accusations, Hanan has repeatedly maintained: "Naturally, if I'm talking to *Ms.* magazine, for instance, I'm more apt to discuss topics that are relevant to the woman who reads it, different than if I'm talking to a journalist from an Arab publication. And by the way, what politician doesn't tailor statements to fit the audience?" Whether Hanan positions herself as an academic, feminist, or politician, she remains loyal to the notion that diverse opinion and opposition within the ranks of the PLO do not necessarily constitute conflict nor automatically create enemies. She maintains that—like other democratic governments—Palestinian society is pluralistic and can survive differing views even as they have to do with the peace process. Where once, she admits, it might have been ideal to strive for total political unity as a means of defeating the

Zionist entity, now the strength of the Palestinian struggle is in its diversity, significant of a growth and maturity in which disagreements don't necessarily end in massacres. Unfortunately, since the beginning of its history; again, just two days after that handshake on the White House lawn; and continuing now as well, that has not been the case.

GAZI MAHMUD ABU JIAB is a senior Intifada activist and a supporter of the PFLP who was first imprisoned by the Israeli authorities in 1969 for life and subsequently released after sixteen years in the 1986 exchange of prisoners orchestrated with the Ahmed Jibril organization. Abu Jiab was arrested again by the Israelis in 1988 for his activity in the Unified National Command of the Intifada and released after six months on financial guarantees, or bail. In an article for the East Jerusalem newspaper *El Kouds,* on May 10, 1992, he disagrees with Hanan on murders of Palestinians by Palestinians: "Often the murders of Palestinians by Palestinians are carried out in shocking ways and in front of the victim's family, in a hospital in front of other patients or in a holy mosque in front of worshippers. This is a clear indication that we [Palestinians] are on the way to losing our human element and to suffering from incurable mental diseases."

According to a study compiled by the IDF, in the seven years since the Intifada began, the number of Palestinians killed by other Palestinians has increased while the number of Palestinians killed by the army has decreased. In 1988, 21 Arabs were killed by other Arabs, while 279 were killed by the IDF; in 1989, 248 Arabs were killed by Israelis, while 138 were killed by Palestinians; in 1990, 119 were killed by Palestinians while 184 were killed by the IDF; in 1991, 82 were killed by the IDF while 194 were killed during internecine fighting; and in 1992, 223 were killed by other Palestinians, while 101 were killed by the IDF.

More recently three high-ranking PLO officials in Gaza, members of Fatah, were the victims of an internal conflict. In fact, the man in charge of all PLO finances within the Occupied Territories, Abu Khalid al-Amla, the same man who fought against Arafat on the side of Syria when the PLO had its base in Tripoli, Libya, is suspected of ordering the murders. Another prominent member of the PLO on the West Bank claims to have been with Arafat in Tunis when news of the first killing reached the PLO chairman. He calls the murders part of an internal struggle within the PLO leadership in which certain members of Fatah are trying to assure their place in the Occupied Territories after the peace accord goes into effect and Israel withdraws from Gaza and Jericho. The primary reason given for the killings was that the victims had formed a new PLO faction in Gaza, called the Pioneers of Fatah, which they refused, after several warnings, to dissolve. "I was sitting with [Arafat] in his bedroom in Tunis," the PLO official explains, "when he received a message from someone in Gaza that they were going to kill one of his men. The chairman's first reaction was disbelief. The next day I was with him again when he got the news that the man had indeed been murdered because he had refused to disband that new faction." While Arafat felt guilty about the murder, he refused to believe that any of his own men were responsible. It was too easy to assume that Mossad had listened in to the conversation in which the man had been warned by aides close to Arafat to dissolve the Pioneers of Fatah and had simply used the opportunity to eliminate a leading PLO activist. "After that first murder," the PLO official continues, "the murdered man's assistant called the chairman to say that he had all the details including the names of the murderers. A few hours later he was also fatally shot. And then, the next day, another close aide also called to say that he knew the names and details of the killings of both men." The official pauses. "That afternoon he was ambushed by masked men as he was leaving his house."

Hana Sinora, a noted Palestinian leader and the editor of the now-defunct newspaper *al-Fajr*, a publication that was financed by Arafat's Fatah, has himself been the victim of death threats from within the PLO for articles he published that criticized the PLO chairman. Sinora is also one of those relegated to the sidelines since Hanan's rise to fame. He is bitter about Hanan, claiming that the only reason she throws herself into the middle of the fray is to increase her visibility and prove her credentials. "She functions on an intellectual level," Sinora says. "She's only good at talking in abstractions about the tragedy of living under occupation. She has never experienced anything firsthand." Sinora claims that Hanan's major attribute is her talent for seducing the media and concentrating more on her love for her own words than the needs of her people: "Sometimes when Palestinian journalists ask her for an interview she'll claim that she's not well or that she's overworked, and then you read a statement she's made to an Israeli newspaper, for example. She's not in good standing with the local Palestinian press because she insists on speaking English. It's a snob thing: She confuses us with her audience in the West when she doesn't even speak our own language."

Michael Kady is one of the founders of the American-Arab Anti-Discrimination Committee. He believes that Hanan, as spokesperson for the Palestinian delegation to the peace talks, while consistently articulate and informed, evoking admiration and respect among tens of millions around the world, failed to garner support from her own people. "But if I were forced to grade her on her shrewdness for capitalizing on opportunities to propagandize for her cause, I would have to fail her." Kady claims that there have been innumerable times when Hanan received openings to "reach out" and bare her soul to the American people to make them understand the Palestinian cause. "And time and time again she reverted back to [being] the restrained academic lecturer. By wowing them with her rhetoric and learning, she left Americans cold and strangely disconnected from our suffering."

Not all Palestinians agree with Sinora or Kady. Imad Iyash, while suggesting that Hanan does not have among her credentials years of physical suffering in either prison or a refugee camp, marvels at her popularity in the United States and the effect it has had on those back in the Occupied Territories. "I was in Houston and Philadelphia to speak to the Arab community," he says, "and all everybody wanted to talk about was Hanan. Americans were begging me to tell them about Hanan, asking for my phone number to contact me to put them in touch with her to make speeches or just to write to her to tell her how much they admired her." While Iyash still voices regret that it was Hanan who gave the Palestinian cause global recognition, he also admits that the cause has taken on positive aspects since her involvement. "I never thought in my life that I would be in this position, from jail to diplomat, making speeches in America for the Palestinian cause. Hanan opened the door for Palestinians to be accepted as people."

THE CONSENSUS AMONG certain members of the Israeli press is not very different when it comes to any intellectual distance that Hanan puts between herself and the rest of the world. Some agree that while her intellect is superior, her delivery is occasionally incomprehensible even to those who speak English fluently. In his office in the newsroom of the Broadcast Center in Jerusalem, Ehud Ya'ari, the Dan Rather of Israeli television, talks about Hanan and her miraculous transition from obscure academic to sophisticated spokesperson for the

PLO. With his blue eyes intense and unblinking behind his rimless glasses, Ya'ari explains: "There are kibbutzniks, peaceniks, Likudniks, and no-goodniks like Mr. Arafat and his band of bums, and then there's Hanan Ashrawi, who holds herself up as an academic, someone above the fray and superior to most of the Palestinians living under occupation, which doesn't help those Israeli ministers who are really working for an agreement."

If Israelis such as Ehud Ya'ari view Hanan as an obstacle to peace, it is because she is an obstacle to peace on solely Israeli terms. With Hanan in the fray, she gives the Palestinians sufficient credentials to eliminate an Israeli edge in any debate.

According to Ya'ari, however, it was not only the Israelis who considered Hanan an obstacle to peace. He recounts an incident that almost cost Hanan her job during the opening days of the peace conference in Madrid.

The fact that the Palestinians were invited to participate in a world forum and allowed to present their own case was a historic event. What was crucial was that the speech delivered during those opening hours of the peace conference would carry more impact and emotion than any other ever presented on that subject. During the frantic hours and days before the opening round of ceremonies, in Madrid, a group of Palestinians including Hanan and the celebrated Palestinian poet, Mahmoud Darwish, labored over the words to be spoken at the opening of the conference by the head of the Palestinian delegation, Dr. Haidar abd al-Shafi. The decision to deliver the speech in English came after days of arguments between Hanan and the leadership back in Tunis, with Hanan finally prevailing because it was primarily the Americans who needed to understand and be convinced of the merits of the Palestinian cause. In the end it was Hanan who translated the entire text from Arabic into English. The response was almost unanimous; there was hardly anyone who either read the speech before or heard it while it was being delivered on international television who wasn't moved to tears. According to Ya'ari, tears flowed as well behind the scenes, but for a very different reason.

Minutes before Dr. Haidar was to step before the television cameras to present his cause, Hanan convinced him to insert the phrase "willing suspension of disbelief" as it applied to the unwillingness of the world to accept the Palestinian right of self-determination. Ya'ari smiles. "Naturally, Mr. Arafat wasn't a student of English literature and didn't know what the hell that meant. After he heard it he was furious, yelling and screaming for forty minutes on the phone, with Hanan crying and threatening to quit. Obviously he was more upset that she had done something without first checking with him than he was about the meaning of the words."

If Hanan doesn't speak the same language in literary terms as the leaders of the PLO in Tunis, or share the same experiences as most of her people living under occupation, she is certainly the ideal spokesperson to appeal to a world traumatized by terrorist actions committed in the name of the Palestinian cause. Months before the peace conference convened, the PLO leadership realized that Hanan had the potential for presenting the Palestinian cause more effectively than it had ever been presented before. If only her words didn't get in the way of the facts; if only she could learn to write and speak simply so that the most apolitical spectator could understand. The turning point in Hanan's career came at the International Press Club in Washington, D.C., after the Intifada began, when she became familiar, and before the opening of the peace conference in Madrid, when she became famous. There were a lot of nervous coughs and baffled expressions during Hanan's speech that evening, but not one question at the end, which indicated that few had any idea what Hanan was talking about. To give an example of Hanan's style before she made the transition from incomprehensible to incomparable, here is a portion of her speech delivered at the International Press Club:

> It [the conference] is an inextricable set of internal dynamics, self-generating as a result of negotiation and a set of external factors between every participant that becomes a contract. The internal dynamic in many ways is a result of the fusion of substance and political position which translates those positions into mechanisms generating momentum and progress. As far as external factors are concerned, we all have cultural historical luggage when we come to the negotiating table.

A highly placed Palestinian leader was in the audience that night, along with an American whose area of expertise was political image making, getting American politicians elected by training them in public speaking and general appearance during their campaigns. His assessment of Hanan wasn't positive. What was positive was that he had been hired by the PLO and had already formulated a plan according to which Hanan would learn how to speak, smile, and move in front of an audience and a camera. And according to that Palestinian, the original idea to hire a political image maker originally came from Secretary of State James Baker and several of his team at the Pentagon. It was Baker and the "Baker boys" who needed to sell the whole idea of a Middle East peace conference with Palestinian involvement to the American voter, who held a predisposed negative opinion of all Palestinians. "They had the basics with Hanan," the Palestinian says. "Western clothes, makeup, education, and cadence of speech. The job now was to get Hanan to come across as more human."

Hanan was a quick study. Three weeks later when the conference convened in Madrid, the world heard a different Hanan, who had even coined a series of expressions that became part of her negotiating jargon. When referring to the relationship between the Israelis and the Palestinians within the context of the Occupied Territories, she called it the "fatal proximity"; when face-to-face dialogue between them was imminent, it became the introduction of the "human dimension"; when describing the involvement of the United States and the Soviet Union—the two original cosponsors of the peace conference—she used the phrase "driving forces." According to Hanan, when the "driving forces" demonstrated a "hands-on" policy, they were "catalysts"; if they made only limited efforts to speed progress along they were "spectators"; while if either side refused to address certain sensitive issues crucial to the dispute, they were accused of lapsing into an "invisible dialogue." Gradually, when the United States and the Soviet Union began to withdraw after the American presidential elections and the collapse of Communism, which resulted in a different set of priorities, Hanan observed, "We started out with two 'cosponsors' before one disappeared and the other became a 'permanent spectator.' "

Hanan spoke about "reciprocity" and "mutuality," meaning mutual recognition between Israelis and Palestinians, and "accountability" as it applied to protection for Palestinians under the auspices of human rights organizations. After a while her delivery became not only comprehensible but copied, as for example, when Margaret Tutweiler, the former spokesperson for the Department of State under Secretary James Baker, admitted, "Hanan's words are so etched in my mind that every time I brief the press or make a statement, I find myself wondering how Hanan would say it."

Not only did Ms. Tutweiler "wonder," but her boss wondered as well. And copied. Secretary of State Baker appropriated Hanan's words in Madrid when referring to the peace talks as the beginning of the "human dimension." Hanan took it as quite natural. "Maybe he understood my invisible message that the human substance was always more my concern than the political veneer," she said simply.

While it is clear that Hanan retained enough of her intellect to remain credible, acquired enough warmth to appear human, and used phrases consisting of not more than two words and words of not more than two syllables to make her speeches and pleas memorable, it still didn't improve her image within her own community.

The impression she gave the more simple residents of the Occupied Territories was of inaccessibility while the more culturally elite, those Palestinians who worked with her at Bir Zeit or served with her on various international peace committees, accused her of having sold out to the Americans. She responds: "A couple of meetings with Baker or Dennis Ross at the Pentagon doesn't make me an American agent. People here are naive; they don't understand the concept of *realpolitik*."

A member of the Palestinian delegation claims that it is not only the nuances of diplomacy or *realpolitik* that cause the misimpression of Hanan among her own people. According to him, if the Americans changed her manner of speaking to reach the uneducated masses, there was no one on the Palestinian side who advised her to stop using convoluted and highly technical terms. "The Americans taught her how to speak for them," he says. "In Arabic her speeches and briefings are still long-winded, belaboring the obvious and making reference to literary figures in English literature. It's obvious that she's more in love with her own words and intellect than with our cause."

Despite Hanan's verbal commitment to feminist issues, which includes her participation in international women's forums, whose agendas are to further women's rights throughout the world, she is also criticized by women. Certain of those women on both sides of the Green Line, whose backgrounds and lives range from the elite in exile to the militant in prison, have different opinions of Hanan concerning her ability and effectiveness in speaking for the cause.

Zahira Kamel explains. "Hanan is a writer, while I support the Intifada on a grassroots basis, mobilizing people and acting on my beliefs. Hanan is the voice, the connection within the Palestinian society—the village people, city people, high officials, laborers, martyrs, all factions—and with the outside world. But just because she doesn't have much contact with the refugees or speak the language of the people doesn't mean she doesn't understand the hardships of the occupation. We all do: It's part of life. I've had many disagreements with Hanan about how to handle the influence of Hamas on the women in the refugee camps."

Zahira not only supports Hanan's contribution to the Palestinian cause but also defends her views concerning the women whose lives are vastly different, living under occupation. "One of the first times Hanan went with me to Gaza we learned that Hamas was threatening women if they didn't cover their heads. Hanan felt we should confront the leaders and resist, while I argued that women should cover their heads if that meant they could go out and work, because if they rebelled they would be forced to stay at home and not come to our women's groups or earn money for their families. I felt covering their heads was a small price to pay, since these women basically want to be liberated from their husbands and freed from occupation. The *chador* doesn't change their feelings. What Hanan believes is that we should have fought the fanatics and taken over the mosques, dared to go there and speak out against the extremists, but that's easy for her to say because she's not actually out there to get shot, stabbed, or beaten. While I agree with Hanan that the mosque is for everyone, not just for the new wave of *mullahs* and clerics who want to turn Gaza into another Iran, it's too late to confront the big issues. Right now we have our hands full with the occupation, so the last thing we need is to call attention to women on the streets. There have been too many incidents where women have been stoned if they haven't complied to the rules of the ultra religious." Zahira smiles sadly. "But again, it's understandable that Hanan acts so brave, since she lives in an urban area and not in a refugee camp. It's hard to imagine the realities some of our women face when life is so very different in Ramallah."

On the subject of women who have achieved prominence in the Middle East, Leila Shahid admits that while there are very few Palestinian women in important political positions, any chauvinism within the Palestinian culture is no different than in other cultures or countries. "In fact," she argues, "the ratio of women who are members of the Palestine National Council is greater than women who are members of the United States Senate or the Israeli Knesset." In Leila's estimation the most important contribution that Hanan has made to the struggle is to give the people back their identity by turning what was considered an existential revolution into a pragmatic political cause. "Hanan reversed years of prejudice to give us back a stake in our own land."

Rula Khalil is currently serving twenty-five years without parole—the maximum penalty under Israeli law for murder—in Tel Mond Women's Prison in Natanya. Rula was convicted of hacking to death an Israeli student in Jerusalem and cutting up his body in small pieces, as well as murdering an Israeli soldier with an ax. From Tel Mond, where Rula is the PFLP representative within the prison, she talked about the common bond that joins all Palestinians. "What has to be clear is that we are all part of the PLO regardless of what faction we belong to or what we decide to do for the cause. The PLO takes care of all of us, whether we are Rula in prison or Hanan on television. I'm fighting for peace here while Hanan fights for peace on the outside, and when I was on the outside I made the armed struggle while Hanan negotiated with words, exactly the way it was in Vietnam when negotiation for peace was accompanied by violence. There isn't a revolution in history that succeeded with only one method. You have to use both to get a peace agreement. Weakness won't do it. The world was asleep until a Palestinian child threw a stone, and that small stone created the women of our struggle, both me and Hanan."

Of course, the prototype for the female Palestinian terrorist is still Leila Khaled, a hijacker and former sex symbol of the Palestinian revolution during the 1970s. According to Richard Murphy, undersecretary of state for Middle Eastern affairs in the Bush administration, Leila and Hanan are the only two notable women to have emerged from the Palestinian struggle. "Leila Khaled was the first woman to bring the Palestinian cause to the forefront of the news, even if she did it in a negative way. But still, it was the beginning of the world's awareness of the Palestinian cause."

Both Leila and Hanan have contributed in different ways to focusing international attention on their cause. Coming from the woman who blew up two aircraft and underwent plastic surgery twice to alter her appearance so she wouldn't be recognized by airport authorities in order to carry out more "revolutionary hijackings," Leila's criticism of Hanan has curiously to do with her role as a woman. Leila says, "Hanan isn't a loving or caring woman, but rather a woman who neglects her family by traveling all over the world." The former terrorist remains a firm believer that being a truly liberated woman means that no area of responsibility should suffer. "Regardless of a woman's job," she continues, "her first responsibility is to her husband and children, and Hanan has obviously forgotten her priorities since she has become so visible." It is with nostalgia that Leila recalls those years when she was as visible a symbol of the Palestinian cause as Hanan is now. "When I was hijacking airplanes," she says matter-of-factly, "I was married to my first husband, who was also a freedom fighter for the cause, so there were no conflicts at home."

Married to her second husband and the mother of two boys, Leila now heads the Palestinian Women's Committee, which is headquartered outside Damascus. No longer in a high-visibility job, she is responsible for improving living conditions for those Palestinians living in UN–sponsored refugee camps throughout the Arab world. Plump and middle-aged, Leila accepts her place in Palestinian history. Nevertheless, her assessment of Hanan and the role she currently plays might be interpreted as not entirely objective. "Times have changed," she admits, "and while some of us had our moment in history, it doesn't necessarily mean that we've given up the fight. The only way we're going to achieve statehood is with a combination of dialogue and revolutionary acts which is something, I believe, Hanan knows." She pauses to push back her dark, wavy hair, holding it away from her face as she concludes, "There's no guarantee that negotiations will liberate Palestine, which means that just as Hanan replaced Leila, it's possible that a younger Leila will replace Hanan."

Dominique Roch, an attractive woman of thirty-five, is an example of "royalty" among Palestinians—those who can trace their roots back to the nineteenth century, when Palestine was under Turkish rule during the Ottoman Empire. Her great-uncle, Alfred Roch, was one of the Palestinians who negotiated with the British during the Mandate and was eventually exiled to the Seychelles Islands for his efforts. Yet she also has her own views, not only about who is qualified to speak for her people in their quest for a state, but also about what exactly are the fair and just borders of that state.

From Paris, where she works as a journalist for Radio France, Roch explained her position. "Hanan is speaking for the refugees in the camps and for the people actually living in the Occupied Territories. For me the reality is that my family will never be able to come back and recuperate the land we lost in Haifa and Jaffa because only the land in the West Bank and in Gaza is under discussion. Hanan is not speaking for me." Yet, notwithstanding Roch's resignation concerning her gains in any eventual Palestinian-Israeli accord, she admits that there have been many positive aspects to Hanan speaking for her people. "Single-handedly," she says, "Hanan turned around world opinion, [so that] we are now perceived as a civilized people with intellect instead of a band of terrorists." Roch recalled the first time people in Beirut became aware of Hanan. "It was right after her appearance on *Nightline*. Everybody in the streets, in the stores, in the cafés, was talking about her; they were so proud when they asked each other who this Palestinian woman was who made the world cry for our sorrow. It isn't necessary to suffer in a refugee camp to understand the feeling of tragedy and sadness that goes with being a Palestinian. I live with it every day of my life in Paris."

Opinions about Hanan from women on the other side of the struggle are as diverse. Some left-wing Israeli women, with whom she has served on human rights committees or marched in peace demonstrations, consider her a sincere advocate for peace and passive resistance. Others who are not politically active but who have watched her for years either on Israeli television or on CNN simply dismiss her as a *farbissineh-klafteh*, Yiddish for a woman who is unfeminine and bitter, while some who are more politically aware view her as the last chance to negotiate with a Palestinian who doesn't have "blood on her hands." Yet, even within a politically sophis-

142

ticated milieu, there is still competition and criticism when it comes to Hanan.

Yael Dayan, novelist and daughter of the late Israeli Defense Minister Moshe Dayan, is a vocal advocate for Peace Now, a left-wing Israeli group that presses for the return of Palestinian land in the West Bank and Gaza, and also a member of the Knesset for the Labor party. She has her own problems with Hanan that are not limited to times spent on opposite sides of a debating table.

Dayan recounts an incident that occurred at the Hakawati Theater in East Jerusalem, when Hanan delivered a speech to a group of Palestinian and Israeli women. "I think the problem is more that Hanan forgets where she is, since she's so used to talking to the Western media or politicians." As was usually the case, after Hanan finished her speech that evening there were questions. "There must have been two hundred people in the room," Dayan begins, "when a Palestinian woman raised her hand, making it immediately obvious that she was very self-conscious about speaking out in public. The woman started by telling Hanan that as a Palestinian she was honored that Hanan spoke for her and then explained that she preferred to ask her question in Hebrew because her Arabic wasn't very good—not unusual for Israeli Arabs to feel more comfortable speaking Hebrew." Dayan shrugs. "Anyway, even educated Palestinians feel self-conscious speaking Arabic in front of Hanan since she speaks it so poetically. How was a simple, uneducated woman supposed to feel?"

According to Dayan, Hanan screamed at the woman in front of everybody. "She insulted her, told her she should be ashamed of herself for forgetting her Arabic roots by speaking the language of the occupation. It was awful. Everybody there was shocked, especially when the woman ran out of the room in tears."

Hanan dismisses the issue with a wave of her hand. "I

don't remember the incident," she claims, "but perhaps I was just fed up with those Uncle Tom Palestinians living under Israeli rule." She looks disturbed. "Yael and I have worked on many committees together for peace and women's rights, but deep down she is right wing when it comes to any peace settlement. Maybe that's the reason for the story."

Dayan responds, "Hanan is sophisticated both negatively and positively, because she's quite adept at hitting below the belt during any debate. But what really fascinates me is how fluid her tongue is and how she talks in a completely different style when she's in Israel or on the West Bank than when she's abroad. She knows how to play the audience to give the impression that she's a moderate, even though she's not more moderate than the others. While I don't exactly identify her as my friend, I'm careful not to make her angry. The big problem with Hanan is that she forces me to take my opinions down a notch or two so we don't get hung up on semantics and can get down to substance. She can be very arrogant."

Nomi Chazan, a member of the Knesset from the Meretz party, has been involved in women's movements within Israel and the Occupied Territories since the beginning of the Intifada. While she is unable to date the beginning of her friendship with Hanan, she can cite the first time they began working together during a women's conference in Brussels in 1989. "We were both attending a meeting where there was an exchange of ideas and a dialogue between Palestinian and Israeli women that was to finish by our drafting a joint statement for peace. It was there that we discovered that we were on the same wavelength."

There are other similarities between the two women that transcend politics, beginning with their age (their birthdays are two weeks apart); they are both academics who have children the same age, and they are both chain-smokers and each married to men who have taken over the daily care of the house and family. "After Brussels, Hanan and I set up two separate movements. I was the force behind the Israeli Women's Peace Net, while she was my counterpart. From the beginning Hanan's rise was meteoric, and the more she did her job, the more confident she became. She was always a quick study. By providing a voice for her people and representing the mainstream, she changed the image and strategy of the PLO although she never pushed herself into the discussion. Certainly I would rather see her heading this whole peace initiative, since I would much prefer having Hanan as my 'enemy,' in quotes, given that she is also my friend. We . . . periodically joke that if everybody would leave us alone in a room, we could finish this whole thing off satisfactorily and quickly."

Hanan has said that although Nomi Chazan is a colleague, friend, and partner for peace, she remains a Zionist. And while Chazan agrees that she is indeed a Zionist, she also maintains that the definition of Zionism has changed with the political times. For Chazan, Zionism resulted in the Jewish national liberation movement, which gave Jews the right to create a state in Israel. By definition Israel should have a Jewish majority, which would preclude Jews ruling over Palestinians. "In ten or fifteen years," Chazan explains, "if we continue to do that, we won't have a Jewish majority, so where is the national movement that we want in our society, which is based on a Jewish heritage, culture, and tradition?"

While both women are striving for a Palestinian state, Hanan considers it more a nominative issue than one of demographics, although both regard it as unethical for any group to deprive another of its basic civil and human rights. "You cannot be democratic for some people," Hanan says, "and not for others." Chazan adds, "One of the major sources of our security in the past forty-six years is that we've succeeded in maintaining a democracy in very adverse circumstances. But we can't continue to be democratic if we don't give people the right to vote and be elected, or keep them in prison without a trial." From Chazan's point of view there are only two options: "Either we check out of the territories or we give the population the right to vote and be elected and everything else under Israeli law, which includes all human rights. But if we do that, we become a bilateral state, which is not something that I want. On the other hand, I don't want to live in a state that is not democratic, and occupation is basically undemocratic."

While Nomi Chazan's definition of Zionism takes into consideration the current political options under discussion, some Israelis remain wedded to what was once a more relevant definition of Zionism. Ariel Sharon, a right-wing politician, and former defense minister who orchestrated the Israeli invasion of Lebanon in 1982, has his own definition of Zionism, which is "keeping your head down when Palestinians launch Katyusha rockets across the northern border from Lebanon." About Hanan, he is dismissive when he says, "The Palestinians need a feminist about as much as Hanan Ashrawi needs a haircut."

Another right-wing Israeli, Yigal Carmoun, the prime minister's adviser on counterterrorism under both Shamir and Rabin, and a former member of the Israeli delegation on the Syrian negotiating team, has trouble referring to Hanan as anything other than "the Whore." When asked to elaborate he makes vague references to a Palestinian lover in London and shopping sprees financed by the PLO. When asked for specifics he is unfortunately unable to provide any for reasons of "security."

Hanan finds the response typical. "When the Israelis decide to close a kindergarten they claim it's for security reasons," she says disgustedly. On the subject of a lover in London, she retorts, "Since taking on this job I haven't been able to sleep alone, I've been so busy, so a lover in London or anywhere else is ridiculous. Anyway, doesn't it count that I happen to be happily married?" And on that subject Emil Ashrawi adds, "If people can't discredit Hanan based on her intelligence, talent, or credentials, they'll make up vicious rumors." When it comes to "shopping sprees" Hanan explains that the entire budget for the Palestinian delegation, including travel, hotel, phone, and fax, is paid out of the Palestine National Fund with checks issued through the Orient House, the East Jerusalem headquarters for the Palestinian delegation. Ronnie Shaked, a former Shin Bet agent and currently a journalist covering events in the Occupied Territories for *Yediot Aharanot,* one of Israel's leading newspapers, explains: "It wasn't only travel expenses that the PLO paid for but also for clothes. The PLO leadership wanted their male delegates to look respectable and wear proper suits and ties so they instructed them to buy clothes and turn in the receipts for reimbursement. It's likely that they gave Hanan the same instructions, which probably accounts for those rumors of shopping sprees."

While Arafat remains in sole control of all PLO finances—a fact that has become a growing source of dissatisfaction among Palestinian leaders throughout the Occupied Territories—the responsibility for daily expenditures during the initial peace conferences in Washington was handled by several of his close aides. Muhammad Ishtayye was one; Salah Zuheila was another, although he was only involved for one or two rounds, and Hamdullah Alul was a third. On the subject of Hanan's expenditures Nabil Shaath offers this comment: "Of all our people who turn in receipts for justified expenditures, Hanan spends the least amount of money. She's a true intellectual, more interested in making headway with the negotiations than in how she looks."

Hanan has consistently maintained that she has never

taken any money from the PLO, neither when she was working full-time at Bir Zeit University nor when she became the official spokesperson for their delegation. In fact, while she was on leave from Bir Zeit, the university continued giving her a salary, money that stopped last September. "The university decided then that I was on leave without pay," Hanan says, "which meant that I spent a lot of my own money while I held the job of spokesperson for the delegation." (She is referring to income derived from several properties in East Jerusalem left to her by her father.)

Most of the other Palestinian delegates were either paid by their respective political parties or made private arrangements with their regular employers. What is certain is that, given the financial hardships suffered by the PLO, part of the displeasure now expressed by those delegates or by leaders within the Occupied Territories is economically based.

IN ONE OF THE FEW instances in which they are in accord, Israelis and Palestinians agree that Hanan is more a creation of the Americans than she is a choice of either the Palestinians as a leader or of the Israelis as an adversary. Most of those on both sides of the struggle who have observed her since her return from the United States to the West Bank in 1972 agree that she came back not only with a set of slogans and ideas from the intellectual left but also with several acquaintances who would prove to be solid political contacts.

Peter Jennings wasn't the only American who noticed the young Palestinian woman. Several Western diplomats in Jerusalem took notice of the attractive, American-educated feminist who chain-smoked her way through official receptions. It was through a friendship with the wife of the British consul, however, that Hanan became a regular guest at the private dinner parties. And it was during one of those dinners that Hanan met Thomas Pickering, who, at the time, was the United States ambassador to Jordan.

According to Pickering, who was fascinated by Hanan's intellect and knowledge of Chaucer and charmed by her refreshing independence, he encouraged her to take the position of dean of the Faculty of Arts at Bir Zeit. Hanan credits another person with that decision. "While he [Pickering] was a big supporter, I credit my husband with convincing me to take on that job, since he himself knew it meant I wouldn't be home very much to take care of the house and children." And Emil concurs. "We had many discussions about Hanan's career," he says, "and there was no question in my mind that she was meant to do great things. It was worth it to all of us that she achieved her full potential."

Mahmoud Nofel, a Palestinian from Ramallah, was a member of the economic advisory committee to the Palestinian delegation and one of the more influential members of the PLO. He is not particularly supportive of Hanan's stellar rise as spokesperson for the Palestinians. "We have a saying here," Nofel begins, "that the person who grows and nurtures something will harvest it. In this case it seems that even though we did the growing and nurturing, it is Hanan who is reaping the glory." According to Nofel, Hanan didn't care about the Palestinian cause before 1980 because she was too busy with her studies in Beirut and Virginia, and before 1987 because she was too busy with her feminist activities. "It was her love affair with the West that made her take notice of what was happening to her own people," Nofel claims.

THE INFIGHTING between the Palestinian leadership inside the Occupied Territories and those who remain financially and symbolically responsible on the outside has been going on since the PLO was founded. If there is any change in the confusion and dissension that are part of the usual operating policy of the PLO, it is due in part to the organization's transition from revolutionary to political to economic. And if Hanan is the current focus of rumors, she is by no means

the first or the last Palestinian leader to suffer the consequences of representing an organization that thrives on back-
biting and intrigue.

Given the changing world order, which forced the PLO
to project a different image and present a new agenda, Israel
made the best deal it could with an organization that was in
no position to make a better one. During different periods of
their occupation of the territories, the Israelis have played a
substantial role in pitting one group of Palestinians against
another. Historically the Israelis have always supported the
weakest link within the Palestinian leadership to dilute the
power of the strongest. Within the Occupied Territories they
have also tried to cement alliances with those Palestinian
leaders who were predisposed toward tacit cooperation,
which would ensure easier living conditions under occupation.

THE ISRAELI ATTEMPT TO CREATE "alternative leaderships"
within the Occupied Territories that would dilute the influence and power of the PLO is a story that began some twenty
years ago. While the majority of those plans failed to depose
Yasir Arafat permanently, what emerged was a temporary
hierarchy of internal Palestinian leaders who became Israel's
initial partners in peace. Ironically even those who recently
acted as Palestinian delegates to the peace conference seemed
to forget that the basic concept for their participation was
not to replace but to represent the PLO. In the end, when it
became obvious to everyone that the PLO still had all the
options to keep its delegates or make them withdraw, to
accept proposed conditions or reject them, the Israelis
changed their focus to the outside leadership, culminating in
a peace accord signed by Yasir Arafat. What the Israelis could
never overcome in their attempts to dilute the power of the
PLO—and what the Americans never understood when they

tried to exclude the PLO from the peace negotiations—was that any leader inside the Occupied Territories was made on the basis of grassroots support. Similarly, it was a reality that Hanan always refused to face. Never for an instant, while she was acting as spokesperson for the PLO or making pronouncements that she was "carrying the PLO on her shoulders throughout all the debates," did she believe that the Israelis would finally agree to direct negotiations with Arafat. Despite all her statements and pleas to the contrary, Hanan believed that she was fighting a lost cause when it came to persuading the Israelis and the Americans to accord legitimacy to the PLO. There had been too long a history of repeated terrorist attacks and infighting within the organization for even such an articulate spokesperson to succeed at convincing the opposition that Arafat had indeed changed his tactics. The only change that occurred was that while the Palestinian people continued to consider the PLO to be their legitimate voice, they did not necessarily consider it to be their sole voice.

CHAPTER EIGHT

ALTERNATIVE LEADERSHIP

FOR YEARS Palestinians have been claiming that the world became aware of their plight only after the PLO emerged as their one authentic leadership. In the early 1970s Palestine and the PLO provided the central theme of the Arab League—specifically, in 1974 during the Rabat summit, when the PLO was first recognized as the sole representative of the Palestinian people. Later the United Nations followed, and then, in 1980, the European Community declared Palestinian self-determination to be one of the main points in its collective Middle East policy. Although the Arab world was determined to utilize the Palestinian cause to destroy the Israeli state, and the Soviet Union had its own agenda for establishing a military and strategic foothold in that region, the result was that the PLO could always count on others to adopt its cause. Yet, despite Arab and Soviet allegiance, the PLO and all other involved parties were aware that without the sanction and approval of the Western world, any settlement of the dispute would never have full legitimacy.

In 1978 civil war broke out in Lebanon, with Christian and Muslim factions fighting to gain control of the country. At the same time Syria took advantage of the opportunity to realize its goal of hegemony in the region by sending in troops to back any Lebanese militia sympathetic to its regime. As the chaos within Lebanon increased, Israel also took advantage of the situation by launching its first military incursion, Operation Litani, as far as the Litani and Awali rivers, to eliminate PLO terrorist bases that were attacking northern Israeli settlements. Gradually the international media included in their reports the number of Palestinian civilians, residents of various refugee camps scattered throughout Lebanon, who had been tortured, wounded, and killed in the fighting.

In June 1981 Israeli Gen. Ariel Sharon was appointed minister of defense in the newly elected Likud government under Prime Minister Menachem Begin. The platform responsible for the Likud victory was not only to drive the PLO out of Lebanon—forcing them into Egypt, Jordan, and Syria—but also to diminish the organization's influence throughout the Occupied Territories. As the fighting in Lebanon escalated and Israeli troop presence increased, the political plan was an eventual peace accord between Lebanon and Israel. Not only would the plan represent the second historic peace agreement between Israel and an Arab nation, but it would also represent a joint effort between the newly elected Lebanese president, Bashir Gemayel, and the Israeli government to rid Lebanon of external forces, specifically Syria and the PLO.

The accord was doomed to fail. On September 24, 1982, Bashir Gemayel was killed in a bomb blast as he delivered a speech to a group of supporters at his party headquarters near Beirut. Any hope for that Lebanese-Israeli peace treaty leading to an end to the Lebanese civil war was destroyed in the rubble of that explosion. What followed, under the command of Defense Minister Sharon and Israeli Chief of Staff Gen. Rafael Eitan, was a final effort by the Israelis to destroy the PLO by pushing Israeli forces all the way to Beirut. The reaction from the international community was double edged; for the first time in its history Israel was perceived as having participated in an offensive military action that went far beyond its recognized borders, while the PLO was suddenly elevated to victim status, viewed by the world as a nation in exile.

AFTER THE WITHDRAWAL of Israeli troops from Lebanon in 1982, Arab states augmented their financial support of the PLO by pouring billions of dollars into their coffers. That annual revenue, coupled with the 10 percent tithing taken every year from each Palestinian who lived and worked throughout the Middle East, made them the richest group of underprivileged people in the world. In fact, while the Palestinians, for the most part, languished in refugee camps, the PLO leadership lived extravagantly throughout the world. But it wasn't until the organization continued to rely on terrorist attacks to make the world aware of its cause that the Palestinians lost their previously earned victim status. As the Western community fell prey to a spree of international assassinations and hijackings, costing numerous human casualties, opinion gradually turned against both the PLO and the plight of the Palestinians.

In its own defense the PLO claimed that it was the focus of a vicious public relations campaign waged by the Zionists and the pro-Israel lobby in the United States. Yet, while insisting that violence was the natural process in any revolution that galvanized the people as well as attracted global attention to a political cause, Yasir Arafat systematically denied involvement with terrorism by blaming renegade PLO factions or covert operations by Mossad. Even Hanan, who always claimed to be opposed to violence, defended the rights of Palestinians living under Israeli occupation to attack targets throughout the West Bank and Gaza. More precisely, she talked about the "complex irony" of the Israelis who, as classic victims of anti-Semitic persecution at the hands of Europeans, had produced a nation of people who victimized others. Despite any attempt to show the political and human injustice suffered by the Palestinian people after the loss of Palestine, however, the West remained firmly on Israel's side, judging it to be a state comprised of people who had survived the most famous massacre in modern history to emerge as a country forced to wage a daily battle of survival against a hostile Arab world.

Shortly after the Israeli withdrawal from Lebanon, a plan to settle the problem of the Occupied Territories was conceived by Menachem Milson, a professor of Arabic literature at Hebrew University in Jerusalem and the former head of the Civil Administration (November 1981–September 1982). The purpose of the plan, known as the Village Leagues, was to create a malleable rural leadership comprising pro-Jordanian Palestinians who would be allowed to take charge of such issues as education and health care. Under the plan, while the Israeli military government would actively continue to curtail PLO influence, it would simultaneously encourage those Palestinians who openly recognized Israel to emerge as more powerful and influential local leaders. The political aspect to this new policy would be to guide those Palestinians toward bona fide peace negotiations with Israel while diluting the power and influence of the PLO. In fact, as far back as 1970, Shimon Peres, one of the main architects of that handshake on the White House lawn, wrote: "Certainly, no political solution is possible as long as there are no West Bank Arab leaders prepared to step forward and publicly declare their readiness to reach one." And in 1982 Yitzhak Rabin, the man who was to shake Arafat's hand on the White House lawn, observed, "The emergence of Palestinian leaders on the West Bank who were openly ready for negotiations with Israel must be seen as a necessary precondition for progress toward peace, whether it be peace according to the plan of Labor or of Likud." But despite the initial optimism and willingness to make the plan work, it was doomed to fail as a result of both confused Israeli policy and fear on the part of certain Arab nations that the PLO would cease to provide cheap labor and willing martyrs.

From the Israeli side, official policy toward this emerging group of local Palestinian leaders was indeed confused. While Ariel Sharon, still functioning as minister of defense, was unwilling to consider the Palestinians' political demands, the position of the Israeli military government made certain decisions that were ambiguous as they affected the ultimate goal of creating viable leaders who would become partners in peace. One incident tells the story.

A group of young Palestinians who had become politically active under the Village Leagues laid the groundwork for a new political organization called the Palestinian Democratic Movement for Peace, which called for negotiations with Israel leading to an eventual settlement regarding the Occupied Territories. Several months later it was the Israeli military government and not the PLO that forbade the group from holding a rally at which they planned to announce the official establishment of their party. Nevertheless, several months later again, when a large group of leading West Bankers informed the Israeli military government of their intention to travel to Amman to meet with Yasir Arafat, permission was granted.

From the other side of the conflict, there were also reasons for opposing the plan—mainly that Jordan and the external PLO leadership were afraid of being excluded from any eventual conciliation between Israel and the Palestinians living throughout the Occupied Territories. Since 1967 Palestinian leaders living on the West Bank and Gaza had always suffered under the oppression not only of the Israelis but of outside

PLO leaders as well, who suspected that they might ultimately exchange their loyalty to the PLO for a better life under occupation. Instead of categorically suppressing those local leaders who obviously enjoyed an impressive amount of grass-roots support throughout the West Bank and Gaza, the PLO external leadership embarked on a plan whereby they would allow those internal leaders to remain visible and viable while controlling their activities by keeping them under the financial auspices of the PLO. Although the PLO allowed local leaders a modicum of independence to serve the community on non-political levels, the stipulation was that their loyalty to the PLO was never to fall under suspicion. It was then that the Arab Summit Conference in Baghdad voted to give $120 million annually for what was termed "steadfastness" in the Occupied Territories. Any organized Palestinian group or union that was affiliated with the PLO could get money for a building project or grants for any one of the universities throughout the territories.

All over the West Bank and Gaza, trade and student unions appeared, professional associations for doctors and lawyers, women's and health groups, and the most important and powerful, a youth committee for social action known as *al-Shabiba,* which accounted for most of the young pro-PLO activists. While the other unions and organizations remained for the most part apolitical, the Shabiba aligned themselves with various PLO factions such as the Palestinian Communist Party (PCP), the DFLP, and the PFLP. For a while, as long as those organizations demonstrated their loyalty to the PLO as well as an apolitical agenda to the Israeli authorities, things went smoothly.

From the Israeli side the situation began to deteriorate only when the military government realized that large amounts of PLO money were pouring into the Occupied Territories and being used for terrorist activities, operating safe

houses, and buying weapons. On the other side, the deterioration was due to the PLO's realization that this new generation of young activists was increasingly intolerant and
impatient with the leadership's efforts to put an end to occupation. The situation was certainly not made any easier
when the Shabiba were given the opportunity to attend Israeli-
sponsored universities only to exit to dismal employment
possibilities.

The Shabiba were members of a generation over whom
fathers and grandfathers had lost control, a youth who wore
their arrests, prison records, and wounds with pride. While
their grandfathers had fled the Jews in 1948 and their fathers
had been driven out by the Israelis in 1967, their refusal to
continue that legacy of loss played havoc on the structure of
the Palestinian family. While the previous generations had
seemingly come to terms with the situation, speaking Hebrew
and, for those who remained, feeling grateful for the chance
to work in Israeli factories and live without war, it was the
Shabiba who stepped in to change the fate of the people.
These were the stone throwers who knew only a dead-end
life under occupation—few ever having had an Israeli friend,
few never having been interrogated by Israeli security forces.
Also unlike their fathers and grandfathers, they had never
been intimidated by Israeli might, witnessing instead the confusion and mistakes made by that elite Israeli Army in dealing
with a civilian uprising such as the Intifada. From the beginning of the uprising, their message was clear: Shoot me, arrest
me, or set me free. More critical was that these young men
were not even frightened by the wrath of the PLO.

The danger of this new generation became more apparent
when they began garnering increasing popularity and support
within the Palestinian population on the West Bank and Gaza.
As Hanan explained it, "There was a collective guilt among
those Palestinians like my father who fled the Israelis in forty-

eight since they never stopped feeling that they were responsible for the loss of Palestine. Up until the Intifada, that was
the generation that handed down to their sons and grandsons
a legacy of shame and defeat that only changed when those
same sons and grandsons took matters into their own hands."
As well as the last two generations of Palestinians living under
occupation, Hanan maintains, a new generation of Israelis
has contributed to the changing atmosphere throughout the
Occupied Territories. If any one event changed the thinking
of that new generation of Israelis, it was the massacres at the
Sabra and Shatila refugee camps during the Lebanon war.
The Kahane Commission was appointed by the Israeli government to investigate Israeli involvement when Phalange soldiers, in reprisal for the murder of Lebanese President Bashir
Gemayel, went into the camps and slaughtered hundreds of
Palestinian civilians. If the shame that permeated Israel could
be compared to the American response to any incident in U.S.
history, it was to the massacre of civilians at My Lai during
the Vietnam War. "Where there was once a fundamental
anger among the Israelis that we existed to remind them of
the injustice they had perpetrated on us," Hanan claims, "Sabra and Shatila and then the Intifada changed that anger into
guilt, which eventually forced a solution to the problem."
What is interesting to note, however, is that the only group
of people who demonstrated en masse in protest of Sabra and
Shatila were neither Palestinians nor other Arabs but Israelis,
who marched in the thousands on the streets of Tel Aviv.

As the Shabiba continued to gain popularity, the PLO
took a harder stand, forbidding them to make any unilateral
decisions and forcing them to act only as intermediaries between the residents of the territories and the government-in-
exile. And at the same time as the PLO cracked down on the
activities and influence of these young leaders, the Israelis
destroyed the PLO's base of operations in Lebanon in 1982,

creating a vacuum that further liberated the Shabiba, making them the dominant political factor in the Occupied Territories.

While still known as PLO supporters, these young radicals emerged as a group of public figures who remained unaffiliated with any particular faction and, on occasion, criticized PLO policy. Eventually the Shabiba expanded to become known as "independent nationalists," or "general personalities," *al-Shakhsiyat al-'aama*, comprised of journalists, academics, lawyers, former mayors, and other notables mostly from the Jerusalem-Ramallah area, whom the Israelis recognized as official spokespeople for the residents of the West Bank. It wasn't surprising, therefore, that when a delegation was eventually chosen and deemed acceptable to represent the PLO at the peace conference, it was these same men and women who were drafted. In fact, one of the most prominent leaders to emerge from that group was Dr. Haidar abd al-Shafi, the head of the Red Crescent Association in Gaza and eventually the head of the Palestinian delegation to the peace conference. Others from the group who found themselves in Madrid in October 1991, along with Dr. Haidar, were Sami Abdullah, an economics professor with ties to the Palestine Communist party; Fraih Abu Meddain, head of the Gaza Bar Association and pro-Fatah; Mamduh al-Aker, a surgeon and urologist, independent politically but bound through friendship to Faisal al-Husseini and Hanan Ashrawi; Saeb Erekat, a professor of political science at Najah University in Nablus, pro-Fatah; Elias Freij, the mayor of Bethlehem, who was considered close to Jordan; Abderrahman Hamad, dean of the Faculty of Engineering at Bir Zeit University, pro-Fatah; Nabil Ja'bari, a dental surgeon and chairman of the board of trustees of Hebron University; Sameh Kanaan, an employee of the Nablus Chamber of Commerce; Nabil Kassis, a physics professor at Bir Zeit; Ghassan Khatib, a professor of economic development at Bir Zeit and the founder of the Jerusalem Media Communications Center, with affiliations with the Palestine Communist party; Sami Kilani, a physics professor at Najah University and a poet, writer, and member of the Palestinian Writers' Union as well as the DFLP; and Mustafa Natsheh, an engineer who was deported to Jordan by the Israelis in 1983, also a member of Fatah. More significant to the potential image of the internal leadership, however, were the members of the steering committee of the Palestinian delegation, as they were the ones who briefed the press or gave lectures on the progress of the negotiations. Serving as head of that committee was Faisal al-Husseini, founder and head of the Arab Studies Society, pro-Fatah; Zahira Kamel, DFLP; Anis Kassel, living in Amman, an expert in international law and the chief editor of the *Palestine Yearbook of International Law;* Rashid Khalidi, a professor of Middle East history at the University of Chicago; Camille Mansour, professor of political science at the Sorbonne in Paris and the former director of research at the Institute for Palestine Studies in Beirut; Sari Nussibeh, professor of philosophy at Bir Zeit University and a leading pro-PLO activist; and of course, Hanan Ashrawi, spokesperson for the delegation.

With the exception of Dr. Haidar abd al-Shafi, who had a large following in Gaza, the Shakhsiyat were mostly intellectuals who lacked a certain grassroots base, making their public standing almost completely dependent on the PLO and their power base among those Palestinians in refugee camps and prisons almost negligible. In fact, large sections of the population resented that the Shakhsiyat spoke on their behalf, branding them "salon liberals" who had spent the years of occupation either hidden away in universities or lecturing outside the country. Although Hanan was considered an outstanding and influential member of that group, she was resented even more than the others on the streets of the West Bank and Gaza. Not only was she an academic and intellectual who had indeed spent years hidden away in Bir Zeit or on lecture tours throughout the world, but she was also a woman. And worse, she was a Christian.

In the pecking order of importance throughout the Occupied Territories, while the Shakhsiyat were clearly the elite, it was the Shabiba who controlled the cafés and the refugee camps. It was the Shabiba who hung around street corners looking to become martyrs while the Israeli Army seemed only too willing to accommodate them. Ironically, weeks before the Intifada broke out in December 1987, the Shakhsiyat had not yet organized into one main group that would become the directing force behind the Shabiba who actually went into the streets to confront the army. The Shakhsiyat were still functioning primarily as individuals whom the PLO exploited as presentable tools to explain to foreign dignitaries and the international media facts concerning the conditions of Palestinians living under Israeli rule.

As the PLO's economic situation worsened and as the Israelis cracked down on daily life in the Occupied Territories, the Shabiba took to referring to the PLO as a "Cadillac revolution gone fat." Gradually those Palestinians physically involved in the Intifada became aware that what they needed was a local leadership not only to keep up anti-Israeli momentum but to explore ways to make life in the territories more economically and socially viable. Whether in fighting a war of attrition against Israel or waging a rebellion against the PLO, the Palestinians on the West Bank and Gaza had, for the first time since 1967, taken their fate into their own hands. Predictably the PLO reaction was swift, an implicit threat that any Palestinians who tried to supplant them would be assassinated.

Sensing the growing hostility between the PLO and the

Palestinian internal leadership, the Israelis analyzed the rebellion as it might eventually create a new Palestinian hierarchy instead of focusing on any long-term political risks from the Intifada. What both the Israelis and the Americans needed was a sign that the seat of power had indeed shifted away from the PLO leadership outside, *al-kharij*, to the local leadership from within, *al-dakhil*. As the Intifada escalated, with no sign of abating, again the Israelis, along with the Americans, began looking for a structural crack in the PLO in order to support emerging leaders on the West Bank and Gaza. Unfortunately there were so many cracks within each different internal faction that it was impossible for any one group to guarantee majority control. Given the Soviet Union's approaching demise into economic disaster, which made it unable to continue supporting client states like Syria or terrorist organizations like the PLO, the Americans decided the time was right to open up a dialogue with the beleaguered PLO chairman. The justification was threefold: to dilute what appeared to be the mounting power of the Palestinians inside the territories who were leading the Intifada, to stop the Intifada, and to force the PLO to set a tone that would bring the rest of the Arab world to the conference table with Israel. After all, historically, Arafat had always managed to pull things together to control his majority faction of the PLO.

One year into the Intifada, on December 15, 1988, Robert Pelletreau, then serving as American ambassador to Tunisia, announced that the United States would begin formal talks with the PLO. Using a microversion of a political theory that was a version of "cross-alliances"—not allowing one side in any conflict to gain too much power as was seen during the Iran-Iraq War—the United States outlined certain conditions that would be the basis for the talks. On December 16, 1988, Ambassador Pelletreau conveyed to the government of Israel what he described as the "talking points," or the conditions set down by the United States for the impending dialogue with the PLO. In reality those "talking points" were nothing more than a variation of the points contained in UN Security Council Resolutions 242 and 338. Adjusted to fit the current American stipulations, they stated that "no American administration can sustain the dialogue if terrorism continues by the PLO or any of its factions." Further stipulated was that the PLO was required to "publicly disassociate [itself] from terrorism by any Palestinian group operating anywhere," and "in the event of a terrorist action by any element of the PLO or one or more of its members, we expect that [it] not only condemn this action publicly but also discipline those responsible for it, at least by expelling them from the PLO."

In a letter dated December 22, 1988, President Ronald Reagan wrote to Prime Minister Shamir, reiterating the conditions set forth in those "talking points," justifying the decision to open a dialogue with the PLO as well as assuring the Israeli prime minister of continuing U.S. support. Portions of that letter follow:

> I would like to add my personal assurances to those already made by Secretary Shultz, that nothing in this decision should be construed as weakening the United States' commitment to Israel's security. . . .
>
> I believe that our dialogue with the PLO potentially can encourage realism and pragmatism within the Palestinian leadership and thus contribute to a comprehensive resolution of the Arab-Israeli conflict, in which the long-term security of Israel can be achieved. . . . I am under no illusion about the PLO. Their words will have to be supported by action, namely a continuing renunciation of terrorism everywhere and disassociation from those who perpetrate it.

And on December 15, 1988, in a letter to Foreign Minister Shimon Peres, Secretary of State George Shultz also wrote of the U.S. commitment to the Israeli state:

> Today, in a press conference in Geneva, Yasir Arafat made a statement in which he unconditionally accepted UN Security Council Resolutions 242 and 338, clearly recognized Israel's right to exist, and renounced terrorism. I have studied the text of Arafat's remarks carefully, and have concluded that this satisfies long-standing American conditions for opening a substantive dialogue. . . . We will also be watching closely the PLO's performance of the obligations it has undertaken as a result of its renunciation of terrorism. . . . We enter this dialogue with our eyes open and our guard up.

Almost as an afterthought, Ambassador Pelletreau informed Israel that the United States accepted Arafat's claim that he did not control the daily violence on the West Bank and in Gaza connected to the Intifada. And, in fact, if Arafat had controlled the daily violence, the United States would never have decided to open a dialogue with the PLO.

Regardless of who controlled the violence connected with the Intifada, the agreement between the parties fell apart when, five months into the dialogue, on May 30, 1988, a Libyan ship attacked the coast of Tel Aviv. The Americans considered this action to be a terrorist attack, unrelated to any violence to do with the uprising. In the case of the Libyan ship, the targets were not only tourists and Israeli civilians who happened to be on that Tel Aviv beach but also the American Embassy.

During interrogation by Israeli authorities, one of the captured terrorists, Mazen Ibrahim Rashid Hijazi, said, "Our mission was to spread the five boats across in a row and to begin to shell Tel Aviv with our 23mm guns and with the Katyushas, which were in our boats. Afterward we would continue to advance and begin firing toward the shorefront and at the buildings in the area with machine guns. When we [had used up] the ammunition of the heavy weapons, we were to land the boats and to begin shooting at people, cars, and buildings and to prevent disruption of the three middle groups, whose mission was to take control of the Hilton Hotel, killing as many people as possible, and to attack the American Embassy."

What was learned during interrogation of the other two captured terrorists, Muhammad Ahmad Aqedat and Ziad Hassan Muhammad al-'Leimi, was that the mastermind behind the plan was Abu Abbas, the same man who gave the world the *Achille Lauro*.

For two weeks following the attack, the American-PLO talks hung precariously in the balance while Washington waited for Arafat to comply with the conditions that had been set down in the "talking points." Specifically, the United States was waiting for the PLO chairman to condemn the attack and expel Abu Abbas from the Palestinian Executive Committee. When there was no condemnation forthcoming nor an expulsion of Abu Abbas, the United States formally broke off all dialogue.

The Intifada continued to rage with the foot soldiers of the uprising, the Shabiba, controlling the streets, and the Shakhsiyat directing the overall tactical operations, both entities functioning completely autonomously from the PLO. It was only after the rupture of the talks with the United States that Arafat finally sanctioned what became known as the Unified National Command (UNC) of the Intifada, or *al-Qiyada al-Wataniyy al-Muwahhada*. The name was merely a formality for the activities that the Shakhsiyat had been doing all along, namely directing the Shabiba so that spontaneous scattered demonstrations became an organized mass uprising. Actually, in the beginning, it was primarily the activists who belonged to the DFLP who were responsible for coordinating all Intifada activity, although later the UNC was made up of the three largest PLO factions in Jerusalem: Fatah, the PFLP, and the Palestine Communist Party (PCP).

Two dilemmas faced the UNC organizers those beginning months of the uprising, specifically whether to choose a public leadership centered around those already-well-known figures of the Shakhsiyat, or to form a clandestine group to direct the violence and strikes. Either option would further doom relations between the inside and outside leadership by promoting an intense and constant struggle between them. There was no doubt that Arafat and his once-most-powerful faction, Fatah, were losing ground, when on January 5, 1988, he failed to draw enough support during a vote in the PLO Executive Committee to set the official agenda of the Intifada. Eventually the UNC, functioning on the basis of parity among the three participating factions was the hand that continued to direct the uprising. Arafat had still not regained control of a rebellion he had made himself part of after the fact.

Contributing to the success of the UNC was the fact that it never recognized one leader nor appointed a chairman. Rather, the group functioned less as a bureaucratic body than it did as a group of coordinating committees that were in constant touch with one another. Unlike the PLO, whose various factions fought among one another for control or to change internal policy, the UNC saw its role as guiding the Palestinian population against Israel. By setting tactical goals and coordinating daily activities, the UNC was guaranteed not to run out of steam.

The method used by the UNC to contact the population was through calls, or *nida'at*, which were either distributed as leaflets or broadcast out of Baghdad on the PLO radio station. Interestingly—and deliberately—most of the representatives of the three factions belonging to the UNC were unknown activists without star quality who could have been replaced without any loss of morale among the people. Again unlike the operating practices of the PLO, which made heroes out of certain leaders, those directing the UNC kept a low profile surrounded by a veil of secrecy, giving the movement an aura of invisibility that only served to increase its impact throughout the Occupied Territories. And, in keeping with its democratic format, the UNC always maintained that it was not in any way part of the decision-making echelon of the Palestinian people. Eventually Arafat came to realize that the UNC "calls" for strikes and violence were unquestionably obeyed by the Shabiba regardless of which leader or faction gave any specific order. For the first time in Palestinian history, leaders managed not to confuse issues or goals by succumbing to internal power struggles. There was a lesson to be learned from the experience, which the PLO ultimately recognized and which led to the members of the Shakhsiyat finding themselves appointed as delegates to the opening Middle East peace conference in Madrid.

CHAPTER NINE

SLEEPLESS
IN MADRID

THE JOKE THAT went around Madrid during those opening
days of the first Middle East peace conference was that
Yitzhak Shamir kept asking where Yasir Arafat was when
he needed him most. As Hanan's media popularity soared,
many Israelis lamented that Arafat had not been allowed to
plead the Palestinian cause, wearing a hip holster, checkered
kaffiyeh, and scruffy beard. The feeling was that the PLO
chairman would surely have evoked the same negative reaction as he did in 1974 when he addressed the United Nations on behalf of his people. Instead, given their ban on any
contact or direct dealings with the PLO, the Israelis found
themselves competing for media points with a woman who
had already captured the sympathy and respect of the world.

For the Palestinians Madrid was a turning point in their
history. Regardless of which faction the members of the delegation belonged to, or whether they had been chosen for
their academic credentials or for their suffering in an Israeli
prison, there was a spirit of equality. When the delegation
arrived in Jericho to cross the Allenby Bridge to Amman to
fly to Madrid, the crowd was euphoric, with adults shedding
tears and children handing out olive branches to Israeli soldiers. For the first time in their history, the Palestinians had

as their spokesperson an articulate woman with a fondness for literary allusion and a talent for making comparisons between the suffering of the Jews at the hands of the world and of the Palestinians at the hands of the Jews. Yet even then, when the atmosphere was so charged with emotion and optimism, Hanan was aware of the enormous task of translating those sentiments into a coherent political message. In order to succeed the Palestinians had to achieve a twofold political gain. They had to make the world listen as they articulated their cause and they had to convince the other Arab nations that they were an independent people striving for a homeland, no longer an excuse to wage war with Israel. "I was a professional," Hanan says simply, "and not an apologist. When I left for Madrid there were so many people crying and telling me that I bore the responsibility for all of them, that I was charged with their fate, which, to me, was the most precious gift. Because of them I knew I had to present our cause with as much feeling and honesty as the people displayed on the day that we left for Madrid. We knew we faced a tremendous challenge to change our image, that people tended to believe the worst of us because of all the years that we had been so distorted. There was a long legacy of stereotyping which we had to cut through to tell the world who we were, not in a defensive way but by affirming ourselves. My way of doing this was to convey things honestly, since I always believed that if you really feel what you live and know who you are, you give people a firm understanding of your own history. More than anything else I knew that if people were going to listen to us in Madrid and recognize us, it had to be based on their perception of my honesty. But all along, right from the beginning, I said that it was only a first step and a very long one—that after Madrid was over and all the fireworks and the ceremonial were done, old habits would resurface and we would still be discriminated against."

Discrimination was not the only "old habit" to be overcome. The seeds of disharmony had been planted even before the delegation's arrival in Madrid.

AS THE PLANE carrying the delegation was making its final approach into Madrid, a stewardess handed out landing cards requiring the usual information about each passenger, including nationality. Albert Agazarian, seated next to Hanan, put down on his card next to the question of nationality, "to be decided in Madrid." His response was picked up by the press and cited during the opening press conference. "Perhaps I was remiss, but at the time I wasn't thinking about Hanan's reaction," Albert explains. "I was so propelled by the excitement of the moment and by being a part of history in the making."

When journalists, equipped with lights and cameras, descended on the Palestinian delegation for an impromptu news conference, Albert made sure that Hanan was the center of attention, squeezing her in front of the battery of microphones to assure that her image was carried throughout the world. "Hanan loved being the center of attention," Albert says, "the press loved putting her there, and I loved doing it, which should have made everything work without any discord." But discord there was. The battle lines were drawn when a journalist in the crowd suddenly waved a copy of Albert's disembarkation card in front of at least five hundred people, asking him to explain what he meant and how his response might affect any predisposition toward peace on the Palestinian agenda. Hanan was furious. According to Albert, as he proceeded to answer the question, Hanan shoved him with her elbow and whispered that she was the spokesperson and the only one to state any political position on behalf of the Palestinian delegation. After the press conference, Hanan took Albert aside and explained that she called all the shots and if he ever again took a political initiative, it would be the last in his official capacity as public relations officer for the delegation. "She warned me," Albert says quietly, "that our relationship would be over if I ever did anything like that again." The tragedy was that as far as he was concerned, the relationship was already over. "That was the moment when I made up my mind that when the conference ended in Madrid, I would quit," he adds.

Albert waited until the conference was over before announcing his intention not to continue on to Washington for the next round of talks. According to him, Hanan called him day and night until five o'clock in the morning for two days to try and get him to reconsider, imploring him to put aside their personal differences for the sake of the cause. Albert recalls, "She hurt me too deeply for me to get over it. There was nothing she could do or say at that point to convince me to work with her again regardless of how many times she apologized."

Albert's decision caused the other delegates concern as well, since all had come to depend on him to keep them on an equal media footing with the Israelis. It was the PLO leadership in Tunis, however, that seemed the most distressed by Albert's decision, because they, too, understood how vital he had been in changing the organization's image. "Sometimes I think that Hanan was more afraid that Arafat would blame her for my leaving than she was worried who would make her look and sound good if I left." He smiles. "It was almost like that movie *Broadcast News*. I took that wonderful voice of hers and that impressive vocabulary and fed her the lines, advised her when to laugh and cry so she would appeal to people's emotions. The world needed to forget about our past and focus only on Hanan." Even after the delegation returned to Jerusalem before leaving for Washington, Hanan still tried to change Albert's mind. Only when Albert stopped taking her calls did Hanan realize that for all her prowess at negotiation, she had failed to convince him how much she needed him. It was then, according to Albert, that Arafat began calling him. "I had several conversations with the chairman until eventually I just unplugged my telephone because I didn't want the temptation of caving in," Albert continues. "But when he couldn't reach me, he began calling my mother to get her to [persuade] me to change my mind."

Hanan is terse about what transpired in Madrid with Albert, unwilling to say more than that there were personal problems stemming from the fact that she was a woman in a position of authority, which forced her to give orders to men. "I found myself in a political arena where I expected to be judged on my merits and not my gender and when I wasn't, I suppose I made some mistakes. But that doesn't excuse Albert for thinking more of himself than our cause when he resigned. Frankly it surprised me, although I still consider him a talented professional. But there's just no room for temperament when people's lives are at stake."

Despite that incident, which marred what was otherwise a euphoric beginning, Madrid was the only moment in Palestinian history in which total harmony existed between the internal Palestinian leadership, the residents of the Occupied Territories, and the PLO government-in-exile in Tunis. It was a time of political purity with an absence of hidden agendas and backroom dealings, when all discussions were reported, recounted, and rehashed on the record and for general consumption. Of the seven participating countries, three—Syria, Lebanon, Jordan—were sworn enemies of Israel, while Egypt, the United States, and the Soviet Union were either old or newly reconciled allies. Notwithstanding any old agendas that might have caused temporary animosity among the seven, everybody worked together toward a common goal: peace in the Middle East with an emphasis on the creation of a Palestinian state.

Not a single Palestinian could recount his or her memories

of those opening days of the conference without including an overwhelming feeling of pride; not a single one could claim not to have shed tears during that historic opening speech delivered by Dr. Haidar abd al-Shafi. Reviewing the speech at the Reina Victoria Hotel in Madrid before the delegation left for the Grand Palace, there was a particular section at which Dr. Haidar paused to tell Hanan, "If I read this, I'll cry," to which Hanan replied, "Then cry; the world will be crying with you."

THERE WAS NO DOUBT that Hanan's prowess as the principal writer of the speech delivered by Dr. Haidar surpassed that of Yossi Ben Aharon, the man who wrote the final version of the speech delivered by Israeli Prime Minister Yitzhak Shamir. Shamir's words were a series of angry remonstrations and historic grievances that, although accurate, set a more unforgiving tone, while Dr. Haidar's words were coated in symbolism and pathos.

We the people of Palestine stand before you in the fullness of our pain, our pride, and our anticipation, for we long harbored a yearning for peace and a dream of justice and freedom. For too long, the Palestinian people have gone unheeded, silenced and denied. Our identity negated by political expediency; our right for struggle against injustice maligned; and our present existence subdued by the past tragedy of another people. For the greater part of this century we have been victimized by the myth of a land without a people and described with impunity as the invisible Palestinians. Before such willful blindness, we refused to disappear or to accept a distorted identity. Our Intifada is a testimony to our perseverance and resilience waged in a just struggle to regain our rights. It is time for us to narrate our own story, to stand witness as advocates of truth which had long lain buried in the consciousness and conscience of the world. We do not stand before you as supplicants, but rather as the torch-bearers who know that, in our world of today, ignorance can never be an excuse. We seek neither an admission of guilt after the fact, nor vengeance for past inequities, but rather an act of will that would make a just peace a reality.

And by Shamir:

We appeal to you to renounce the jihad against Israel; we appeal to you to condemn declarations that call for Israel's annihilation, like the one issued by the rejectionist conference in Tehran last week; we appeal to you to let Jews who wish to leave your countries go. And we address a call to the Palestinian Arabs: Renounce violence and terrorism. Use the universities in the administered territories, whose existence was made possible only by Israel, for learning and development, not agitation and violence. Stop exposing your children to danger by sending them to throw bombs and stones at soldiers and civilians. Just two days ago, we were reminded that Palestinian terrorism is still rampant, when the mother of seven children and the father of four were slaughtered in cold blood. We cannot remain indifferent and be expected to talk with people involved in such repulsive activities.

Madrid became not only a symbol of acceptance for the Palestinian people but also a sign that the PLO was finally willing to adhere to the rules of conventional diplomacy. If there was any resistance within the Palestinian population, it was said to be only among those minority factions that continued to call for a *jihad* to settle any territorial disputes. Still, despite the harmony and high hopes shared by all members of the Palestinian team, there wasn't one who wasn't aware of the almost-schizophrenic transition each was forced to make. Each one had his own story.

SAMEH KANAAN, the delegate who had spent seventeen years in an Israeli jail for setting explosives inside Israel, said, "I went from prison, where I couldn't talk to other prisoners, to Madrid, where I met with heads of state and diplomats. When was the last time a Palestinian was allowed to walk into a foreign embassy without being suspected of terrorism?" he asked.

Certainly not since March 1, 1973, when eight Palestinians, all members of Black September, a faction of Fatah, burst into the Saudi Arabian Embassy in Khartoum during an all-male farewell party thrown by the Saudi ambassador, Sheikh Abdullah al-Malhouk, in honor of the departing U.S. chargé d'affaires, George Curtis Moore. Three men were murdered by the terrorists: American Ambassador Cleo Noel, George Curtis Moore, and Belgian diplomat Guy Eid. Times were changing. "In Madrid," Kanaan continued, "I felt that we were part of the world for the first time when we were invited to the Spanish Embassy and the ambassador bent down to kiss Hanan's hand."

At the height of the violence in 1988, Mamduh al-Aker, another delegate and a urologist from Ramallah, was accused of belonging to the UNC and writing the leaflets that fueled the Intifada. In a manner reminiscent of countless other incidents, he was invited to the Civil Administration across from Hanan's house for a meeting, at which he was promptly arrested and detained in solitary confinement in a boxlike cell with just enough room to sit with his knees pressing against his chest and touching his chin for six months. After Aker was released and appointed to the delegation, the Israeli ambassador to the United Nations, Zalman Shoval, made a statement on television in which he cited by name certain members of the Palestinian delegation, including Dr. Aker, whom he claimed were terrorists. "When I found myself in Madrid," Dr. Aker recounted quietly, "Frank Sesno from CNN asked me to appear on a show with Ambassador Shoval." It was Aker's moment of revenge when he interrupted Shoval's discourse on how pleased he was to be sharing the spotlight with such an esteemed Palestinian leader. On worldwide television Dr. Aker asked Ambassador Shoval when he had changed his opinion of him, since he had only recently branded him a terrorist. Sesno caught on quickly and invited Aker to explain. "Are we not a people with rights?" Aker asked with dignity. "Do we not have the right to be charged with a crime when we are imprisoned and not just incarcerated under your laws that allow you to keep us in jail for months at a time without seeing a lawyer or having a fair trial?"

Saeb Erekat, the Palestinian delegate who wore the black-and-white-checkered *kaffiyeh* during the opening press conference in Madrid as a symbol of his connection to the PLO, recalled an incident that happened to him shortly before he left for Madrid. On his way to Jericho to pick up his mother-in-law, his car was stopped by three Israeli soldiers driving in an army jeep. According to Erekat the soldiers, who were no more than eighteen or nineteen years old, took his identity card before they pushed him up against a wall. In response to his question of just exactly why he was being detained, Erekat was slapped in the face twice, kicked in the back, and forced to stand against the wall for more than two hours before he was suddenly released. "If I were twenty years younger," Erekat claims, "or even fifteen years younger, I would be out throwing Molotov cocktails after that experience at anything that was called Israeli." What Erekat also maintained throughout all the negotiations, both in Madrid and in Washington, was that if the Palestinian conflict had been with any other people other than the Jews, it would have been solved long ago. "I used to teach Jewish history," he adds, "something that I stopped doing because everything was constructed to keep them as the world's victims. For me it became a lie, an erroneous image, since they had long ago become the aggressors while we had become the victims."

The Americans' policy during that week in Madrid was to accord official recognition only to the negotiating delegation and not to the rest of the Palestinian team. Even though the Palestinians had set up their own statutes, which included the recognition of the guidance committee as part of the official delegation, when Hanan arrived in Madrid she discovered that she had no accreditation. "We didn't get tags or security," she explained, "which meant that when we arrived at the airport, only the fourteen members of the negotiating team were recognized. The Spanish officials who met us informed Faisal and myself that we didn't have official status, and when we asked why, they said that the Americans had only given those fourteen names."

What that oversight meant in real terms was that neither Hanan nor Faisal nor any of the other unofficial advisers to the delegation could even approach the Palace of Justice where the conference was being held. "Initially we didn't even have accreditation to get to the press center because we didn't have the proper tags to enter IFEMA [the Madrid press center]," Hanan continued.

Hanan's response to the oversight was to deal with each problem separately and usually by instinct. While it was never a question of having an official welcome from the Spanish dignitaries—nobody particularly cared about the pomp—it was imperative that the guidance committee had official accreditation to be able to move around. "The first day I decided to hold a press conference right on the street, since I couldn't even come close to where there was a setup with microphones and cameras. There were hundreds of journalists who simply followed me and set up their equipment where I stood, which made the security guards furious. But I didn't care. I told them that I had to talk to the press and that's what I did— just stood in the middle of the street and held a press conference."

It took only one such happening for the Americans to understand that the woman speaking for the Palestinian delegation was not about to be excluded from the center of the action. Nor would she allow anyone to intimidate or discourage her from doing her job. Within minutes of that impromptu conference, the official policy changed and Hanan and the others were issued press cards which at least enabled them to enter IFEMA. For Hanan, however, it was an unsatisfactory accommodation. "It was insulting," Hanan recalls, "because it was a lie: We weren't press. But I had no choice. I took the card and put it in my pocket. I never even put it on but just went to IFEMA anyway." While Hanan had succeeded in getting permission to move around freely in the press center, there were still no security guards or police escorts for the woman who was receiving anonymous death threats every day. "Our intelligence maintained that the threats were coming from both sides who were against the peace talks, radical factions of the PLO and right-wing Israelis."

On the evening of the opening press conference Hanan; her assistant, Suhair Taha; Faisal al-Husseini; and Albert headed for the press center in an ordinary rental car. Stuck at every light, with traffic backed up for miles and crowds lining the streets, they were forced to abandon their car and continue on foot toward IFEMA. The press ended up waiting hours for them to arrive. "It was very strange to me," Hanan remembers, "that Faisal and myself had to push through on our own when the Spanish security forces told us specifically that we were the target of several assassination plots." Notwithstanding death threats, improper accreditation, and non-recognition as part of any official delegation, there were even more obstacles to overcome before the Palestinians could communicate their cause on an equal basis with the other participating delegations.

IF HE HAD BEEN ASKED to describe his job during the first conference that opened in Madrid on October 30, 1991, Albert Agazarian would have said "kingmaker." Or, as it fit the person who was the object of his efforts, he would have perhaps said "queenmaker." From the moment the lights snapped on for the biggest show on earth in the Middle East since the Israelis took six days to change the map in 1967, Hanan was primed, packaged, and portioned out to the world. While the plight of the Palestinian people had gained notoriety over the years, it had never gained acceptance in the aftermath of some of its most famous terrorist attacks: the dumping of the lifeless body of U.S. Navy diver Robert Stethem from the door of a TWA aircraft onto the tarmac of Beirut International Airport; the murder of Leon Klinghoffer aboard the cruise ship *Achille Lauro;* the murder of thirteen Israeli athletes by masked PLO terrorists during the Munich Olympics.

With Madrid came the perception that the PLO had changed from a group of freedom fighters or terrorists, depending on political opinion, to a group of intellectuals. Even the cynical international press corps, which had always chosen to interview the PLO leaders who spouted revolution rather than rhetoric, embraced the "new Palestinians" in Madrid as heroes. Within the structure of the PLO, groups such as the PFLP, the DFLP, or the Popular Front for the Liberation of Palestine, General Command (PFLP-GC),* which were once considered renegade factions of Yasir Arafat's al-Fatah, were suddenly transformed into political parties. Where once those renegade groups were considered Arafat's sworn enemies, when they broke off from the mainstream to maim, kill, and attack members of rival factions, they were suddenly positioned as equal within the PLO parliament, armed not with weapons but with letters of assurances from Western leaders, letters of invitations to peace conferences from the American secretary of state. From the moment the Palestinians entered into the peace talks, each faction that fell under the umbrella organization of the PLO was referred to as part of the PLO's "pluralistic" form of government, having the right to both a dissenting opinion and a vote. Hanan took the position that just as the Israelis had the ultrareligious Gush Emunim, the party that had come out against any conciliation with the Palestinians, the PLO had Hamas and other fundamentalist factions that were also against any compromise with Israel. Ever vigilant to nuance and public relations, she took great care to explain how it was not the image of the PLO that had changed but rather the world that had never chosen to accept anything but negative propaganda about the PLO. With Albert at the helm, handling all press and public relations, and Hanan at the microphone, pointing out all the good work the PLO had done for widows, orphans, and revolutionaries in the way of summer camp, food, medical treatment, shelter, and education, it was a combination that had to succeed. The one issue that remained baffling about that fundamental change in PLO policy, however, was why the old guard in Tunis, whose

*Ahmad Jibul formed the PFLP General Command in 1968 after breaking away from George Habash's PFLP.

names and faces were synonymous with terror, had not been replaced by those new PLO leaders whose names and faces were synonymous with academia. One explanation given was by President Reagan in his letter of assurance to Prime Minister Shamir: "Our dialogue with the PLO potentially can encourage realism and pragmatism within the Palestinian leadership and thus contribute to a comprehensive resolution of the Arab-Israeli conflict." Another explanation was the fact that Arafat, despite his defects and failures, was the symbol of the struggle, maintaining a sense of unity and Palestinian nationalism. If changes were to occur and a new permanent leadership was to replace the original founders, Arafat would undoubtedly be perceived as the George Washington of any newly created Palestinian state.

WITHIN HOURS of arriving in Madrid, Albert realized that the best way to project the Palestinians' transition from terrorist organization to political entity was to put Hanan in the starring role. He devised a formula whereby a supporting cast always surrounded Hanan during each televised news conference: one American; one Zionist American; one person each from France, Germany, and the United Kingdom; two Israelis, one from the Labor party and one from Likud; and three Arabs—from the Maghreb, or North Africa, another from the Gulf, and a Palestinian from the Occupied Territories. "She was a quick study," Albert says, "believe me. She would walk into a press conference and handle the setup beautifully. But who made the setup? Me, that's who, and that's what killed her every time."

Yet Albert swears that while he never cared about glory when it came to his professional accomplishments, he expected a modicum of respect and appreciation. "I was the one who coordinated everything in Madrid that put the Palestinian cause on top of the list of world injustices," he states matter-of-factly. "It was me who created that love affair with the media, for the first time in our history, that made everything euphoria all the way. It was me who launched Hanan's star. It was me who had all the contacts with the foreign press all through the years whenever they'd come to Jerusalem and want to go out drinking or be briefed on background information."

Minutes before that first emotional press conference, Albert discovered that he had hundreds of friends and acquaintances among the journalists. "It was like you send out postcards all your life," Albert explains, "and one day you find yourself in a room with all those postcards and you're amazed. Did I send out all these cards, you ask yourself?" His expression changes suddenly to one of regret. "Naturally it didn't help my relationship with Hanan when she saw the camaraderie between me and all those reporters. What was ridiculous was that she was actually jealous, since that's what public relations is all about and that's what was needed to make Madrid a success from the Palestinian point of view. I needed to make heroes out of villains, and believe me, it wasn't easy!"

The night before the conference opened, Albert took a cab from the Hotel Reina Victoria to IFEMA, the press center where each delegation had its headquarters, three-room suites serving as both hospitality and communications centers. He intended to inspect the rooms assigned to the joint Palestinian-Jordanian delegation, checking the configuration and seating capacity for the opening press conference scheduled for that afternoon. While the space was freshly painted, with brand-new carpeting and furniture, the chairs and tables were still wrapped in plastic and not a single telephone or piece of office equipment had been delivered. Albert was shocked at the lack of organization on the part of the chief of protocol appointed by the Spanish government—and even more furious at himself for not checking everything out days before. Heading down the hall, he walked until he reached the rooms assigned to the Israeli delegation. "I needed to see what ammunition my enemy had at its disposal," he explains.

It was one-thirty in the morning, and Albert's worst fears became realities when he walked into the Israeli suite and saw thirteen people sitting at fully functioning computers with as many laser printers spilling out paper, tables piled high with printed material and stationery, and telephones hooked up in every corner of every room, including several mobile phones and special long-distance beepers. Everything in the Israeli press room was the latest state-of-the-art equipment. "Compared to the Israelis, we had nothing. It was like throwing someone on a court to play in a championship tennis tournament and forgetting to give him a racket," Albert says.

It was two o'clock in the morning when Albert raced back to the hotel and found Señor Martos, the chief of protocol, who was busy making last-minute arrangements for the opening of the conference, which was only seven hours away. The conversation was short and to the point, as Albert explained that the Palestinian delegation needed telephones, fax machines, computers, laser printers, and stationery. He was so anxious that there was a note of hysteria in his voice as he asked Martos just how the Palestinians were meant to manage the most important press conference in their history without so much as a microphone. The Spaniard didn't bother to remind Albert that it had been up to each delegation to provide its own equipment. Dignified and understanding, Martos nonetheless made it perfectly clear that it was too late to either purchase or rent the necessary equipment and have it delivered in time for the opening press conference. After all, this was Spain and not New York or Washington: People took their time. Companies didn't even open until ten o'clock and closed at one o'clock for a three-hour lunch/siesta. If Señor Agazarian expected miracles he was dreaming. Not only wasn't Albert dreaming, but he had a keen-enough memory to quote an article that had appeared in the morning newspaper about how the coming week was going to be the only one out of the entire year when Spain actually functioned. If the country had been able to set up IFEMA in less than ten days in preparation for this international media event, Albert told Martos, what he was asking for, as he put it, was "basically garbage."

In a country where efficiency was never a credo and procrastination was a way of life, Martos could only promise his best. While he rushed off to try and mobilize Madrid, Albert walked to a telephone to call one of the advisers to the delegation, Rashid Khalidi, who headed the Middle East Studies Department at the University of Chicago. By then it was almost three o'clock in the morning.

After Khalidi finally roused himself to pick up the phone, Albert launched into a detailed description of the situation before falling silent to listen to Khalidi's response. Shocked to hear that Khalidi's primary concern was the cost of all the equipment—his only advice was that before anything could be ordered, Faisal al-Husseini had to approve every expenditure—Albert put down the phone. By now having appropriated the hospitality desk in the lobby, Albert dialed Husseini, waking him out of a sound sleep as well. Unlike Khalidi, all Husseini had to hear was that the Israelis were operational while the Palestinians had nothing more than freshly painted walls, brand-new carpet, and a couple of chairs and tables still wrapped in plastic. Before Albert could even broach the subject of cost, Husseini instructed him to get whatever was necessary, however and wherever, before the conference officially opened in the morning. As it turned out, old contacts went a long way during those hectic early-morning hours when Albert was scurrying around to remedy a nightmare scenario.

A sensitive man who lists his memory as one of his most

formidable assets, Albert claims never to have forgotten either
a kindness or a slight. Once a tour guide in Jerusalem, he
held special memories of a certain young Chinese-American
woman whom, along with her elderly aunt, he escorted
around the Old City years before. At the time money had
been a problem for the young woman, who worked as a low-
level employee for the U.S. Department of State in Washington while her aunt was retired on a small pension. As Albert
explains it, "The issue wasn't money, because it was pleasure
enough teaching someone who was so interested in every
cultural detail and nuance. The woman soaked everything up
like a sponge, she was brilliant."

Albert took a special interest in the State Department
worker, spending long hours lecturing her on the city's history
and showing her treasures in small out-of-the-way churches
and convents that were not included on the regular tour. In
the end the woman's memory proved as keen as Albert's. She
never forgot her first trip to Jerusalem or her tour guide.
Impressed by his knowledge of history, charmed by his sense
of drama, and touched by his generosity, when Molly Williamson returned to Jerusalem years later as the American
consul general, Albert Agazarian was the first person she
called. "I was amazed that Molly even remembered me,"
Albert says. "But she did, and later on, she was the one person
who helped me organize our delegation so we could keep up
with the Israelis."

Molly Williamson, still the American consul in Jerusalem,
was also part of the diplomatic entourage in Madrid for those
opening ceremonies. Without a thought to how she might
react, Albert did the unthinkable and picked up the phone to
call her. "I told her simply that we were stuck and even though
the Spaniards promised to help, I needed a guarantee of at
least basic equipment." There wasn't the slightest hesitation
before Molly agreed to lend Albert equipment from the Amer-

ican Embassy in Madrid—off the record, of course, since if anyone found out that one of the senior American diplomats had raided the embassy for the Palestinians, it would create not only an international incident but a media nightmare. Albert wasted no time before he was already on the way out with what he considered "basic equipment." Laughing, Albert remembers, "I carried the stuff myself, along with three or four junior secretaries from the embassy, back to the hotel—in the middle of the night for God's sake—computers, telephones, everything. We didn't finish until the sun was coming up."

While the opening ceremonies were scheduled to begin at nine o'clock in the morning, Albert hadn't yet slated the hour for the first press conference. He was busy working in the suite, connecting printers to computers and directing the technicians supplied by Martos where to install the telephones, when he heard the commotion. Before there was time even to throw a switch to make everything operational, hundreds of journalists were crowding into the room, surrounding Albert and demanding to see Hanan. "Obviously Hanan wasn't there because she had no idea the press would descend on us like that," Albert explained, "so I told the journalists to come back at two o'clock in the afternoon and I'd guarantee that she'd be there then." When he finally managed to get everybody out of the room, he got a message to Akram Hania, the man who handled all press relations at PLO headquarters in Tunis and who was currently functioning as the liaison between Arafat and the delegation in Madrid, that he had scheduled the first press conference for two o'clock. The press wanted Hanan. "I was being squeezed," Albert admitted, "but I loved it. This was my blood."

There were two press centers at IFEMA, one room that held seventy people and another that held two hundred, plus a room called the Core, which was reserved for the Americans, Russians, and Spaniards to make statements between and after each round of talks. The two officials in charge of communications for the Americans were Kenton Keith, the former cultural attaché in Cairo, responsible for the whole Middle East; and Chris Knowles, the cultural attaché in Tel Aviv. Albert wasted no time in contacting the pair, explaining that although it bent the rules, he absolutely needed to use the Core room, since the number of journalists would exceed two hundred, the maximum for the larger of the rooms assigned to the delegations. What bothered both Knowles and Keith was not so much borrowing the Core room as it was breaking the rules, which clearly stated there were to be no press conferences before the talks officially convened on Wednesday. This was only Tuesday. Challenged by yet another obstacle and thriving on being a rule breaker, Albert recounts the conversation that followed in the lobby of the Reina Victoria on that morning before the conference officially convened.

"Tell me, Chris," Albert said. "If members of my delegation want to visit my office, there are no ground rules about that, are there?"

"I don't see why not," Knowles said cautiously.

"And if there's a journalist who asks something of a member of my delegation, is that banned?"

"I don't see why," Knowles said, glancing at Keith who by then understood exactly what was happening.

"And if my office gets too crowded," Albert continued, "can't I stand outside in the hall?"

Knowles started laughing. "I like you," he said as he started walking, "but instead of just standing in the hall, why don't I show you another courtyard?" He stopped to look at Albert. "But I didn't tell you anything."

Elated, Albert followed. "You sure didn't!" he said.

The men walked down one flight of stairs to an empty

room that looked large enough to accommodate at least four hundred people. "How's this?" Knowles asked.

Albert didn't waste any time. "I need a microphone," he announced.

Knowles looked indignant. "We can't supply things like that," he replied before adding, "but why don't you try the NBC studios. I bet they've got lots of microphones."

What followed was pandemonium. When Hanan, Faisal, and Dr. Haidar abd al-Shafi arrived ten minutes early, they were besieged by the press. As it turned out, that moment would be the indicator of the press reaction each time that Hanan appeared for the duration of those talks in Madrid. When Albert realized that the trio was literally unable to move, he did what any self-respecting and irreverent public relations person would do: he held the press conference for the Palestinian delegation right there on the street with Hanan, Faisal, Haidar, and thousands of journalists. It made a beautiful picture. It was then that Hanan, a woman, a Christian, and a little-known academic, began to recite her first words as the official spokesperson for the Palestinian delegation. The subject had been unplanned and it was only because Albert learned that the press would question her on an event that happened the day before that he provided Hanan with any warning.

On the day before the conferences opened in Madrid, the headlines screamed of a Palestinian youth who had been killed by the Shin Bet. "All the more reason for a peace agreement," Albert announced, as journalists swooped down on him in the Hotel Reina Victoria minutes before Hanan appeared. Following Albert's suggestion, Hanan spoke quietly. "This incident should only serve to remind us of our enormous responsibility and how seriously we must take our job since lives on both sides of the struggle are in our hands." From there she launched into an emotional plea for a Palestinian

homeland. Hanan's image ended up on the pages of *Time,
Newsweek,* and *Paris-Match.*

From the moment the conference opened, there wasn't
anyone, from Middle East pundits to Middle American house-
wives, who wasn't aware of what the Palestinians considered
their inalienable right of return to the lands under Israeli
control. By the time Madrid was over, Hanan had already
made an indelible impression on the world as the voice of
reason for the Palestinian cause. And, by the time the peace
conference was preparing to move to Washington to continue
the talks, a larger plan was already evolving that would bypass the efforts of those chosen to negotiate a solution.

CHAPTER TEN

RAJA, AKRAM,
AND BELAT

R AJA* WORKS AS A WAITER in one of the most luxurious hotels in East Jerusalem. Born, raised, and educated in America, he is a Palestinian who speaks Arabic with an American accent and English like a kid from the streets of New York. A big fellow with an appealing space between his front teeth and a fondness for wearing a beret cocked on one side of his head and a trench coat that trails to his ankles, Raja resembles an escapee from *Casablanca*—the movie, not the city. He talks and acts tough, challenging any Israeli policeman or soldier who dares to approach him for identity papers or a traffic violation to do so at his own risk. Raja is a volcano constantly on the verge of eruption. His one weakness—and the only human being in his life who reduces him to a romantic, sentimental hulk—is his lovely half-French, half-Lebanese girlfriend. Playing King Kong to her Fay Wray, Raja meets her and leaves her with a "Love ya, babe."

Raja was born in Michigan, where his father and two of his uncles had a small restaurant. In 1992 the father, along with his wife, a secondary school teacher, decided to return to their home in Nablus with their son and daughter. Currently Raja's father owns a taxi and a small dry-cleaning store in Nablus.

The decision to move back hadn't been easy. Raja and his sister had grown accustomed to a tranquil life in suburban Detroit, raised more as average American kids than Palestinians caught in the middle of a conflict. While the family was realistic about the consequences of living on the West Bank during the ongoing Intifada, everyone in the family had agreed that a new era in Palestinian history was near. What Raja didn't count on was that the violence that once seemed so distant would touch him so personally.

Soon after returning to Nablus, Raja enrolled at al-Najah University, where he took courses in engineering. With his knowledge of English and his outgoing personality, it wasn't long before he managed to get a job on weekends at that prestigious hotel in East Jerusalem, serving mostly English and American tourists. But even before that, within weeks of returning, Raja became involved in the turmoil that fueled the uprising. For a while Raja even had his own rules about just how far to go. "I used to stop the other kids from stoning an Israeli bus with settlers if there were children on board," Raja remembers. "It worked like this," he explains. "The spotter would stand further down the road and make the sign that an Israeli car or bus was approaching, get ready to throw stones or Molotovs. I was always the one who stopped the others from attacking children." Grinning his jack-o'-lantern grin, Raja continues, "Until one day I found myself throwing stones at children, knowing that I could kill them or hurt them really bad. But all of a sudden I didn't care. I was numb, and that really scared me." What caused Raja to change his policy when it came to harming children in the name of the Palestinian cause began on a quiet evening near the main square in Nablus.

On the West Bank, whenever there is a clash between Palestinians and the Israeli Army, a chain of events has occurred. Beginning during a debate at the conference table in

Washington, continuing in Tunis and Jerusalem, where political decisions affecting the peace process are made, it usually results in an act of violence in the territories, perpetrated by either side. It didn't take Raja long to learn the rhythm of any demonstration, where the army arrived with jeeps that rolled down the middle of town to cart people off to jail, or the Shin Bet appeared in their white unmarked vans. On that particular evening when Raja was walking near the Nablus town square, he was the lucky one.

Raja describes his friend Belat* as a sweet and funny kid who was thin and gawky with a mop of brown hair and a face full of freckles. "Belat was my best friend from the moment I arrived in Nablus," Raja says. "We lived near each other and went to al-Najah University together." While Belat's family lived near Raja's, the parents were not particularly close; the relationship was mostly between the children, who participated in community projects together and hung out at the same pizza parlor in town. If any members of either family had something in common, it was the fathers, who had both been born shortly after the loss of Palestine in 1948 and the creation of the State of Israel, survived Jordanian occupation to suffer through the Arab defeat in 1967, and lived in fear for their children during the Intifada. Raja's father, who had been exposed to a world away from the West Bank, found life under occupation oppressive, while Belat's father remarked on more than one occasion that under Jewish rule there were more conveniences, beginning with indoor plumbing and ending with modern equipment in the local hospital. Despite their cultural differences, what the two men also shared was a subtle loss of control over their sons, who had become part of the foot soldiers of the revolt. Both Raja and Belat were examples of those Palestinians born after 1967 who, when it came to their future dreams, had no other frame of reference except growing up under Israeli occupation. They

193

were the baby bombers of the Occupied Territories, no longer prepared to bring attention to their cause by dying in foreign cities throughout the world. Instead they were determined to bring the focus of the revolution back to where they envisioned an eventual Palestinian state.

As Raja and Belat strolled through Nablus that evening, they decided to meet another friend, a sixteen-year-old named Akram*, who lived in a refugee camp nearby. Akram was a tough kid whose father had been killed during a confrontation with the army several years before while his two older brothers had been deported to Jordan for anti-Israeli activities. Suddenly an army jeep appeared followed by an unmarked white van, both vehicles turning the corner and screeching to a stop near where the boys were walking. Several men with weapons drawn jumped out of the van, calling Belat's name, making it instantly clear who was their target. Without further warning the men aimed and fired their weapons directly at Belat. Raja remembers counting five rapid rounds before his friend fell to the ground in a pool of blood. Within seconds after the shot were fired, everyone in the immediate vicinity raced toward the wounded boy, the Palestinians who had been milling around the town square and several who had been outside their houses nearby. A doctor happened to be in the crowd of people who gathered. Pushing his way through, he fought to reach the wounded boy.

Raja describes the scene. "The doctor didn't wait for permission but bent down to take Belat's pulse. It was weak, but he started screaming that he was still alive and that if he [was to have] any chance, he had to treat him right away." Belat's assailants, whom Raja describes as the "death squad"—agents who cruised the West Bank disguised as Palestinians, looking for those suspected of throwing stones or Molotovs or worse—pushed the doctor away. Instead one of the soldiers attached to an army unit picked up Belat's feet, while another grabbed him under the arms and dragged him over to their jeep. By then it was obvious that Belat was dead, as he lay sprawled across the back seat with his head dangling from the side of the vehicle. And that was exactly how the soldiers drove the body around Nablus until dark. "It was a message," Raja says angrily. "Look what happens to you if you demonstrate or throw stones."

It was Akram's idea to hold a mock funeral for Belat—not that it was an original plan, since ceremonies for Palestinians killed either by the army or Shin Bet were common. Rarely did the Israelis allow Palestinians to hold proper funerals for fear they would turn into massive demonstrations or riots. "When someone dies," Raja explains, "the authorities take the body to the morgue and do a postmortem before they either bury it themselves in a mass grave in Jericho or tell the family they can hold a secret funeral at night, with no more than five family members present."

Raja remembers Akram telling him that he would arrange to get the symbolic coffin and have it draped with the black, green, and red Palestinian flag, organize supporters from within the refugee camp, and have the pamphlets printed that would advise everybody as to the time and place for the demonstration. Raja also recalls that Akram made him promise that if anything happened to him, he would take care of his mother, as he was the last son left at home. Without him, she would be all alone. "Akram knew what he was doing was dangerous," Raja says. "If the Shin Bet found out he was the one organizing the funeral, he would be their next target."

On the day of the mock funeral, the army was everywhere, in some cases using megaphones to round up demonstrators while in others, already engaging in violent clashes with civilians. The procession was making its way toward the center of town. Raja was walking next to the coffin near Akram, who was acting as a pallbearer, holding up one side next to half a dozen other Shabiba who were in the procession. Again without warning, a group of Shin Bet dressed as Palestinians in the crowd suddenly drew weapons, two of them pouncing on Akram. Raja turned and ran blindly down the street, through the throng of demonstrators, down several more streets, until he raced into an alley. Soldiers with weapons drawn were right behind him. Turning around, Raja saw that Akram had broken away as well and was running in the opposite direction, disappearing down another alley with the Shin Bet following. Shots were fired, and Akram fell. Within minutes, more soldiers blocked off both sides of the alley so no one could get through to help the injured boy. "At the time I didn't know what happened to Akram," Raja says quietly. "All I could think about was how dumb it was that I ran into that alley, not even thinking that it wouldn't have an exit." As it turned out, unlike Akram, Raja was trapped in a dead end with four armed soldiers coming at him. "I knew I had it then," he says grimly.

Raja was beaten with fists, sticks, and the butt of a rifle, his right arm twisted back with a metal crowbar until it broke, his left shoulder shattered when he had sense to move so a blow intended for his elbow missed, instead dislocating his clavicle. Bleeding and barely conscious, Raja was dragged about two meters, to where the soldiers had left their jeep and where Raja's parents happened to be standing. Thrown into the back of the vehicle, Raja remembers little else. "Even when I was in and out of consciousness," Raja says, "I remember seeing my parents running after the jeep, following us to the police station."

The army didn't drive Raja directly to the police station, however, but rather circled around town for about fifteen minutes or so, he claims, in an effort to disorient him. "I just remember going around in circles and I still had no idea where I was or what happened to Akram. I didn't even know that

196

I was bleeding so bad—I thought I was perspiring." When Raja finally arrived at the police station, his parents were already there waiting. "That's when I went to wipe my face and saw my sleeve was covered with blood, and that's when the pain set in." While he was being handcuffed, Raja was aware that his father was pleading for his release; as he was taken upstairs for interrogation, the last image was of his mother crying. "After they dragged me upstairs," Raja remembers, "I asked one of them for a glass of water and got kicked in the mouth." Seated in the interrogation room, Raja was warned that he would be shot or imprisoned if he didn't confess to a series of crimes or at least give the names of others who had committed those crimes. "They told me that my father would be interrogated as well if I didn't talk, but I figured, what more could they do except kill me, and at that point, with all the pain, it was almost a welcome alternative." Finally, after about three hours, in which Raja was held in solitary confinement in the police station, he was released on bail. "When they brought me downstairs my parents were still there, my mother was still crying, and my father was still begging the police to let me go."

After Raja was released, his parents put him into the car to drive to the American Consulate in Jerusalem to report the incident. "After all, I was an American citizen," Raja says, not without irony, "which was what I was trying to tell the soldiers and the police all along." He shrugs. "Anyway, when I got there, I couldn't even write to fill out the forms, so many bones were broken or bruised in my hands." It was his father who filled out the forms before the family headed to the hospital, where Raja's injuries could be treated. "There were about forty people in front of me that day," Raja recalls, "with broken arms and smashed skulls." He still didn't know about Akram.

Later that night, after Raja was home in bed, he heard

the news. Akram had been left to bleed to death in that alley. "That was the moment I made up my mind," Raja says quietly, "that I didn't give a damn about stoning Israeli children."

As Hanan wrote in the Madrid speech, it is sometimes necessary to make an imaginative leap to transcend the pain of the moment. "Anger generates energy," she adds, "and that clouds the constructive reaction, which shouldn't be violence but rather a peaceful solution which we must achieve. If not, the victim or the victim's family are doomed to become the captive of their own pain to justify any action that falls under the category of retaliation."

While the reality remains that Belat and Akram are dead, the purpose of any participation in the peace negotiations—as Hanan has always maintained—has been to prevent more children from getting killed. For Belat's and Akram's mothers, a solution—land, global recognition, and respect—will never make it better for them. "It's one thing to lose your children," Hanan concludes, "and another to lose your humanity."

Stephen Pearlman

IN 1989 STEPHEN PEARLMAN* left his home and family— mother and father and two sisters—and his job as a social worker in New York, to live permanently in Israel. He chose a relatively new community called Maale Adumim just over the Green Line. On June 17, 1989, only three months after arriving, Stephen set off on one of his weekly nature hikes in the hills overlooking Jerusalem, an enjoyable way to get to know the country. With a backpack containing maps, a camera, and a commando knife, Stephen carried only a shepherd's walking stick he had found in an Arab market in East Jerusalem.

Ashrawi and her Shabiba guards, Ramallah, 1992. *(Courtesy Zoom)*

Israeli protesters burning tires in Ramallah. *(Courtesy Zoom)*

Left: Palestinian delegate Sameh Kanaan leaving for Madrid. (*Courtesy Zoom*)
Right: Suhair Taha, Ashrawi's former assistant, daughter of "Captain Rifat," 1992. (*Barbara Victor*)

Hanan and Emil Ashrawi, saying good-bye in Ramallah before the Washington peace talks. (*Courtesy Zoom*)

Ashrawi and Dr. Haidar abd al-Shafi at a press conference
in East Jerusalem. *(Courtesy Zoom)*

Zahira Kamal taking food supplies to 415 deportees stranded across
the Israeli border in "no-man's-land" in Lebanon. *(Courtesy Zoom)*

Dr. Mamduah Aker having his papers checked at an Israeli checkpoint between Ramallah and Jerusalem. *(Courtesy Zoom)*

Stephen Pearlman.*
(Courtesy Shin Bet)

Akram*and Belat.*
(Courtesy Shin Bet)

Pearlman's photo of the hills overlooking Jerusalem. (Courtesy Shin Bet)

Pearlman's photo of his own shoe as he lay dying after the attack
by Akram and Belat. *(Courtesy Shin Bet)*

Pearlman's body after Israeli settlers found him in the hills
overlooking Jerusalem. *(Courtesy Shin Bet)*

An Israeli bus after an attack by Palestinian terrorists
with stones and Molotov cocktails. *(Courtesy Shin Bet)*

The interior of the bus, the charred bodies of casualties
outlined by police. *(Courtesy Shin Bet)*

A map of Tel Aviv found on the bodies of Arab terrorists. *(Courtesy Shin Bet)*

Somewhere near the Arab village of Herbril Jafal Eldin, Stephen met up with two Palestinian boys on their way to buy fruit in Borkin, a neighboring Arab village. What amused Stephen were the T-shirts the boys wore that had PEACE written on the front and the big "ghetto blaster" they carried. He stopped to chat, mentioning that he was from New York and a new immigrant to Israel, keen on exploring the surrounding villages. But what seemed to fascinate the Palestinians more than Stephen's story of where he came from were his topographical maps and his camera. They asked him to explain how to read the maps and then asked if he could take some pictures of them. They would give him their address and maybe he could send the pictures, or perhaps they could even meet up again next week. One of the boys, who said he was from Nablus, had the idea that if they went to higher terrain, they could take better pictures of Jerusalem. Pearlman quickly agreed and set out, leaving his knapsack behind, following the boys to an area they claimed offered a spectacular view of the Old City.

The younger of the pair lingered behind while the boy from Nablus, with Stephen in tow, began the climb to the next plateau. When they reached the cleared area that looked down over the city, Stephen walked to the edge of the precipice to marvel at the view. The boys had been right: The panorama was indeed spectacular. In the meantime the boy who had stayed behind had already managed to go through Stephen's knapsack, where he found the commando knife. Hiding it behind his back, he approached.

The weather was beautiful that day, sunny and warm with a clear view of the Old City. Stephen opened the maps and began explaining to the boys how to gauge distances and calculate altitudes. They seemed to grasp everything quickly, asking intelligent questions in halting English until one of them reminded Stephen that he had promised to take photographs of them. Why not right there, since he could also get a shot of Jerusalem behind them?

The attack happened without warning. One minute Stephen Pearlman was enjoying the company of his new friends; the next minute the boy with the knife stabbed him in the back, piercing a lung. Though severely injured, Stephen managed to hit him in the head with his walking stick. While the injured boy scrambled to his feet, the other one grabbed the knife and stabbed Pearlman again in the back and the neck as his accomplice picked up a rock and smashed it into the side of his face. Bleeding, Stephen sank to his knees before collapsing on the ground. Leaving him for dead, inches from his knapsack, maps, and camera, which had fallen during the assault, the pair ran back down the hill. But Stephen wasn't dead. Lying in a pool of blood, he still had enough strength to crawl over to his knapsack, open it, and pull out a jacket, and put it on. But more incredible was that he was conscious enough to reach for his camera. Aiming in front of him, Stephen captured a picture of his own shoe before pulling out the film and hiding it in his shirt pocket. Near death, Stephen somehow remembered that he had taken pictures of his murderers.

About an hour later, when it finally occurred to them that Stephen had taken photographs of them, the two Palestinians returned. Finding the camera off to the side of the body, they picked it up, unaware that the film had been removed, and ran back down the hill. Several hours after that a group of Israeli settlers found Stephen Pearlman's body and, turning it over, discovered the roll of film that he had managed to tuck away in his shirt pocket. They gave the film to the authorities.

Two days later an Israeli undercover unit that routinely patrolled Nablus spotted Belat strolling down the street with an unidentified friend, who turned out to be Raja. Emerging from their unmarked car, they called out Belat's name. When he turned around they shot him. A week after that, during the mock funeral for Belat, another undercover team cornered Akram as he helped carry the symbolic coffin through the streets of Nablus. Chasing him into a nearby alley, they shot and killed him.

CHAPTER ELEVEN

—————

THE TURNING POINT

THE MOST CRUCIAL MONTHS for Hanan during the peace negotiations in Washington were November and December 1992. Not only was she at the height of her media popularity, but she was working eighteen-hour days, debriefing her delegation, racing around the Pentagon from office to office, trying to put pressure on the Americans to force a breakthrough in the talks, while simultaneously clearing everything with the PLO leadership in Tunis. More crucial an activity during those months was her involvement in arranging secret meetings between two Israeli academics, high-level Israeli government officials, and members of the PLO. She seemed to function at her best when she was intervening to solve problems that others considered hopeless.

Hanan held court at the Ritz Carlton Hotel in Pentagon City, Virginia. The hotel, set in the middle of a three-level glass-and-chrome shopping center near the Pentagon in Arlington, Virginia, served as headquarters for the Palestinian delegation. Newly constructed, the approach to the building itself was blocked off by a series of concrete barricades where work was in progress to widen the road. Inside the hotel, security men with walkie-talkies lounged on wingback chairs or stood around the newly refurbished lobby among reproductions of Early American antiques and grandfather clocks decorated with spread-winged eagles. The dimly lit cocktail area in the lobby, completed just that week, quickly became the mecca for informal gatherings of representatives and advisers attached to the delegation or journalists conducting interviews.

Upstairs in a three-room suite on the sixth floor, the air was thick with cigarette smoke, and tabletops were covered with trays of used coffee cups, half-eaten sandwiches, faxes, and piles of foreign newspapers. Television sets throughout the suite were tuned soundlessly to CNN. The extra telephone lines that had been installed meant only that many more requests for interviews could reach Hanan, coming from as far as Australia and as near as the CNN studios in Washington. Hanan's assistant, Suhair, an attractive Palestinian woman of twenty-five with a perpetually suspicious expression, rarely left her side. Speaking alternately in Arabic and English, Suhair fielded calls from journalists who were asking, pleading—demanding—interviews or at least a comment on the day's events. Usually Hanan would ignore the ringing phones unless Suhair held up the receiver—the caller relegated, sometimes for half an hour, to the other side of the hold button—until Hanan took the call or waved it away with her hand. She was always dressed smartly in tailored suits and silk blouses, accented with scarab earrings and bracelets, and an array of rings on her fingers. The only hint that she was ever exhausted were her swollen feet, shoes kicked off, propped up on a table or chair when she sat down. The image of Hanan in repose was always the same, nervously chain-smoking and drinking coffee, grabbing chocolates for energy, and carrying on several conversations at once with the endless procession of delegates who streamed in and out of her suite. When she took a rare moment to relax, she would enjoy chatting with Suhair, welcoming any subject that had nothing to do with her current problems in Washington.

Despite all the changes within the hierarchy of the PLO

and the power struggle between the internal and external leadership, there were indissoluble links. Past leaders of the Palestinian struggle had connections not only to their own families but to the families of their fallen friends. Not unlike in the Mafia, it remained a duty to care for the wife and children of a revolutionary who had lost his life in the course of trying to liberate his land. The world of the Palestinian refugee, though spread throughout the Arab lands, was small; people were related by blood, marriage, or violence. Even Yasir Arafat, whose real name was Abd al-Rauf Arafat al-Qudwa al-Husseini, was a cousin of Haj Amin al-Husseini, a second cousin of Faisal al-Husseini.

Hanan had hired Suhair in Amman on her way to Madrid for the opening peace talks. Under an Israeli law, whereby Palestinians between the ages of eighteen and twenty-five were forbidden to return for nine months after exiting the Occupied Territories, at the last minute the woman who was slated to be Hanan's assistant decided not to cross the Allenby Bridge into Jordan. It was a law that was meant to discourage Palestinians who were of a certain age from making contact with terrorists in Lebanon or Jordan, leading to their participation in terrorist activity in Israel and the Occupied Territories. Suhair, a resident of Amman, had been in the crowd of well-wishers on the Jordanian side of the Allenby Bridge. It was a fortuitous coincidence, since she immediately volunteered to step in and take the job. Within an hour the young woman had permission from the Palestinian Embassy in Amman, where she worked as an assistant for the PLO representative, to take an indefinite leave of absence and accompany Hanan to Madrid. As Suhair explained it, "It was an honor to work for Hanan and take part in such a historical occasion." Now, in Washington, Suhair intended to follow Hanan back to Ramallah for the Christmas break. After a five-year absence she had finally been granted a visa to return to East Jerusalem and Hebron to visit relatives and friends. According to Suhair, until then she had been unable to obtain the required visitor's visa, issued by the Israelis, on the basis of what she described as "the Israeli policy to discourage Palestinians from returning to their land." The visa itself was expensive for the average Palestinian, costing about three hundred Jordanian dinars, or about two hundred American dollars. How often or if at all a Palestinian could come home and visit depended on his or her political affiliations and/or the general climate of violence throughout the Occupied Territories. During a lull in the telephone calls, Suhair explained, "I was banned from coming into the territories because my father had been a political figure, although as a child, I was allowed to come home more often."

In between the chaos, while Suhair relaxed with Hanan in the suite, she talked about her childhood in Jerusalem until the family had been forced to leave. According to Suhair her father was murdered by the Israelis in Tel Aviv in 1972, after which the family was expelled to Beirut. While she gave few details about her father's murder, she was extremely verbal in her opinions on the potential success of the peace conference. Admittedly, while she had an inherent mistrust of the media as she claimed they were consistently biased against Palestinians, branding them as terrorists each time a "revolutionary act" was committed to liberate Palestine, she was proud that Hanan had managed to improve that image. It was a subject that touched her deeply, since after the death of her father, she had had a succession of surrogate fathers who had been branded as terrorists and subsequently murdered by the Israelis. "There are so many life-and-death orphans born out of this struggle," she said. But there were other kinds of orphans—and widows—born out of the struggle as well: the women and children whose husbands and fathers were spending so much time away from home in Washington trying to come to an agreement.

During those months since the euphoria of Madrid,

Hanan kept hearing from the Palestinian delegates that they spent most of their days hanging around hotel corridors during the peace talks, making small talk with the Israelis, who had instructions from Jerusalem to discuss only the venue for the next round of meetings. Saeb Erekat, a delegate, remarked on several occasions that his twin daughters hardly recognized him anymore when he returned to his home in Jericho for brief visits. If anything positive came out of that time spent away from home and the lack of progress in Washington, it was that delegates on both sides bonded while they discussed feelings, told jokes, and exchanged photographs and news about their respective families. Mamduh al-Aker, the delegate from Ramallah who spent six months in prison without being officially charged with any crime, and who confronted Zalman Shoval, the Israeli ambassador to Washington, on CNN, recalls a particular anecdote from an afternoon in one of those corridors during the negotiations.

It was difficult for Aker to forget his time spent in prison when he had been held incommunicado, unable to contact either a lawyer or his family. Admittedly, it colored his reactions in Washington when he met with Israeli delegates between sessions. Dr. Aker's constant impression was that they operated in the same way as the Shin Bet during the time he was held in jail, a "good cop–bad cop" routine that was designed to destabilize him. After a while, he grew immune to their efforts, viewing all of them—bad or good—as the same. None was his friend; all were his enemies. "One of the Israeli delegates during a round of talks introduced himself to me on a personal level," Aker recalls, "which was part of the tactic. He told me that he knew I drove an Ascona because he also drove one. It seemed that we shared the same mechanic." After a while it became a habit to chat with the Israeli with the Ascona, who also happened to be the legal adviser to the delegation. Each time there was a break or a deadlock in the talks, when delegates on both sides were obliged to wait for orders from Tunis or Jerusalem, the men would find each other in the corridor. "He used to express his personal views," Aker continues, "telling me to be patient with his government, that the deadlock wouldn't last, which was what reminded me of my time spent in prison, when one guard was kind and the other was brutal."

It was on a particular occasion during a lull in the meetings when the subject of human rights was on the agenda. According to Dr. Aker, General Danny Rothchild, one of the Israeli delegates and the man who was responsible for all military operations throughout the Occupied Territories, would sit in the meetings, jacket off, sprawled out, smoking, and with an expression of boredom on his face, "as if he was just listening but saying to himself that we would never get anywhere, that it was all a waste of time." There was a heated debate about administrative punishment, deportation, house demolition, and administrative detention without charge, all topics that touched Dr. Aker personally. Ely Rubinstein, the head of the Israeli delegation, defended those practices by claiming that precedent for them had been set during the British Mandate in 1945. From the Palestinian side, it was pointed out that when the British left the region in 1948, they had summarily canceled those regulations, which made it strictly irrelevant that the Israelis had decided to reinstate them. "We even wrote to the British Parliament to confirm that those mandates had been rescinded in 1948, and we received an answer that they had been," Dr. Aker says. "We even had the proof in our hand."

When the meeting finally broke up that day, Aker was unable to contain himself. He was emotional as he rushed up to his new Israeli friend. "Listen, you're a lawyer, just for the sake of my own sanity, forget we're on the delegation for a minute," Aker pleaded. "Just as a human being, can you really accept someone being arrested and not charged, without even being given the right to call a lawyer?" Tears welled in Mamduh Aker's eyes. "It's just the two of us, off the record," he continued. "Tell me honestly, you're a man of the law, how does that fit into your lexicon?" Aker waited while the lawyer, visibly uncomfortable, finally looked him in the eye and said quietly, "No, I can't accept it, I can't accept it at all." Clutching his hand and shaking it, Aker replied, "Thank you, thank you, at least now I can walk away knowing that we're not both crazy."

While those newly cemented friendships and that newfound mutual respect made good personal-interest stories, from a political point of view, to report to the people back home in the Occupied Territories that there were still no concrete results was to invite disaster. Hardly anyone wanted to remember that Hanan had predicted from that first day, when buses filled with the Palestinian delegation crossed the Allenby Bridge in Jericho for Jordan and the trip to Madrid, that any agreement would take months, maybe even years, to reach. Back then, when people held to the widespread belief that things would move quickly since never before had Palestinians been given the opportunity to express their cause before an internationally recognized world forum, she had been accused of being unnecessarily pessimistic. Now, more than a year later, mumblings could be heard throughout the territories as to whether the leaders who had gone off to Madrid were still worthy of the people's trust, or if the rejectionist positions of Hamas and other radical factions opposed to the talks were not justified after all. For Hanan, who was well aware of all the potential repercussions stemming out of deadlock in the talks, the only hope was that certain secret channels that she had helped to arrange would benefit the official negotiations in Washington. Providing each side with a partner for peace was the only alternative to combat those violent factions that were against any potential peace accord.

BEGINNING IN 1989, before Madrid, Hanan had been involved in talks between Yossi Beilin and Avram Burg, men loyal to Shimon Peres within the Labor party; two unknown academics, Yair Hirschfeld, an eccentric forty-nine-year-old professor of Middle East history at a minor Israeli university; and Ron Pundik, thirty-eight years old, who had recently received his doctorate and was looking for a job; and several prominent Palestinian leaders from the Occupied Territories. The first meeting Hanan arranged between the men, later called the "proximity talks," was held at the Notre Dame Hotel in East Jerusalem. Earlier, Hanan had set up other "proximity talks" in Holland where she tried to get several Israeli officials to agree to meet with several members of the PLO. Although the talks in Holland were to be sponsored by an ex–foreign minister from the Socialist party, Max Vanderstuhl, a man who had close contacts with the Israeli Labor party, they never led to any direct talks. "That was one channel I really got to know well," Hanan says, "which led to Yossi Beilin and later on Yair Hirschfeld and Ron Pundik sending messages back and forth through me to our leadership in Tunis." Yair Hirschfeld was also knowledgeable about several secret channels. In the fall of 1992, he had been involved in a study financed by the European Community, on the political and economic conditions in the Occupied Territories. In connection with that study, Hirschfeld had been meeting with Palestinian activists in East Jerusalem and Ramallah but primarily with Hanan, with whom he was discussing the "typical fair dream of an academic—economic development as a basis for potential compromise."

While the "proximity talks" in Holland failed, they nonetheless prompted Professor Hirschfeld to ask Hanan if she could arrange for him to meet with a PLO official during an upcoming trip he was making to London. After checking with Arafat, who seemed in favor of any secret meetings that would lead to an eventual agreement, Hanan contacted Ahmed Suleiman Kriah, Arafat's director of finances (known by the nom de guerre Abu Ala), who, also as a member of the Palestinian steering committee, would coincidentally be in London at the same time as Hirschfeld. Hanan gave him Hirschfeld's number in London. "Yair was supposed to be staying with relatives in London, but when he got several calls from people identifying themselves as members of the PLO in Tunis, he decided to move to a hotel."

Also in London at the same time happened to be a Norwegian sociologist named Terje Rod Larsen, whom Hirschfeld knew and in whom he confided about his secret meeting with the PLO official. Larsen was the head of the Norwegian Institute for Applied Social Sciences in Oslo, while his wife, Mona Juul, was a senior Norwegian diplomat with experience in the Middle East. (Her first foreign post had been in Cairo.) When Larsen understood the purpose of the meeting, he suggested that if both men felt there was a chance to further the dialogue, he was certain that the Norwegian government would provide both sides with full facilities to continue in Norway under full security and secrecy.

Hirschfeld's first meeting with Abu Ala took place over breakfast in Larsen's hotel, the Forte's Crest St. James, followed by another meeting that night in the café of the Ritz Hotel. Also in London for the steering committee meetings was Yossi Beilin, whom Hirschfeld contacted to report that Abu Ala was interested in broad bilateral talks with Israeli officials. While Beilin operated under the constraints of the Israeli law, then not yet repealed, which forbade any Israeli contact with members of the PLO, he told Hirschfeld unofficially that he could send him a report of the meeting, which he would read, but that he could neither comment upon nor advise. While Hirschfeld could offer no guarantees, he did take it upon himself to assure Abu Ala that there might be people in the new Labor government who would be willing to act as a channel for future meetings. Up to that point, the only people on the Palestinian side who were aware of the London meetings were Hanan; Yasir Arafat; Abu Mazen, an aide close to Arafat; Hassan Asfour, another close aide to the PLO chairman; and of course Abu Ala. It was then that Hassan Asfour told Hanan that if the talks continued, there was a general feeling in Tunis that she should be brought in as one of the chief negotiators. "The problem with that," Hanan adds, "was that I was so visible and the main criterion was to keep things secret, so that in the end it was decided that I should be left out." On the Israeli side only Yair Hirschfeld and Yossi Beilin were aware of the London meetings. Until then, while Foreign Minister Peres was uninformed of Hirschfeld's meetings with Abu Ala, Prime Minister Rabin might have been briefed by Mossad. The leak may have come about because of Adnan Yassin, a Mossad spy who had been planted within the ranks of the PLO in Tunis and was arrested shortly afterward.

At the same time as Yair Hirschfeld and Abu Ala were meeting in London, and several days before the official talks in Washington were scheduled to break for the winter recess, Hanan decided to meet confidentially on her own with U.S. Deputy Secretary of State for Near Eastern Affairs Dan Curtzer. The purpose of the meeting would be to try to persuade the State Department official that without the PLO, there were only limited possibilities of coming to any agreement. It was time to mend fences. All along, from the beginning of the first contact at the Notre Dame Hotel in East Jerusalem between Israelis and Palestinians, and more pointedly after the London meetings, Hanan maintained that while she was in favor of any secret talks that would lead to peace, the talks should not be kept secret from the Palestinian delegation. Further, she understood that by then the delegates were basically functioning as a "front" to deflect what was really going on behind the scenes. "Nothing could succeed without the PLO, that was clear, but I told Abu Ammar that the delegation had a right to know, since they couldn't maneuver. Not only couldn't they maneuver, but they had a complex set of accountabilities. What I didn't want was for the delegation to feel used, which was exactly what happened in the end. I wanted Abu Ammar to tell everybody, without going into detail, that secret talks were going on, and to explain that they should try their best while remembering that they were there as the visible negotiators. It was obvious to me that by the time those secret meetings were going on regularly, the PLO didn't want any progress made on the Washington channel because it [had become] clear that any progress . . . would happen directly between the PLO and the Israelis."

Still, despite her displeasure with Arafat, Hanan, during her meeting with Deputy Secretary Curtzer, raised several issues that were ultimately settled during the secret talks in Oslo and subsequently incorporated in the DOP that was signed on the White House lawn. According to Hanan the two main obstacles to any peace accord between Israel and the PLO were the ruptured dialogue between the PLO and the United States and the PLO's fear that other Arab nations would cement an agreement with Israel first, relegating the Palestinian cause once again to obscurity. Opening her statements with a warning, Hanan informed Curtzer that any attempt to delegitimize the PLO would lead nowhere, that "the PLO was the only group with the ability to deliver and the only group that had the sanction of the Palestinians living in the Occupied Territories."

Concerning any reopening of a dialogue between the PLO and the United States, Hanan expressed her belief that it would do a great deal to alleviate the tremendous anti-American sentiment that was rampant within the Occupied Territories. What she conveyed to Curtzer in plain terms was that any progress that had been made in legitimizing the PLO had been seriously set back by the PLO leadership itself. "There was the Abu Abbas issue," she admitted, "as well as other problems, of which the chairman is aware. There is also the Gulf War crisis and the PLO decisions that have harmed the PLO's image."

Curtzer's response was succinct. "It's like bad old music," he said. "What rings through is the organizational integrity of the PLO versus progress toward realizing national aspirations. When organizational integrity is pitted against progress, without realizing national aspirations, then organizational integrity takes precedence. This does not sell well in the United States." With regard to the requirements for any resumption of dialogue, Curtzer reiterated that the policy of the United States had not changed.

In response Hanan raised the following question: "In dealing with the rift between the suspension of the dialogue, if the Abu Abbas issue is resolved, and the issue with respect to other terrorist activities that are close to the chairman is resolved, will it clear a deck or will it clear the entire deck?"

Curtzer answered, "It would clear a deck but not all the decks, since the PLO's Gulf War activities would have to be dealt with." Additionally Curtzer reminded Hanan that while there was anti-American sentiment among Palestinians, there was also a reversal of attitudes against Palestinians within the general American public.

That was unfortunate, Hanan told Curtzer, since "the PLO," she said, "is much more flexible than the people within the Occupied Territories. They will not allow the PLO to be self-effacing and are greatly displeased when the PLO makes concessions to Israel or to the Americans. The Palestinians in the territories are more hard-line than the PLO itself." Hanan went on to say that the real hurdle was the attempt to remove the PLO from the peace process. "Anyone who is not PLO-designated cannot move politically," she warned.

Curtzer spoke for President Bush when he replied, "President Bush is prepared to act and has substantial standing, domestically and internationally, but he is not prepared to deal with Tunis because it is a nonstarter. The United States is prepared to deal with people like you because you're intelligent and deeply affected by the conflict and want to overcome the obstacles." In addition the deputy secretary mentioned that while he couldn't officially accept direct messages or questions from the PLO, he took and understood all questions raised by Professor Ashrawi as relayed on behalf of the PLO.

In concluding the meeting, which lasted more than two hours, Hanan advised Curtzer that if "something was not delivered within a few months, there would be serious changes on the ground." The message was received and the implication was obvious when Curtzer replied, "The United States is afraid of Hamas and also afraid of the consequences of not acting. We only have a moment."

The moment came without warning when negotiations ground to a hopeless deadlock in December, after Israel expelled 415 Palestinians to a stretch of no-man's-land on the northern Israeli border with Lebanon. All the deportees were accused of belonging to Hamas and Islamic Jihad in Gaza, organizations responsible for the increase of brutal murders of Israeli citizens, including the ax mutilation of a Shin Bet agent in an East Jerusalem "safe house," a residence reserved for informers to meet with Israeli security agents.

Images of buses filled with the deportees, handcuffed and

hooded, were shown to the world as they made their way at dawn in a long procession toward Lebanon. What Prime Minister Rabin expected was that the Lebanese government would allow them to pass across the border into Lebanon as they had always done in the past, to join other Hezbollah groups that were scattered throughout Beirut and the Bekaa Valley. Unfortunately for Israel, Rabin had misjudged the serious intentions of the newly formed Lebanese government to put the country back in civil order. The last thing the Lebanese needed was another group of militant pro-Iranian Palestinians to reignite the violence.

The world was divided into two camps of opinion, those who were horrified by the mass deportations, which were branded as the ultimate example of typical Israeli "collective punishment" against Palestinians living in the Occupied Territories, and those who viewed the deportees as the ultimate example of a group of radical Palestinians who were blocking the peace process. Following Arafat's lead, Hanan and the others involved in the talks adhered to the official PLO party line when they announced that there would be no further negotiations until the 415 Palestinians were returned. The implicit instructions from Tunis were that any date set for future talks would only further incur the wrath of the Hamas members who remained in residence on the West Bank and in Gaza. On the one hand, never before had Yasir Arafat found himself in such a weakened position, given the Americans' continuing refusal to deal openly with the PLO; on the other, never before had so much global opprobrium been heaped on Israel for expelling so many men for what was said to be violence perpetrated only by a few. The reality of both situations was quite another story.

In defense of its action the Israeli government claimed that during the last three months of 1992, the Shin Bet uncovered a terrorist operation comprised of more than fifteen hundred members of Hamas and other Islamic fundamentalist groups. The group known as the Hamas military arm also included men who had already been deported to Lebanon in the past. Following the arrest of one of the leaders of the organization, Jawad Bahar, it was discovered that the group would meet in mosques or safe houses they had rented in Gaza, where they would plan their attacks. One of the methods for calling a meeting would be to scrawl the time and venue on the back of a shoe closet in a certain mosque. More than two hundred thousand dollars had already been smuggled into Hebron to bankroll the operations where the group also trained in the use of firearms. Of these fifteen hundred men, the Israeli government chose those whom they deemed the most "hard core" and who had been responsible for some of the more deadly terrorist attacks on civilians. In some cases those civilians included Palestinians whom Hamas accused of collaborating with the Israelis.

Another reality that emerged during that period—apparently higher on Arafat's agenda than supporting those deported Hamas members—was to continue engaging in the secret negotiations that had begun in London, still behind the backs of the official Palestinian delegation. What only Hanan and a small group of people knew at the time was that despite the tense political climate throughout the Occupied Territories, peace was in the air.

BY THE TIME Hanan arrived back in the house on Radio Street from Washington in December 1992, she was suffering from severe exhaustion and a bad case of the flu. Neither her frail state of health nor her fatigue, however, prevented her from meeting long into every night with local Palestinian leaders, who were concerned about the increasing violence that raged through the Occupied Territories. Since the opening conference in Madrid, few people could have learned so much as fast as Hanan did, under what she once referred to as "combat conditions." Whether it was projecting the appropriate image of the Palestinian people for seasoned reporters or giving the correct response to political pundits, Hanan rarely faltered. Animated on command, she routinely flashed her most charming smile when delivering bad news—whether it was refusing an interview or rejecting a proposal on behalf of her delegation—or demonstrating outrage when confronted with reports of Palestinian casualties at the hands of the Israeli Army. In reaction to incidents of Palestinian violence against Israeli civilians, however, it was just as routine to watch her retreat behind an impassive mask, not quite justifying the violence yet somehow leaving an observer with the impression that as long as a settlement remained elusive, unfortunate but unavoidable atrocities would continue. Implicit in her words was the warning that time was running out before more radical Palestinian factions, such as Hamas or the Islamic Jihad, would launch their own brand of "negotiations."

While most of the violence throughout the Occupied Territories that winter could be attributed to an escalation of the Intifada, given the deportation of the 415 Hamas members, attacks were also directed at the Palestinians involved in the peace negotiations. More critical, Arafat's popularity was decreasing to the point where local leaders were actually calling for his resignation. Even Faisal al-Husseini, usually reluctant to make statements that went against the official party line, addressed a group of Palestinians in Jerusalem and announced, "We are facing a total collapse of our existing institutions, which might be the signal to form a national salvation government."

That blatant internal PLO strife produced the naive hope on the part of the Israelis that Hamas might finally forget about killing Jews and concentrate on eliminating the Palestinians who were members of opposing factions. Encouraged as well by the growing dissension within Palestinian ranks, Israel also held to the notion that a conciliation with local leaders might entice the Gulf States to resume financial aid to the PLO if the organization would replace Arafat as its leader. Without Arafat, and with a new leadership within the Occupied Territories, Israel would feel comfortable with an accord that would lead to an eventual Palestinian state on yet another of its borders. But just as naive as those Israeli hopes was the belief among certain Palestinian leaders that Arafat would simply fade into oblivion after decades of power to make room for a group of local upstarts to claim the glory.

As Hanan recovered from the flu, her way of relaxing would be to talk about herself, a subject she claimed always to avoid. On the one hand she seemed to take her fame for granted, having accepted the position of most popular sound bite in the Western media, while on the other she seemed to have a horror of profiles, in-depth articles, and books that recounted her life. Sitting in the music room on Radio Street, she often caught herself on television or pored through all the articles about her that appeared in the press, yet, con-tradictorily, she would wonder out loud why there was so much "fuss made about a woman who was nothing more exciting than academic."

There was something Kafkaesque about the atmosphere around the house on Radio Street that Christmas. While the peace talks were stalled and people were dying each day throughout the West Bank and Gaza either at the hands of the army or terrorists, and more than four hundred Palestin-ians had set up a makeshift camp somewhere in the snowy foothills of the Shuf Mountains in Lebanon, Suhair arrived in Ramallah with a three-piece set of Louis Vuitton luggage, wearing designer jeans, gold bangle bracelets, and Ray·Ban sunglasses. She was there to help Hanan, between making the rounds of family and friends in East Jerusalem and Hebron.

CHAPTER TWELVE

SUHAIR

SUHAIR IS A NEW BREED of Palestinian princess, a description formerly reserved for the daughters of oil-rich sheikhs. While she describes herself as the daughter of a revolutionary who is forever inscribed in Palestinian history, had her father not been murdered by the Israelis, Suhair, her three sisters, and her mother would be living average middle-class lives within the framework of Israeli occupation. Instead they are supported by the PLO leadership, given jobs with generous salaries within the hierarchy of the system, either as Yasir Arafat's press secretary (Rydah Taha, Suhair's oldest sister) or as Hanan Ashrawi's assistant during the peace conference. Still, the pain and suffering that Suhair feels about being Palestinian she describes as a legacy passed down from generation to generation, not unlike an Olympic torch that is passed from athlete to athlete. What Suhair wears almost as a badge of suffering despite the Vuitton bags, Ray·Ban shades, and gold bangle bracelets, is how painful school vacations were after her family was exiled from Jerusalem and living in Beirut. All the other little girls could go home to visit their families. Suhair had no home she was able to visit, her family lands having been confiscated by the Israelis after 1967.

Sitting in Hanan's music room on Radio Street, Suhair produces photographs from her wallet and proceeds to explain that one sister is studying in Amman; another is attending college in Washington; Rydah, of course, is based in Tunis and is temporarily living out of a suitcase. Proudly holding up a picture of her mother, a beautiful woman who, Suhair explains, has suffered bouts of depression since the death of her husband and now spends her time taking aerobic classes and fretting over her daughters. "My parents were madly in love," Suhair adds quietly. "I have memories of my father carrying my mother into their room every night." The last photograph Suhair takes from her wallet is of a handsome man who bears a striking resemblance to a young Desi Arnaz, with his black hair combed into a pompadour, a radiant smile, dimples, and spectacular white teeth. It is a picture of Suhair's father taken shortly before his death. Still, Suhair remains mysterious concerning the details of her father's murder at the hands of the Israelis.

What Suhair did explain was that her father had been a tour guide in Jerusalem until 1967 and had been accorded the highest honor any Muslim could achieve, which was to be guardian of the key to the Church of the Nativity. Traditionally the key was given by a high Christian official to a Muslim worthy of keeping it in his possession except for Christian holy and feast days. "My father held the key until the Israelis took it from him, when they forced us to leave Jerusalem after the war broke out in sixty-seven." What Suhair also mentioned, although she claimed she was too young to remember precise details, was that she always felt that something was missing from her life, a sense of growing up within a family and a society in which tradition was so important. "Which is why I've made a vow that my own children will never suffer the same kind of feelings of loss that I did as a child." Apparently the moment had come for Suhair to talk about those Palestinians who had functioned as surrogate fathers after her own father's death.

"Kamel Nasser was the first," she began. "He was a Palestinian poet who was also murdered by the Israelis in Beirut. Abu Jihad was another father for me who was murdered by the Israelis in Tunis in front of his whole family, and then there was Abu Iyad, who was killed by someone from the Abu Nidal organization, which everyone knows is a cover for the Mossad." It was an impressive list.

While Kamel Nasser was indeed a renowned Palestinian poet, he was also the PLO's chief spokesperson in Beirut as well as the deputy to Abu Yussef (Muhammad Yussef al-Najjar), a leader of Black September, one of the men who carried out the murder of the Israeli athletes during the Munich Olympics. Kamel Nasser, along with Abu Yussef and another Black September deputy, Kamal Adwan, had been ambushed by Israeli commandos at their apartment in Beirut, shot more than eighty times by six different automatic weapons.

Abu Jihad, second in command to Yasir Arafat, was also a Palestinian hero, one of the founding members of the PLO and widely regarded as Arafat's natural successor. The architect of terrorism within the Occupied Territories that held Israel in its grip for more than two decades, he was killed by a group of Israeli commandos from the Sayaret Malkal, an elite commando unit, while in front of his wife and two children in his villa at PLO headquarters in Tunis. In one of his rare interviews with an American journalist, Abu Jihad was quoted as saying, "The Kalashnikov [Soviet-designed AK-47 assault rifle] is our only language until we free all of Palestine." In the recent years before his death in May 1988, Abu Jihad had developed close ties to the military and intelligence organizations of many Arab governments, especially those in Libya, Syria, Jordan, and Algeria. Highly secular in his outlook of the world, Abu Jihad had been an admirer of Mao Zedong and had received intelligence and military training in China during the early 1960s.

Finally Abu Iyad, the roly-poly, talkative PLO leader, also one of the founding fathers of the organization, had moved up to second-in-command after the death of his lifelong friend, Abu Jihad. While his title was officially minister of defense of the PLO, Abu Iyad gained his fame and notoriety as the leader of Black September and as the mastermind behind the Munich massacre. Since he was killed while visiting the home of another PLO notable, Abu Tol, who headed the PLO secret service and who was killed during the same attack, it was believed that the men were the victims of an internal dispute.

Still, the question of the murder of Suhair's father, the Jerusalem tour guide who had been so honored during his short life, remained unanswered. But before Suhair could explain the connection between her family and three of the most famous Palestinian terrorists, Hanan interrupted to ask if she shouldn't be leaving for her appointment at Dr. Scholl's foot center in West Jerusalem. It seemed Suhair was suffering from an ingrown toenail, and since there were no podiatrists on the West Bank or even in East Jerusalem, the obvious solution was to be treated at Dr. Scholl's. "Suhair has an appointment with an Israeli doctor," Hanan announced, "and I'm a little worried about her going there alone when it's dark."

With all the internecine fighting between different factions of the PLO, and the Israeli Army's increased vigilance throughout the Occupied Territories given the suspension of the peace talks, it was more dangerous than ever to make the trip from Ramallah to West Jerusalem. Since the Intifada began in 1987, it had been unsafe to drive a car with yellow Israeli plates into the Occupied Territories for fear of getting stoned, and just as unsafe to drive an Arab car with blue plates through certain ultrareligious Israeli neighborhoods or settlements. The trip, therefore, from Ramallah to Jerusalem entailed an Arab taxi as far as the American Colony Hotel in East Jerusalem, where an Israeli-Arab taxi, identifiable by the number 9 at the beginning of the serial numbers on its roof, would make the rest of the trip into West Jerusalem.

During the drive through Ramallah with me, Suhair discussed everything from her foot problems to her opinion on the validity of the Holocaust. "I've studied the Holocaust in great detail," she said, "and frankly, it's a big exaggeration. Maybe Jews *were* killed, along with a lot of other people, during the course of the war, but never any mass extermination of six million. That's Zionist propaganda."

During the ride through the neighboring cities of El Biryeh and Bet Hanina, Suhair seemed calm, although she grew anxious as the cab approached Jerusalem. Talking about the apprehension she felt each time she entered the city, she claimed it was a glaring reminder how it was no longer a part of her lost country but rather a hostile environment controlled by a foreign entity. The genesis of her feelings about Jerusalem had to do with her father, his death, and her own feelings of depression that have never left her. As the Ramallah taxi pulled up at the American Colony Hotel, and we stepped into an Israeli-Arab cab for the ride into the western sector of the city, Suhair talked more about her father. Again it was all related to the loss of Jerusalem, which turned his life around so that he became obsessed with politics almost to the exclusion of his family. "My mother used to ask him if he loved her more than anything else in the world," Suhair said, "and he would tease her that perhaps there was another love he had which was almost as big. My mother would get jealous and demand to know who it was." Suhair smiled sadly. "You see, my mother's name is Jamel, so my father used to say that both his loves had names beginning with a *J*, Jerusalem and Jamel, and maybe he did love one just a bit more than the other, since one was a lost love."

As the cab made its way through the heavy rush-hour traffic toward Dr. Scholl's Foot Center on Jaffa Street in West Jerusalem, Suhair became agitated. "I hate coming here," she said. "I can't pretend to be anything but jealous that this city doesn't belong to us anymore. Look at the faces—these people are all strangers to me." She paused before speaking in a barely audible voice. "I'd be a liar if I said that I didn't hate the Israelis for killing my father."

SUHAIR HAD COME to the West Bank on this particular visit not only to see friends and family but also to visit her father's grave in Hebron. She talked about experiencing a moment of tension as she knelt to put flowers at the tombstone. "A group of Palestinians gathered on the hill just above my father's grave in a kind of protective circle. When I explained that I was his daughter, they understood." Still, she had said nothing concerning the circumstances under which her father had died in Tel Aviv, or anything about what he had done for the revolution that would accord him posthumous hero status. "He's not the first Palestinian to be killed in cold blood by the Israelis; it happens every day here," Suhair said simply as she stepped out of the car for her appointment with the Israeli podiatrist. It wasn't until she reappeared, limping slightly but relieved that her toe was finally proclaimed cured, that the real story of her father emerged. Finally it became clear why Ali Shafik Ahmed Taha was so revered as a hero of the Palestinian revolution.

During the years that the PFLP committed its bloody attacks on Israeli and Western aircraft, Habash hired a Palestinian named Waddia Haddad as his "operational genius." While it was Haddad who devised some of the most daring PFLP's terrorist attacks, it was a handsome and mysterious man named Ali Shafik Ahmed Taha who actually carried out those attacks to their successful conclusion.

Recruited in 1967, Taha operated under the name of Captain Rifat and, with his first endeavor, became something of a legend in the area of hijacking civil aviation. His illustrious career with the group began as the commander of the hijacking operation that diverted that TWA aircraft over Algiers en route from Rome to Tel Aviv. It was also Captain Rifat who masterminded the hijacking of that Lufthansa 747 that was diverted from New Delhi to Athens, on which Joseph P. Kennedy, Jr., the son of slain senator Robert F. Kennedy, was a passenger. Serving not only as a commander and a militant, Captain Rifat was also a brilliant negotiator, having convinced Lufthansa after the drama was over to pay a ransom of five million dollars along with annual "protection payments" to guarantee the airline safe passage in the skies. But the most spectacular attack came on September 6, 1970, when Captain Rifat planned and executed the multiple hijacking of three planes that were subsequently blown up and destroyed at Beirut Airport and at Dawson's Field in the Jordanian desert. It was in Tel Aviv, however, that Captain Rifat's career eventually ended, during his most daring and dramatic hijacking.

On May 8, 1972, Sabena flight number 517, en route from Vienna to Tel Aviv, was hijacked during the end of the flight and ordered to land at Lod (Ben Gurion Airport) in Israel, where negotiations would begin. Twenty-four hours after the hijacking, and with the aircraft still sitting on the ground in Tel Aviv, Israeli commandos from the Sayaret Malkal, under the leadership of Lt. Colonel Ehud Barak, stormed the plane. Ali Shafik Ahmed Taha was killed instantly in the bloody firefight that ensued aboard the aircraft.

A hero of the Palestinian revolution, Suhair's father certainly shared some of the responsibility for two decades of tension between the PLO and Jordan—following Black September in 1970, when King Hussein expelled thousands of Palestinians from what had become known as Fatahland—that ended with King Hussein disengaging from the West Bank in the fall of 1989. During the Cyril Foster Lecture at Oxford University on October 19, 1989, which King Hussein delivered, he stated: "By disengaging from the West Bank, Jordan has enabled the PLO to cast aside its suspicions and engage us and the world community in a serious dialogue about its vision of the future." Hussein's words would prove to be the beginning of a global Middle East peace initiative that would end in Oslo.

CHAPTER THIRTEEN

THE HOUSE
IN BORREGARD MANOR

WITHIN THE PLO, to keep a secret is punishable by obscurity; to divulge it is a mark of prominence. Within Israel, to keep a secret is impossible.

Yossi Beilin was the Israeli official who informed Shimon Peres that an unknown academic named Yair Hirschfeld, along with one of his students, Ron Pundik, from Hebrew University in Jerusalem, had broken the law and were currently engaged in meetings with Abu Ala, a close Arafat adviser and the head of the PLO economics department. It should not be left unwritten that as the one Palestinian who was aware of the almost-bankrupt condition of the PLO, Kriah was determined to see the Oslo negotiations end in a peace accord. Without it Kriah knew that nothing could be done both to improve Arafat's dwindling popularity within the ranks, and to bolster the image of the PLO throughout the world. Whether by just another coincidence or as the result of an ongoing debate, on January 19, 1993, the Knesset formally repealed the law forbidding Israelis to enter into direct contact with members of the PLO.

On January 21, 1993, the first official session took place between the Israelis and the PLO under the auspices of Terje Larsen's research institute, with Mona Juul acting as the liaison to the Norwegian Foreign Ministry. As a cover the participants agreed to pretend for the world, and especially for the press, that the meeting was a conference to consider the results of the institute's field study on living conditions in the Occupied Territories.

At the time Hanan was still back in Ramallah doing her part in fighting a two-front war—against those Palestinians who were opposed to the mainstream PLO, and against the Israeli authorities and right-wing civilians, who were also opposed to the mainstream PLO. For the time being her role in, or knowledge of, what was going on in Norway was limited. When her friends Hassan Asfour and Akram Hania informed her periodically that "things were moving along with the secret negotiations," she claimed that she always believed they were limited to the economic aspect of the problem. "At the time I was convinced that because Abu Ala and Yair Hirschfeld were involved, the talks were contained within the context of an economic conciliation, which we all hoped would eventually lead to a political solution. Actually I wasn't that inquisitive, because I always thought and said publicly that the only way we could ever have results was if the Israelis and the PLO sat down and discussed issues face to face." Her feeling right along was that either the Madrid framework needed to change so that the PLO could meet officially with the Israelis, or the talks would be deadlocked forever. After all, only the PLO had the real authority to make any decisions on behalf of the Palestinians.

While Hanan continued to toe the PLO party line for the general public by advocating a boycott of the peace talks until the 415 Hamas members were brought back from Lebanon to Gaza, behind the scenes she worked toward a very different objective. Most of her time was spent trying to convince members of those "rejectionist" factions to put aside the issue of the deportees so that the PLO could once again resume talks with Israel. She was nothing less than a one-woman lobbying effort as she participated in continuous rounds of meetings with representatives from dissenting PLO factions, on behalf of Arafat and his quest for peace. The more militant "rejectionist fronts," such as the DFLP and the PFLP, while maintaining their opposition to the peace conference, remained solidly inside the realm of consensus. While outwardly against any conciliation, they were nonetheless prepared to go along with any decision that Arafat made concerning the talks. Hamas and other Islamic fundamentalist groups, however, were violent challengers not only of the PLO leadership but also of Palestinians whom they regarded as collaborators—those who were "soft-selling" the concept of a Palestinian state on any less than all the land of Israel, with Jerusalem as its capital.

Abu Ala arrived for that first meeting in Oslo, with two of his aides, Hassan Asfour and Maher al-Hurd, an economist who was a graduate of the American University in Cairo and spoke fluent English. Yair Hirschfeld arrived with Ron Pundik. The expenses for the Palestinians were paid by the PLO, while expenses for the two Israelis (who were unofficial and therefore not covered by their government) were paid by the Norwegian institute.

For that initial encounter, Larsen and Juul wanted to find a secluded, tranquil setting in which the participants would feel more relaxed than if they were seated around a formal conference table in an office. They found the perfect location about sixty miles east of Oslo, in Sapsborg, where a friend owned a luxurious white country house surrounded by forests.

BORREGARD MANOR had been the summer residence of Norwegian kings during the Middle Ages. There were working fireplaces, simple furniture, and enough cozy rooms so that all the participants could sleep under one roof and take all their meals together in the dining room. The manor staff was informed that the guests were academics who would be collaborating on a book. Evn Aas, who usually worked as the trainer for the Norwegian women's speed-skating team, was put in charge of coordinating the schedules and meetings for all the participants. It was Aas's responsibility to make the necessary arrangements for the Palestinians and Israelis to be driven in separate, inconspicuous rented cars from Oslo airport to Borregard Manor. It was also Aas who was charged with the responsibility of inviting Jan Egeland, Norway's deputy foreign minister, to join the group for lunch on the first day. After lunch Egeland drove back to Oslo, while the guests of the manor secluded themselves in a large room for their first official/unofficial meeting.

It was during that first encounter in Borregard Manor that Abu Ala suggested that the past should never be brought up between them. While his words were sincere, they were also directed at one of his aides, who had opened the discussion by citing UN Resolutions 242 and 338. "Let us not compete on who was right and who was wrong in the past," Abu Ala said. "And let us not compete about who can be more clever in the present. Let us see what we can do in the future." The first session lasted more than eight hours.

Three weeks later the participants reconvened for a second session. While the Israelis had been reporting unofficially to Yossi Beilin, now they reported to him officially in Jerusalem, while the Palestinians continued to brief Yasir Arafat in Tunis. It was Hirschfeld's idea to outline in broad terms a joint program, which took the form of a declaration of principles. The declaration envisaged free elections in the Occupied Territories and the gradual establishment (first in Gaza) of an interim autonomous regime. Hirschfeld outlined a number of guidelines that would make the plan palatable to Palestinians living under occupation, especially those in Gaza.

On an emotional and political level, Gaza meant nothing to anybody except the Arab leaders who had consistently pointed to it throughout the years as a glaring sign of Israeli occupation, especially since several hundred thousand Palestinians lived there in abject squalor and misery. Even before the outbreak of the Intifada, Gaza had been a mass of buildings overlooking narrow alleys and piles of garbage, ruined streets, and eroded agricultural land. The Israeli authorities had ignored that reality almost as much as the Palestinians had, although each side blamed the Intifada for the deterioration. The truth was that the Intifada only caused an existing situation to worsen as the arrest of terrorists took precedent over the maintenance of public services.

Agreement between the parties in Borregard Manor—particularly those concerning jurisdiction over territory, Jerusalem, and arbitration—was not reached on all the issues presented by Hirschfeld. The principle of "gradualism," a staged withdrawal of Israeli forces, was a new concept for both Palestinians and Israelis. What it meant was that during the first two or three years, the process of Israeli withdrawal could be halted or even reversed if the situation became either violent or a security risk for the Israelis. To Yossi Beilin's surprise the Palestinians accepted the premise of gradualism. It was a completely new agenda. Even in the Camp David autonomy plan contained in the 1978 agreement, there had never been such a built-in stipulation.

In March, two months after the secret meetings in Oslo began, the Norwegians informed the United States of their existence, presenting a draft of the declaration of principles worked out by Hirschfeld, Pundik, and Abu Ala. Although the Americans were supportive, they were not particularly optimistic, having been burned before, specifically during the U.S.-PLO dialogue in Tunis that had broken off after the terrorist attack committed by Abu Abbas, which Arafat refused to denounce. Still, after U.S. Secretary of State Warren

Christopher read the report provided by the late Norwegian Foreign Minister Johann Urgen Holst, he encouraged the Norwegians to continue. It should not be left unsaid, however, that according to one of Secretary Christopher's aides, the American secretary of state had trouble adjusting to the fact that the Norwegians were apparently succeeding where the Americans had failed.

Five more informal meetings took place between March and May, usually over long weekends at Borregard Manor and other secluded country houses in the area. It was during one of those meetings that Abu Ala threatened to walk out if Israel refused to send in official representatives from the Labor government. In response Larsen flew to Israel to consult with Beilin, who personally assured him that Hirschfeld was now authorized to conduct "prenegotiations." By early May, after the seventh round of meetings in Oslo, Peres proposed to fly to Norway to conduct the talks. Rabin disagreed, however, and instead decided to send Uri Savir, the newly appointed director general of the Foreign Ministry, along with Yoel Singer, a legal expert, to Borregard Manor.

The presence of two unaccredited academics had helped create an atmosphere of relaxed and friendly discussions in which probing more than negotiating was the order of business. However, with the arrival of Singer and Savir, the first official representatives from the Israeli side, the atmosphere and context of the talks changed. Suddenly there were tense moments between the parties, threats to walk out, and passionate fights, until finally Savir and Abu Ala went into seclusion, emerging at last with a first-step plan that would set Hirschfeld's DOP in motion.

It was a historic and emotional moment when Savir and Abu Ala announced that each side was prepared simultaneously to recognize the other's right to exist. For the Palestinians it had been a major obstacle since in 1988 the PLO officially proclaimed an independent Palestinian state on the West Bank and Gaza without any mention of the right of Israel to exist within recognized borders. And for the Israelis, given their inherent fear and hatred of the PLO, it was an enormous step toward peace.

By May 1993, both Rabin in Jerusalem and Arafat in Tunis were paying less attention to the bona fide peace negotiations in progress in Washington and more to the events unfolding in the luxurious farmhouse on the outskirts of Oslo. It was also decided during that time that Paris would be the ideal city in which to hammer out the final details of what became known as the "Oslo draft."

DANY SHEK, the spokesman for the Israeli Embassy in Paris, was not only a Peres confidante but was also a close political protégé of the Israeli foreign minister. Any Paris secret meetings approved by Peres would automatically come to the attention of Shek, who would act as liaison. Savir, Singer, and Abu Mazen went to Paris and checked into the Bristol Hotel.

All through the night, drinking nothing but black coffee ordered from room service, the parties negotiated nonstop in suites 117 and 118 in the Bristol Hotel, except for lengthy long-distance telephone calls made by each side, either to Tunis or to Jerusalem for instructions. On his way to Damascus to apprise the Syrian president in person that a deal was about to be reached between Israel and the PLO, Arafat was unreachable. Finally, at three o'clock in the morning, negotiations were on the verge of breaking down over a section of delicate wording in the agreement, having to do with the PLO's guarantee of Israel's right to exist. But by six o'clock in the morning, Prime Minister Rabin in Tel Aviv received a phone call from Paris announcing that there was a deal. Room service at the Bristol was summoned again, this time for a bottle of champagne and six glasses. Now only two problems remained: to persuade the Americans to allow the PLO chairman to travel to Washington for the signing ceremony, and to persuade Rabin to appear alongside of Arafat on the White House lawn. Still, before any ceremony in Washington could be arranged, Arafat needed to solve his own problems.

During a five-hour meeting with Hafez al-Assad, the Syrian president accused the PLO chairman of betrayal for making an agreement with the Israelis before a comprehensive agreement had been reached on the Golan Heights. There was no turning back. Despite Assad's displeasure Arafat had already agreed to recognize Israel, renounce terrorism, and state that the clauses in the Palestinian covenant calling for the destruction of Israel were invalid. And, in what was probably the most important concession, Arafat agreed to sign the letter of intent with Israel as "chairman of the PLO" rather than as "president of the state of Palestine."

More than any other reason, it was Arafat's title on the document that caused Farouq Qaddoumi, the PLO foreign minister, to boycott the meeting in Tunis. Sitting behind a rectangular table with a photograph of the al-Aqsa Mosque in Jerusalem hanging on the wall behind him, the PLO chairman pleaded with his colleagues to allow him to sign the Oslo draft as agreed on by both sides. In the next room Norwegian Foreign Minister Holst waited. Finally he was summoned. By a margin of nine to four, and with only a PLO photographer to record the moment, Arafat signed the two letters of intent that Holst removed from his brown leather briefcase.

From Tunis, Holst traveled to Jerusalem, where he had a breakfast meeting with Foreign Minister Peres. In that same brown leather briefcase, he carried a draft of the agreement. Yitzhak Rabin had already signed his name, preceded by a "sincerely," formally and finally recognizing the PLO as the legitimate representative of the Palestinian people. Whether or not the PLO would continue to be the "sole" representative of the Palestinian people remained to be seen. Clearly Arafat's biggest problem was any negative reaction among Palestinians living throughout the Occupied Territories, as well as those within the ranks of the PLO in Tunis.

From Jerusalem, Holst, accompanied by Peres, flew to a U.S. naval station in Point Magu, California, to brief Secretary of State Warren Christopher. Within hours Christopher relayed the news to President Clinton.

DURING THE SECOND ROUND of talks in Oslo, Hanan left Ramallah for Washington to participate in the tenth round of the official Mideast peace talks. It was then that the Americans presented Hanan, who continued to function as the direct link between the Americans and the PLO leadership in Tunis, with a draft of a declaration of principles concerning something called the "Gaza First" option. Over the course of approximately sixty hours, Hanan met with the American team—Aaron Miller, Dennis Ross, and Dan Curtzer—and then alone with Secretary of State Warren Christopher. From the inception, what Hanan deemed as unacceptable issues in that document had to do with the American reluctance to include in the discussions Jerusalem as the capital of any Palestinian state; Israeli troop withdrawal from those areas that were to be placed under Palestinian auspices; the implementation of UN Resolution 242—the right of return of Palestinian refugees scattered throughout the Arab world; security; and geographic and territorial jurisdiction. The complete text of UN Resolution 242, adopted by the international community on November 22, 1967, stated as follows:

> The Security Council; expressing its continuing concern with the grave situation in the Middle East, emphasizing the inadmissibility of the acquisition of

territory by war and the need to work for a just and lasting peace in which every state in the area can live in security; emphasizing further that all Member States in their acceptance of the Charter of the United Nations have undertaken a commitment to act in accordance with Article 2 of the Charter: 1. Affirms that the fulfillment of the Charter principles requires the establishment of a just and lasting peace in the Middle East which should include the application of both the following principles: A. Withdrawal of Israeli forces from territories occupied in the recent conflict; B. Termination of all claims or states of belligerency and respect for and acknowledgement of the sovereignty, territorial integrity and political independence of every State in the area and their right to live in peace within secure and recognized boundaries free from threats or acts of force; 2. Affirms further the necessity A. for guaranteeing the freedom of navigation through international waterways in the area; B. For achieving a just settlement of the refugee problem; C. For guaranteeing the territorial inviolability and political independence of every State in the area, through measures including the establishment of demilitarized zones; 3. Requests the Secretary-General to designate a Special Representative to proceed to the Middle East to establish and maintain contacts with the States concerned in order to promote agreement and assist efforts to achieve a peaceful and accepted settlement in accordance with provisions of this resolution; 4. Requests the Secretary-General to report to the Security Council on the progress of the efforts of the Special Representative as soon as possible.

According to Arafat, even back in 1967 UN Resolution 242 was a formula conceived by the world as a victory for expediency. Those who promoted 242 encouraged Israel and the Arab nations to bury the Palestinian problem permanently by implicitly denying that the Palestinians had the right to self-determination, referring to the Palestine problem as a "refugee problem." In 1993, according to Hanan, when the Americans talked about the "right of return of Palestinian refugees scattered throughout the Arab world," they were very busy, as she put it, "being more Catholic than the pope when it came once again to protecting Israeli rights."

The American response to Hanan's reservations about the document was to state that each side had the right to raise whatever issue it chose. Hanan smiles. "Of course, when we raised the issue of Jerusalem," she explains, "the Americans thanked us for raising it but told us quite simply that at that point it was not up for discussion." When Hanan argued that a commitment concerning Jerusalem was imperative and had to be included on the agenda, the Americans refused to make any promises. When she insisted that there must be implementation of UN Resolution 242 to make the agreement viable, the Americans claimed that whatever agreement was reached would automatically constitute an implementation of 242. "We told the Americans that was illegal. What happens if we came to an agreement that violated 242? Would that also constitute an implementation of 242? And they said it would. Our response was that it would not, since 242 has a very clear explanation, and we wanted implementation of the specific wording contained in that specific resolution." There were other problems as well.

HANAN INSISTED on beginning discussions immediately concerning linkage between the interim and permanent phases of Israeli withdrawal. The Americans took the position that any discussion of permanent status would only undermine the interim phase. In response Hanan wrote out an entire list of reasons why "early empowerment" wouldn't work if isolated from an eventual and total withdrawal. Her rationale was simple.

The precise definition of "early empowerment" was such spheres of authority as education, health, social welfare, labor, tourism, and direct taxation. The PLO had always believed—which is why Hanan and the Palestinian delegates had fought against it from the beginning of the talks in Madrid and then in Washington—that "early empowerment" in isolation could become merely a transfer of tasks rather than a takeover of authority. For Hanan "early empowerment" was simply another way of giving the Palestinians autonomy instead of statehood. "On instructions from Abu Ammar," Hanan explains, "and as far back as the ninth round, we introduced the Gaza-Jericho option for full statehood." In essence, for the PLO the Gaza-Jericho option was to be the first step toward full statehood encompassing the entire West Bank. "When the Americans heard that," Hanan continues, "they laughed."

If the Americans laughed when they were presented with the Gaza-Jericho option, they were even more incredulous when Hanan put forth the plan of bringing in Palestinians who were members of the Palestine Liberation Army (PLA) to act as the police and security forces. "They hit the ceiling," Hanan says. "They told me that this was an otherworldly matter, and when I wanted to start thinking in worldly [terms], I should let them know."

The rationale behind bringing in Palestinians from the outside to be in charge of security was that technically they had neither allegiance nor loyalty to any particular faction within the Occupied Territories. The PLA was considered a bipartisan group, trained and recognized as the peacekeeping army for every faction contained in the PLO and represented on the Palestine Executive Council. But even with the PLA overseeing security, Hanan maintained that an international peacekeeping force was also essential. The irony was that while the Americans rejected the presence of the PLA, Hanan already knew from her contacts in Tunis that the Israelis were prepared to accept Palestinians from the outside as the official police force. Although unhappy about giving any Palestinians—even those functioning as an internal security force—the right to bear arms, the Israelis considered members of the PLA to be the least of all risks, given their distance from on-the-ground involvement with various factions. Also at that time, the Americans had not yet been apprised of the progress of the secret talks in Oslo. "I knew certain points would be acceptable to the Israelis," Hanan explains, "because there were other secret channels I was aware were going on, besides Oslo, where those points had already been accepted. But since the Americans knew nothing, they set up paradigms and then expected us to behave according to a pattern which didn't work with us because it was typically American. What they didn't understand was that they couldn't just set up a process and then control it. It had to have a dynamic of its own, based on an interchange between us and the Israelis and including the requirements of that specific region. It was not the American position that counted."

As Hanan continued battling it out with the Americans in Washington, she concluded that they were unprepared to make any concessions that would meet even the Palestinians' minimal demands. The American position was that they were merely setting forth the Israeli position. In response Hanan consistently argued that Israel was only presenting a maximalist position, which would eventually end up somewhere in the middle in order to reach a realistic accord. Still, the Americans refused to entertain the notion that the Israelis would accept anything different than what they (the Americans) were proposing to the Palestinians. And the only items the Americans would entertain for discussion were "early empowerment"; factional transfer of such responsibilities as education and health; and transfer of land, but only as it pertained to management rather than actual Israeli troop withdrawal. According to Hanan, even the term "withdrawal" was unacceptable, since it pertained to the withdrawal of the military government and a dissolution of the Civil Administration (rather than full withdrawal of troops)—basically the Likud, right-wing position. "The Americans took such a hard line with us that we [decided] that it was time to stop meeting with them until we went to Tunis to consult with our leadership."

But by the time Hanan was about to leave for Tunis to consult with Arafat, the letters of intent had already been signed, formalizing the principles agreed on during the Oslo talks. Still unaware of any concrete agreement, Hanan nonetheless announced in a weary tone of voice hours before her departure, "We believe that Chairman Arafat is making too many concessions to the Israelis." Her statement was in reaction to Arafat's neutral response concerning the hard-line bargaining position the Americans had taken in Washington. Unknown to Hanan, what the Americans were telling her in Washington was already old news to the PLO chairman. Still, Hanan made no further statement before her arrival in Tunis as to what those "concessions" were and why they had prompted her and other West Bank leaders to speak out against Arafat before meeting with him personally.

When Hanan, Faisal al-Husseini, and Saeb Erekat were already behind closed doors with Arafat in Tunis, in a further show of dissension, Mahmoud Darwish—the celebrated Palestinian poet who, along with Hanan, wrote the Madrid speech—resigned from the PLO parliament. Citing Arafat's unilateral decision making, which bypassed the Washington delegation, Darwish claimed that his resignation was also precipitated by Arafat's consistent mismanagement of PLO finances.

While Arafat's methods of running what was supposed to be a democratic organization had apparently not changed over the years, something definitely had changed within the PLO structure. In 1993, when Hanan and the others spoke out against their leader, the repercussions were quite different than they had been in the past when a Palestinian leader within the Occupied Territories spoke up against the leadership's decisions or policies. In the old days the response had always been a severe warning followed by assassination. Now, with a distinct possibility of realizing the dream of a Palestinian state, the stakes were even higher. But, backwards as usual, the PLO palace coup was staged by the king and not the subjects.

CHAPTER FOURTEEN

IN RESIGNATION

WHEN HANAN ARRIVED in Tunis to meet with Arafat, her immediate suggestion to the PLO executive committee was to go, point by point, through the document that had been presented to her in Washington in an effort to show the Americans why it was unacceptable. "Abu Ammar's response was that it wasn't worth the effort, and I should simply tell the Americans that it was unacceptable without giving them any specific reasons." While Hanan argued that it was bad negotiating strategy not to give reasons, Arafat, joined by Nabil Shaath, continued to disagree. "The instructions I got directly from Abu Mazen and from Abu Ammar," Hanan maintains, "were not to give anything in writing to the Americans but only to discuss territorial jurisdiction and the issue of Jerusalem." What Hanan didn't know was that Shaath had already prepared a written draft in response to the position the Americans had taken during her Washington meetings, outlining the PLO position regarding territorial jurisdiction and the issue of Jerusalem. What Hanan also didn't know was that both Arafat and Shaath disagreed with her about presenting anything in writing, not only because Shaath intended to do it himself but because they knew that the Oslo agreement was on the verge of being signed. In retrospect

Hanan is still critical of the fact that she was excluded from all the facts and continues to maintain that while she knew there were several secret channels working in conjunction with the Washington meetings, she was completely unaware that anything specific or concrete had come to fruition. "The PLO was supposed to be a democracy, and I was supposed to be a representative of the leadership, so there shouldn't have been secret meetings without telling those of us involved in the visible meetings that there was something else going on, even if we weren't apprised of all the details. After all, we weren't puppets," she adds. Which was exactly what she said to Arafat during another meeting later that evening.

It was also during that later meeting with Arafat that Hanan was informed that Secretary Christopher; Danny Strauss, an aide; and Dennis Ross were planning a trip to the Occupied Territories. Still, Hanan believed that American presence in the Occupied Territories would help facilitate the continuation of those deadlocked meetings in Washington. Arafat, Nabil Shaath, and Akram Hania, however, understood that the American secretary of state was coming because of the progress in the Oslo meetings.

It came as a surprise to Hanan, therefore, when, during their second meeting, Arafat contradicted his previous instructions by informing her that she was to explain point by point to the American delegation arriving in Jerusalem why the terms they had presented in Washington were unacceptable. Nevertheless, he insisted that nothing was to be put in writing. Rather than question his sudden change of mind, Hanan was relieved that the PLO chairman seemed finally to accept her suggestion. Hanan and Husseini returned to the West Bank in preparation for the meetings with the Americans, while Shaath left Tunis for Egypt.

Again unknown to Hanan, Arafat telephoned Shaath that night in Cairo, instructing him to have the draft translated from Arabic into English to give the Egyptians, with the understanding that they would pass it along to the Americans. Shaath agreed.

Within hours the Egyptians received part of Shaath's draft, which they provided to Dennis Ross. While the Americans were already aware of the Oslo document, the draft that Ross and later Secretary Christopher expected to see was an amended version (changes made by the PLO) of the Oslo DOP.

On arriving in Jerusalem, Hanan was greeted by Dennis Ross, who announced that he already had portions of Shaath's draft and understood, also from Shaath, that she would turn over the complete document. If Hanan was surprised, she didn't let on. "I repeated Abu Ammar's instructions when I told Dennis that there was nothing in writing," Hanan says quietly, "although I was prepared to discuss territorial jurisdiction and the issue of Jerusalem." Predictably Dennis Ross was upset, since he had been assured by officials in Cairo as well as by his own government that a complete draft response would be handed over by Hanan on his arrival in Jerusalem. While Hanan continued to maintain that she had nothing in writing to present to the American delegation, it became obvious to her that the reason Ross kept insisting was that once again Arafat had given contradictory orders to someone else. Still, she refused to believe that anything had been done on purpose to undermine her negotiating power. It was only after Ross left, however, that Shaath faxed Hanan a copy of the draft that he had prepared and that Arafat had instructed him to give to the Egyptians, in English, to be handed over to the Americans. Moreover, at that late date Shaath asked Hanan for her input and suggestions.

The most glaring gap in the Shaath document concerned the issues of settlements which, in Hanan's opinion, produced an automatic self-destruct mechanism. While the document called for the Israeli army to withdraw from Gaza and Jericho, it also gave the army the right to stay to protect those settlers who would also be allowed to stay. The plan was only to negotiate the fate of the settlers during the interim phase of the agreement but not to provide definitively for them until a permanent accord was reached. "It was obvious that the people who wrote the document didn't live under occupation," Hanan explains, "because a freeze on all settlements wasn't included nor was the release of prisoners, which are the two main issues that would have given the document credibility throughout the Occupied Territories." As far as Hanan was concerned, the external leadership in Tunis had looked at the situation from a distance, seeing settlements as merely dots on a map as opposed to real impediments to any future Palestinian state. "Abu Ammar was thinking strategically and in terms of long-term political gain," Hanan maintains. But instead of reacting to the duplicity within her own organization, Hanan focused solely on the problems in the draft. "That was when I told Abu Ammar that I judged the draft to be incomplete," Hanan maintains.

When Arafat sidestepped her criticism of Shaath's draft and repeated yet again that nothing was to be given in writing to the Americans, his reaction made little sense to Hanan. Further confusing were his new directives to Hanan that she was now to discuss the Gaza-Jericho option with the Americans as well as prepare a complete security draft concerning the presence of the PLA police force in Gaza and Jericho. "My instructions then from Abu Ammar," she continues, "were to discuss Gaza-Jericho only as they pertained to early empowerment and the reasons why that option wouldn't work in that specific formula." In essence Arafat was ordering Hanan to discuss what had been negotiated in Oslo without bothering to tell her anything about Oslo. Again unknown to her, by then the Americans had full knowledge of the Oslo accord in all its complexity, which was the basis for Dennis Ross's response during their meeting the following morning.

HANAN WAS OUTRAGED during that morning meeting when Ross suggested that the functional responsibilities such as health and education would be turned over to the Palestinians, while the budget and other related financial matters would stay with the Israelis. What was being offered the Palestinians, in Hanan's view, was nothing more than a transition within a transition, which undermined the three-year Washington negotiations. In essence it was an agreement that had all the elements of failure written into the interim phase from the beginning. According to Hanan the option would fragment the law and risk becoming a permanent-status agreement, which would mean that a Palestinian state would be forever limited to Gaza and Jericho. "Unless we had a full political agreement with framework and commitment as a first step," Hanan explains, "it would be a disaster."

Obeying Arafat's instructions, Hanan wrote and faxed her paper to PLO headquarters in Tunis on the Gaza-Jericho option. Arafat responded only by reiterating that she was not to submit anything in writing to Secretary Christopher when she met with him personally in Jerusalem. Several hours after receiving Arafat's faxed instructions, Hanan received another fax from Nabil Shaath, requesting her suggestions and input on yet another draft he was writing that pertained to the Gaza-Jericho option and early empowerment. "Since I was still operating under Abu Ammar's original instructions not to put anything on those subjects in writing, I ignored Nabil's two faxed requests for my written input."

On the evening before Hanan was scheduled to meet with Secretary Christopher, Hanan was at Faisal al-Husseini's house in East Jerusalem, discussing the issues on the agenda that were scheduled for discussion with the Americans. Again a fax came from Shaath, covering the issues of Gaza-Jericho and early empowerment, this time with Arafat's signature on it, giving Hanan precise instructions to deliver it the following day to Secretary Christopher. It was the same document Shaath had sent her the day before, requesting her input and suggestions. More concerned about the contents than she was baffled by Arafat's constantly changing instructions, Hanan picked up the phone to call Tunis. "I read it," Hanan recounts, "and even though it was signed by Abu Ammar, I wasn't satisfied with it." Hanan's justification was that since she had chosen to obey Arafat's instructions about not putting anything in writing for the Americans, she had ignored Shaath's request for her input the previous day as well as his second request for input. What she found, however, was that she was suddenly in possession of two documents that she had insufficient time either to review or to correct. "I simply refused to submit it," Hanan says, "which of course provoked Abu Ammar."

The response from Tunis was immediate. Arafat accused Hanan of disobeying direct orders. Hanan defended her actions by explaining that it was only out of concern for the PLO chairman's historic responsibility to a document that contained so many glaring gaps that she had refused.

After the phone conversation with Arafat and her repeated refusals to submit any written document to Christopher, Hanan left Husseini's house. It was only later that night, at home in Ramallah, that she finally sat down and prepared a draft DOP based on the fax that had been sent by Nabil Shaath, which Arafat had signed.

The next morning the meetings resumed. Hanan was asked once again by Secretary Christopher to present the document, and once again she refused. Patiently she explained to the American secretary of state that there were still problems with the document, which for reasons that had to do with time constraints wouldn't be ready until the next day. "We told Christopher that while Abu Ammar wanted us to hand over the document, we felt that it still wasn't in final form and for that reason we refused. We simply needed more time to make the necessary changes."

The Americans were furious, pointing out that while Hanan and the others had always insisted that the PLO was their sole leadership, they were suddenly refusing to comply with their instructions. "We don't understand this," Christopher told Hanan. "We understood from your leadership that you had a document to give us, and now you're telling us that you have nothing!"

Unruffled, Hanan answered, "Abu Ammar's instructions will be honored, we are just working on some technicalities and issues having to do with Gaza-Jericho and a confederation with Jordan." Within minutes Arafat was on the phone again from Tunis, accusing Hanan of mutiny.

Two days elapsed between meetings, during which Hanan faxed Arafat all the amendments and changes she had made, including her reasons for refusing to present the original document. However, during the time that Hanan was busy rewriting, correcting, and faxing Tunis, there were no lack of volunteers from within the Palestinian leadership on the West Bank willing to present the document to Secretary Christopher in its original form.

Said Kanaan, a successful Nablus businessman with loyalty to Yasir Arafat, was one of those prepared to step in and present the document. In fact, the man whom Kanaan credits with making him aware of the document, as well as of Hanan's position to present it, was Sameh Kanaan (no relation), the former prisoner and member of the Palestinian delegation. "Sameh called Egypt," Said recounts, "to tell Nabil Shaath in no uncertain terms that I was prepared to deliver the document to Christopher if Hanan continued to refuse." Kanaan further claims that he not only volunteered to present the document to Christopher but actually, later that same day, received a call from Arafat in Tunis, instructing him to call a press conference and announce that if Hanan continued to hesitate, he was prepared to act in her place. Instead of calling a press conference, however, Kanaan contacted Agence France Presse (AFP) in Jerusalem, providing them with details of the internal PLO dispute over the document. "It was a message for Hanan and Faisal," Kanaan claims, "because I knew that Faisal had close contacts with Agence France Presse and someone there would leak the information to him." Faisal got the message. What was clear to Hanan was that someone had to present that document to the U.S. secretary of state. And for obvious reasons that someone had to be a Palestinian from within the Occupied Territories, since officially the Americans still had no contact nor were they engaged in any direct negotiations with the PLO. The last thing Arafat needed was to show the world that there was dissension within the ranks of the outside PLO leadership. Thus, Arafat hesitated in allowing Kanaan to substitute for Hanan, even if he did order him to call a press conference. As for Said Kanaan, he continues to insist that it was the result of his action in contacting AFP in Jerusalem that prompted Hanan to rush to turn over the document to Christopher. According to Hanan, however, she turned over the document to Christopher only after she had made the changes that she deemed necessary and faxed it to Tunis for Arafat's signature. "After Abu Ammar faxed back the signed document," Hanan says, "I agreed to submit it to Christopher, but I also told him that along with it, he would have my resignation."

FOR THE FIRST TIME since Hanan emerged as the spokesperson for the Palestinian cause, she made no effort to keep her displeasure with Arafat to herself. For the first time in all the recent years in which she claimed the maturity of the PLO was in its ability to survive a pluralistic political system, she seemed to be testing that system. What remained to be seen was how many more Palestinians from within the leadership claque on the West Bank and in Gaza would join her. As it turned out, when Hanan boarded that plane for Tunis to offer her resignation, Faisal al-Husseini and Saeb Erekat were on that plane with her to offer their resignations as well, for what they cited as "internal issues."

The official justification that Hanan gave for her decision to resign was accountability. "When a government sends instructions to its delegation, and the delegation refuses to honor those instructions," Hanan explains, "there must be accountability in the form of a hearing." Even Dr. Haidar abd al-Shafi, who had been with Arafat since the founding days of the PLO, was suddenly talking publicly from his home in Gaza about the lack of democracy within the PLO structure, calling for a collective leadership. "My resignation had to do with the way things were being run," Hanan continues, "I felt there was a division between the inside and outside leadership, and it was my job as a representative of the people to bring certain issues out into the open."

According to witnesses, when the trio arrived in Tunis, before anyone said anything, Husseini rushed up to Arafat and hung his head. "I'm here with my neck at your disposal," Husseini announced. "If you want to kill me because you believe I made a mistake when I threatened to resign, go ahead." Later Husseini claimed that he offered his resignation only to protect Arafat's image, which would have been ruined had he signed off on a document that gave away so much to the Israelis. Hanan, on the other hand, was neither fearful for her neck nor concerned about Arafat's image. From the moment she arrived in Tunis, her main objective was to present her study of the Gaza-Jericho option with all its drawbacks and persuade the PLO chairman to make the necessary changes.

Later that night Arafat summoned her to his study to explain how he envisioned the Gaza-Jericho option. "I see a withdrawal from Gaza and Jericho," the chairman began in a distant voice, "with early empowerment throughout the rest of the Occupied Territories. I see bringing in Palestinians from the outside, a national authority in Gaza and Jericho, and the possibility of a confederation with Jordan. I see the PLO in Gaza and Jericho moving toward direct negotiations to liberate the rest of our land." It struck Hanan as more than curious that suddenly Arafat seemed to be accepting early empowerment for the rest of the Occupied Territories after he had always fought against it.

What followed that night in Tunis and into the next day were long discussions and debates, with Hanan remaining steadfast in her insistence on tendering her resignation. And while Husseini might have had second thoughts about challenging Arafat, both he and Erekat followed Hanan's lead by not withdrawing their resignations. All three returned to the West Bank to wait for Arafat's next move.

ON AUGUST 8, the day before Hanan's eighteenth wedding anniversary, she was summoned to Tunis for another meeting with Arafat. "I told Abu Ammar that it was my anniversary," Hanan explains, "and that I wanted to spend it with my husband and children. But he insisted that Sunday was the only day there was a direct flight to Tunis." Hanan and Emil, along with Amal and Zeina, celebrated their wedding anniversary on Saturday, August 7. On Sunday morning, August 8, Hanan, for the first time in years, took a direct flight from Ben Gurion Airport in Tel Aviv to Tunis instead of traveling to Amman Airport for the connecting flight. If nothing else the reception that she received at the airport was a small

victory, quite different than what she had previously encoun-
tered when she arrived at Ben Gurion years ago and was
detained and searched before being allowed to depart. On
this occasion, however, the Israeli in charge of VIPs at Ben
Gurion rushed out to greet her personally and usher her
through security.

Arafat wanted to deal with Hanan's resignation as a matter of form, acknowledging that she had resigned, after which
she would retract the resignation. Instead Hanan insisted on
a fair hearing in front of the entire PLO executive committee,
where she intended to present a list of grievances concerning
all the issues that, in her opinion, had gone wrong during the
three years of negotiations in Madrid and Washington. "I
wrote down all the problems," Hanan explains, "and I told
Abu Ammar that he had to take them seriously." It was then
that Hanan let Arafat know point-blank that if he hadn't
wanted the official negotiations to work, he should have told
that to the delegation instead of changing strategies and terms
with no warning or explanation. In fact, from the beginning
the main criticism of Arafat from within his organization had
always been that he gave double instructions. "We needed
one working process," Hanan adds.

On August 9, 1993, Hanan was accorded her audience
before the PLO executive committee to present her list of
grievances. Afterward she went into a private meeting with
Arafat. It was only then that Hanan realized that something
was going on. "I told him that he looked very mischievous,"
Hanan says now, "as if he was hiding something." Still Arafat
admitted nothing to his spokesperson, although he began
once again to give Hanan his perceptions of how Gaza and
Jericho would work within the political structure of any potential agreement. "Actually, everything Abu Ammar told me
that day was very close to what was being worked out in
that document of principle in Oslo," Hanan says. Neverthe-

less, when Hanan returned to Ramallah the next morning, though she suspected something, she still had no idea that a secret channel was not only working but that a DOP was close to completion.

On August 19 the DOP was initialed by the Israelis and the Palestinians. On August 21, two days later and just twelve days after she left Tunis, Hanan received a phone call from Hassan Asfour and Akram Hania from Tunis. Informing Hanan that certain details that could not be discussed by phone had to be communicated to her right away, they strongly suggested that she, along with Husseini, return immediately to Tunis. "When I arrived in Tunis on a Thursday night," Hanan recalls, "Akram met us at the airport and told us everything." According to Hanan her first reaction was surprise, since it was a miracle that the secret had been so well kept on both sides of the Green Line. "But when I got over the shock and read the document," Hanan says, "all I could see once again were the gaps."

It was to Abu Mazen, the man who actually signed the DOP, that Hanan complained about the wording in the agreement concerning the dismantling and/or freezing of the settlements. They were the same two points that had stopped her from submitting the document to Dennis Ross and Secretary Christopher in the first place. Ironically it was Abu Mazen who asked Hanan to return to the West Bank and try to talk to the Americans and the Israelis in an effort to change the wording. "And while you're talking to the head of the military government," Abu Mazen added, "see if you can get him to agree about releasing the prisoners."

Hanan returned to Ramallah and immediately requested a meeting with Gen. Danny Rothchild, the man in charge of the Civil Administration. But Rothchild refused to consider making any changes in an agreement that had already been initialed. "I didn't blame him," Hanan says, shrugging, "but the amazing thing was that those were the very points that we had been discussing in Washington during the eighth to eleventh rounds, human issues concerning prisoners and deportees, and here we had an initialed agreement that we couldn't change."

Still, there were points in the agreement that were positive. In all fairness, Hanan admits that those were the points now incorporated in the agreement that neither the official delegation in Washington could achieve nor could she during those long sessions with the Americans. "We couldn't get recognition or implementation of 242, or the dismantlement and dissolution of the Civil Administration, elections, or the issue of Jerusalem on the agenda for permanent status, along with the participation of East Jerusalem residents in the peace talks. Abu Mazen managed to get all of that as well as the return of displaced persons. So there were important and strategic redeeming issues in the agreement." When asked to comment, however, her words were telling when she kept referring to the Oslo Accord as only a "symbolic breakthrough." Sighing, she says, "It happened so quickly that nobody really had a chance to evaluate the repercussions, at least not yet."

From a personal point of view, Hanan was concerned that too much responsibility was being placed on her and other internal Palestinian leaders to mobilize enough support from within the Occupied Territories so that people would accept the agreement as it was written. Her most important task was to convince the population that it was only a first step in what would be lengthy negotiations culminating in a Palestinian state that would ultimately include the entire West Bank. "We knew we faced the task of setting up institutions to implement the agreement and form our national authority," Hanan explains, "and we knew we would have to be very careful because we needed the people's support."

It was one thing for Hanan to have pleaded a case for Arafat's legitimacy and acceptance and quite another to acknowledge his inclusion in a negotiation that had always depended on his absence to succeed. Suddenly Hanan found herself succeeding in what she had set out to do from the beginning, namely in forcing both the Israelis and the Americans to negotiate directly with the PLO, and specifically with Arafat as its leader. But for the Palestinians who lived in the Occupied Territories, those who had conceived the Intifada, waged the battles on the streets, or done battle around a negotiating table in Washington, Hanan's accomplishment and Arafat's acceptance diminished their own importance. It was a case of mixed emotions concerning Arafat on the part of the Palestinians that contributed to their negative feelings about the accord. It was also a case of mixed signals on the part of the rest of the world when it came to accepting what was portrayed as a profound change in PLO thinking.

THE WHOLE BASIS for accepting the Palestinians into an international peace negotiation and eventual accord with Israel depended on a global belief that the organization had changed its agenda from terror to diplomacy. The conditions for accepting the Palestinians as an independent entity—a people capable of cementing an agreement with Israel—depended on an absence of any allegiance and debt to the rest of the Arab world. In each case Arafat is the leader who not only conceived and advocated the PLO's terror agenda but who also allowed his people to be utilized by the rest of the Arab world as an example of Israeli inhumanity, which in turn justified the Arab agenda of the destruction of Israel. If Hanan succeeded in convincing the world that the PLO and Yasir Arafat had indeed changed, perhaps she has not quite convinced herself or those Palestinians who represented their cause in Madrid and Washington and adopted a new platform long before Arafat changed his own. Ironically, while Arafat had finally joined the ranks of legitimate leaders, officially recognized by Israel and the United States, in the history of the Palestinian struggle, those political achievements could ultimately cost any leader support and popularity among his own people. It happened to Hanan. It would happen to Arafat.

CHAPTER FIFTEEN

LIFE AFTER OSLO

ACROSS FROM HANAN'S HOUSE on Radio Street, there is a constant traffic jam and long queues of Palestinians waiting for permission to cross into Israel for work or for humanitarian reasons, such as visiting an ailing parent or consulting a doctor. At the end of a long day, in front of the Civil Administration Building, the last of a group of Palestinians finally give up the wait, dejectedly turning away without a permit or perhaps news of a relative still held inside the compound. If anything has changed throughout the Occupied Territories after Oslo, it is an absence of optimism given the unchanged situation on the ground. The temptation to take down the brand-new sign in Jericho that reads WELCOME TO PALESTINE and replace it with a sign that reads WELCOME TO THE REAL WORLD is almost overwhelming. The delegates who set off for Madrid more than two years ago to negotiate a peace accord have a weary look in their eyes and an aura of cynicism as they discuss their future and the dismal economic situation that prevails. Not only is the PLO a bankrupt organization that has experienced difficulty in supporting a government-in-exile, but it is now faced with the prospect of finding the billions needed to build a state. If the people living throughout the Occupied Territories retain any of their spirit now, it emerges only when they speak out against their leadership, criticizing Arafat, for the first time without measuring their words, either to the foreign press or to one another. While days and nights are spent discussing what it takes to build an infrastructure and a state, they remain confused and unsure as to where to begin.

The feeling of euphoria on departure day for Madrid, when Palestinian children gave olive branches to Israeli soldiers, has reverted to discontent and violence. The momentum from the Intifada is gone, and where once there were collective goals to stone, strike, or even slaughter, they are replaced now by random acts of violence that do little to break the back of the Israeli Army. These acts do, however, adversely affect world opinion. The atmosphere only provides an excuse for the Israelis to keep the borders closed between the territories and Israel, increase the number of checkpoints throughout towns and villages, and in some cases turn a blind eye to armed settlers taking the law into their own hands.

Inside the jails the Palestinian prisoners whose release has been ignored under the terms of the Oslo Accord threaten to set themselves on fire to send a message to Arafat that they are the new victims of his peace. It is not the first time that Arafat has chosen a political philosophy that encourages pragmatism instead of humanism by ignoring the daily hardships of his people. In this interim stage accord, the differences between what the Palestinians envisage and what the Israelis intend is vast. The Israelis want the transition to be cautious and gradual, while the Palestinians expect an instant state. Yet there are advantages for both sides under the agreement. Where once there was mutual need between Arafat and Hanan, a similar need now exists between Israel and the PLO to break the Arab economic boycott of Israel and reinstate Arab financial aid to the PLO.

Concerning the members of different PLO factions, if anything unites every Palestinian, it is that all blame their leadership rather than one another for accepting so much less territory in this interim stage than what was anticipated during the long months of negotiation in Washington. Yet again there was a method in Arafat's apparent willingness to accept so much less than he had always proclaimed he expected. While accepting the Gaza-Jericho option, he knew that something else was needed to make the agreement palatable to his people, a symbol of a city within the West Bank that would be seen as the beginning of taking back all the territories occupied by Israel. While Jericho gave the people a fig leaf to cover accusations that the PLO betrayed the West Bank, even the complete Gaza-Jericho option was not as it appeared on the surface. King Hussein was given a guarantee by Israel that the Allenby bridge would remain under Israeli control, denying Palestinian access to Jordan from Jericho. The Israelis, while agreeing to withdraw troops from Gaza and Jericho, maintained the right to have the army present to protect those settlers who would remain.

When the date for the beginning of withdrawal from Jericho and Gaza was set in Oslo for December 13, 1993, it was far enough away to seem possible to achieve. What should have been anticipated was that failure to keep to the schedule would provoke a more violent response among residents of the West Bank and Gaza than if an agreement had not been reached at all. If Palestinian children exhibited unabashed optimism when their delegates first left for Madrid, after the handshake on the White House lawn, adults were just as optimistic: They began planning to build hotels and tourist attractions in Jericho, an official residence for Arafat, and housing projects in Gaza. Not only was the Madrid show blown out of proportion, but the White House handshake was beginning to seem as if it had been nothing more significant than a glorified photo opportunity.

THERE IS A PROFOUND naïveté in the Palestinian people that might be called innocence if they didn't have a history of violence. Even the delegates who got a taste of the machinations and maneuvering that goes into a peace negotiation seem surprised by the lack of change in their daily lives. For more than fifty years the Palestinian people demanded freedom until they realized that recognition of rights was a two-way street. Now, with independence approaching, the reality of their own society confronts them, devoid of any economic or political agenda or platform for human rights and liberty. Soon it will no longer be possible to blame an occupying force for denying them basic entitlements. Rather, it is their own structure that makes it difficult to make the transition from struggle to statehood.

Within the external leadership there is a feeling of isolation after their expulsion from Beirut and their initial exclusion from the negotiations at the insistence of the Israelis and the Americans. This feeling caused them to make a deal that fell far short of satisfying all the people in their various situations throughout the West Bank and Gaza. Within the Palestinian leadership throughout the Occupied Territories, there is a feeling of entitlement since they were the ones who risked their lives on a daily basis each time they even said the words "PLO," or raised the Palestinian flag. While there is a transition from political to economic, with the Intifada producing the adrenaline and hope for the people to survive, there is now yet another wave of leadership that is destined to appear after this transition period ends, one that will be in charge of a more permanent solution.

Albert Agazarian, in his capacity as public relations director of Bir Zeit University, has already witnessed a shift in

leadership on his own campus. Viewing Bir Zeit as a micro-
cosm for the Occupied Territories, the population on both
sides of the Green Line waited for the results of student elections at the university to see which PLO faction would emerge
as the majority. For the first time in Hamas's history, a conciliation was affected between it and the more mainstream
PFLP and DFLP, giving them 51 percent of the vote over
Arafat's Fatah. If nothing else the results sent a clear message
to Arafat that while he was now considered the legitimate
representative of the Palestinian people, he was not necessarily considered the sole representative. Curiously, the Palestinians were more disturbed by the election results at Bir
Zeit than the Israelis. One high-ranking Israeli military official
said, "Every time there were elections in the past and Hamas
lost, they stood next to the winners with smiles on their face,
since they always lost with forty-nine percent of the vote. The
win was no big surprise."

Still, while Agazarian believes that the Hamas win allows
a greater potential for violence, he still believes that Arafat's
leadership is uncontestable. And although Agazarian agrees
that the "sacred cow" of the issue is indeed security, he offers
that as the prime reason why it is crucial for the people to
assure Arafat's position as leader. "If he has a donkey under
him," Albert says, "he will ride; if he has an Arabian stallion,
he will ride more comfortably. It is the job of others to make
sure that Arafat rides an Arabian stallion; it is up to the people
to make sure the vehicle he is riding is a good one." On the
subject of Israel's continued resistance to making the agreement work, he adds, "It is like a woman who is expecting
her first baby and even before the head of the baby appears,
someone says, 'This baby will give you a hard time, this baby
will flunk his exams, this baby will kill you for his inheri-
tance,' all these negative predictions about the baby before it
is even born. The Palestinian people are put under a spotlight

before there is even a state, which makes the whole thing absurd and unfair."

Other Palestinians, like Mamduh al-Aker, have made the decision not to continue as delegates to the peace negotiations in Washington. What he battled for and what he believed in, according to Aker, is gone, leaving him incapable of defending an agreement that he sees as a failure. "It is difficult to think in abstractions when I'm suddenly confronted by a reality that falls far short of the dream," Aker says. Opposed to Arafat's concessions to the Israelis in the agreement, he maintains that in order to understand why the PLO leader acted as he did means to understand the condition of the PLO during its period of post–Gulf War isolation, which includes its financial problems, and the general mentality of exile that has permeated the organization since its inception. Still, Aker insists it was a mistake. "Our leadership should have waited and exhibited more self-confidence to get what they wanted from the Israelis. They could have achieved a better deal, maybe not dramatically better, but certainly better than what we have, even if it . . . is already signed." Curiously, in the aftermath of the Gulf War, the party line throughout the Occupied Territories was that while the PLO was "officially" against the Iraqi invasion of Kuwait, the response by American and other foreign forces was considered inappropriate. Hanan said many times, "It is inconceivable that the world liberated Kuwait and never bothered to liberate the Palestinian people from under Israeli occupation."

Both Sameh Kanaan and Imad Iyash, who have emerged as influential leaders in Nablus, believe that while there is still an important role for the PLO to play in any transition to statehood, there is a need for fresh leaders. Kanaan says, "My concern is that there's this obsession by our leadership in Tunis to come back as soon as possible and take charge. I don't want Arafat to run in the elections but rather wish that he would step down and remain as a figurehead without involving himself in the daily running of our new state."

Those Palestinians who lived under Israeli occupation for their entire lives and participated in the peace negotiations prior to Oslo feel that they have grown to understand the Israeli mentality and inherent attitudes more than those Palestinians who have lived in exile, specifically the PLO in Tunis. According to Imad Iyash, what Arafat thinks he needs more than anything else is loyalty, which is the reason he is choosing those leaders who have worked with him all along in exile. Simply put, the PLO chairman has enough problems with Hamas and other fundamentalist groups that he can't afford to risk a rebellion within his own ranks. "He is forced to bring in all the corrupt leaders only because he has to keep the support of his own internal factions in order to maintain the support of the Israelis," Iyash explains. "All of a sudden, we've got the Israelis in agreement with our external leadership because they've made the best deal they could for themselves. Now it's up to us on the inside to exploit that agreement." The party line that keeps coming out of Tunis is that those on the inside will have to wait for elections to find out who will be in charge. "We are not like the male bee," Iyash adds. "We have no intention of rolling over and dying after making love."

Zahira Kamel, who also has no intention of continuing as a delegate to the new round of talks, believes that while there were certain elements in the agreement that had to be postponed, such as the issue of settlements and Jerusalem, there should have been a status quo as it had to do with those issues, in other words, no additional construction of Israeli houses on the West Bank or Gaza. "Unfortunately," Kamel explains, "the way the agreement is written gives the Israelis a free hand to do what they want for the next two years." While the Palestinians claim the continuing presence of the settlements is an excuse for the Israelis to maintain a military presence, the Israelis counter that the increase of terrorist attacks by Palestinian "rejectionist" fronts force the army to remain.

Mary Hass, who still makes the rounds of the refugee camps in Gaza, finds that the conditions have become even worse. "The Israelis are flagrantly continuing their Judaization of Palestine by continuing to close off portions of the West Bank."

There are arguments on both sides. To open the borders, eliminate the checkpoints, and stop the closure of the Occupied Territories would only encourage more violence from radicals on both sides of the Green Line. Attacks on Israelis by Hamas and other PLO extremists would continue; as settlers, with rifles slung across their backs and revolvers on their dashboards, would continue to drive through Arab towns and neighborhoods, waiting for a stone thrown at a car to open fire on any visible target. Along with the violence, Nomi Chazan is concerned with the political repercussions of failure as it concerns the initial phase of the agreement. "If the accord fails," Chazan warns, "there will almost certainly be a Likud victory in the next elections. Labor and Meretz will be voted out, and that would be a disaster for everybody."

What is certain is that a lack of political accord would encourage increased violence. While a right-wing victory in Israel would delay, at best, or ignore, at worst, any progress already made toward effecting a transfer of territory, the same fear exists on the other side. If the Palestinians themselves fail to establish their state by putting in the right people to organize institutions or eliminate the daily hardships of life suffered in the camps, the risk would be that a radical power, such as Hamas, would step in to turn things around. Curiously, there are Palestinians who now agree with many Israelis

that a confederation with Jordan—a dirty word in the aftermath of Black September in 1970—is the only way a Palestinian state could survive. The consensus among those
Palestinians, however, is that King Hussein should have been
briefed about the Oslo meetings before any DOP was signed.
"One of the tasks should have been to keep King Hussein
and other Arab leaders apprised," Mamduh al-Aker believes,
"since officially they were our partners in peace."

While many of the original Palestinian delegates to the
peace conference have resigned and gone back to their jobs
and former lives, Faisal al-Husseini has emerged with the
"Jerusalem portfolio," which gives him a wider base of support and recognition in the international community. After
the end of the second meeting in Cairo between Rabin and
Arafat on October 6, 1993, Husseini made the following
statement: "We have decided, among other things, to make
a special committee for Jerusalem." The press asked Rabin
to confirm that there was any kind of special committee for
Jerusalem. Rabin denied that any such committee existed.
Two days later, Minister Moshe Shahal, the minister of police
appointed by Rabin, met with Husseini in the private apartment of Faisal's assistant, Mr. Sassoon, allegedly to "check
out some aspects of security to ease up the situation in Jerusalem." When confronted by the Israeli press, Shahal said,
"Faisal came to see me in civilian clothes, no guards, in an
old car, for an informal meeting." And when asked the same
question by the Arab press, Husseini replied, "It was only a
preliminary meeting concerning the issue of the future of
Jerusalem, since we agree that we need experts and agendas."
Since then certain high-ranking military officials call the continuing meetings the "ongoing no committee on Jerusalem."
Still, even though Husseini has been rewarded with a prestigious job, he has consistently come out against Arafat having
any official role in any future Palestinian state.

Despite the widespread anti-Arafat sentiment throughout the Occupied Territories, most Palestinians realize that the PLO structure is needed to absorb within the new Palestinian state those Palestinians who are currently living in exile. At the same time they maintain that the internal leadership should work out any details with Israel as they affect the daily lives of the people. Taking over negotiation or implementation of the agreement, however, costs money, which the internal leadership sorely lacks.

The unreality of the economic situation is evident when Palestinian leaders voice the hope that not only Americans but also Japanese will pay to develop the West Bank and Gaza. "The Japanese should pay because they have been buying Saudi and Kuwaiti oil for very low prices," Said Kanaan says. "They should compensate the Arabs by supporting the Palestinians." It is a far-fetched dream. Sameh Kanaan, another delegate who has refused to continue on in any negotiation, believes that the Palestinian people who shaped the Intifada are the ones who should direct their own fate. "I'm worried about the future," he admits.

From the Israeli side there is also widespread disappointment in the agreement. A highly placed Israeli military official in the Occupied Territories is concerned that if Arafat doesn't hold elections in the Occupied Territories, any emerging Palestinian state will be viewed by the Western world as no different from the 134 other Arab dictatorships that already exist. As it stands now, according to him, all the "dead gaps" incorporated in the agreement make it extremely complex to execute. "Contrary to the Camp David Accords," he explains, "there is nothing resembling a no-man's-land between Israel and any future Palestinian state. There is no buffer zone separating the two territories. We are nose to *tochas* with the Palestinians." Further, according to this official, the main problem is security. "There are about five thousand Israeli settlers in Gaza alone," he continues, "half of whom carry weapons, which means there are approximately 2,500 Uzis being transported daily between Gaza and Israel. In order to defend these people, there are approximately 1,000 soldiers, also carrying weapons, making a total of another 1,000 Uzis and other weapons moving in and out of Israel every day. On the other hand, there are approximately 800,000 Palestinians, 200,000 of whom are of age to throw stones and carry weapons. What this means is that any small incident can easily escalate into a big one."

Another critical barrier to the agreement, according to a spokesman from Prime Minister Rabin's office, is the potential economic failure of the DOP, given that the Palestinians have to build a real state with a concrete infrastructure. "They need approximately twelve to fifteen billion dollars over a five-year period, and so far, all they have managed to raise is one billion dollars in cold cash with another one billion dollars in pledges."

Other Israelis believe that the main defect in the Oslo paper is that it was created by two academics who don't understand the problems in the field. What was especially vague was the question of Palestinian "safe passage" between Gaza and the West Bank. "What exactly is safe passage?" Yigal Carmoun wonders. "If an Israeli policeman stops Palestinians on a main road, is he allowed to search or arrest them?"

What is also unclear in the DOP is if the PLO actually represents all Palestinian Arabs, since there is no guideline in the agreement about the almost one million Israeli Arabs living in Israel. It remains undefined if the PLO represents those Palestinians on the same basis as it does the people living throughout the Occupied Territories. The fear among the Israelis who are against the DOP is that Arafat will eventually make a move from behind the curtains of the West

Bank and Gaza into Israel, on the pretext of governing all the Palestinian people.

Last there is the problem of mutual recognition, which was supposedly solved at the twenty-fifth hour in the Bristol Hotel in Paris, when Arafat finally agreed to state formally that the PLO recognized Israel's right to exist. Until now, however, he has yet to change the PLO covenant, which calls for the destruction of Israel. Following the meeting in Paris, Arafat claimed that he needed more than two-thirds of the vote in the next PNC to dissolve the covenant, and the PNC wasn't scheduled to convene before the DOP was signed.

FROM A POSITIVE ASPECT, despite its delayed beginning, the Oslo declaration of principles has done a great deal to improve Israel's relations with the United States. Since the document was signed, the United States has committed to giving Israel computer technology, access to American satellite installation information, and advanced planes such as an up-to-the-minute version of the F-15E fighter plane, a strategic aircraft that can carry bombs as far as Iran and that has previously been only in the hands of the American Air Force. Additional aircraft, F-16 surplus planes once used by American forces throughout Europe, have also been sold to the Israelis for a tenth the original price, or five million dollars instead of fifty million dollars per aircraft. The rationale for these sales and technology is that if the DOP works, it is by definition the difference between retreat and redeployment. Written into the agreement is that Israel will still be holding forces around settlements in Gaza. But the question of success remains an emotional issue rather than one that is measurable in terms of American aircraft and computer technology or Palestinian flags and olive branches.

Once Palestinians were forbidden under Israeli law to hang Arafat's picture in their homes. Now that the law has changed, most of those same Palestinians have taken Arafat's picture down. Imad Iyash explains, "Arafat is not what he was for me twenty years ago when I went to prison for setting explosives in Israel."

It has taken almost half a century for the Palestinians to make the transition from victim to revolutionary to politician, and for Israel to make the transition from victim to oppressor to withdrawing occupier. What remains to be written is how much time it will take for both entities to accept the present reality while remaining open to any future transition. As sad as those scattered graveyards of junked cars throughout the West Bank and Gaza are those former Palestinian revolutionaries and Israeli military heroes who are unable to step back to allow a new breed of leaders to emerge.

Arafat speaks for himself now when he negotiates with Israel, which means that Hanan is no longer the focus of criticism since she has resigned as the official spokesperson for the PLO leadership. Through Hanan's efforts and the progress made in the negotiations, ending with an accord between Israel and the PLO, Arafat has earned the distinction of being one of the most criticized voices in the Occupied Territories.

CHAPTER SIXTEEN

ON HER OWN

IT IS DUSK on Radio Street and the muezzin can be heard across the loudspeakers from the mosque, calling people to evening prayer. Hanan is preparing to leave the house to pay a condolence call on a friend, a colleague at Bir Zeit University, whose only son, Rami, was shot and killed yesterday by a group of soldiers. The story on the West Bank is that the army appeared at Rami's school in response to a group of angry Israeli settlers who reported a stone-throwing incident. Charging the courtyard, the soldiers fired and wounded one of Rami's friends. As the boy bent down to comfort his friend, another soldier fired. The bullet hit Rami in the chest. Rami, fifteen years old and without any prior criminal record, died instantly. The army issued a formal apology to the family. Hanan puts it this way: "Israel is a state with a government and a structure and yet they are unable to control the behavior of the settlers and the army. On the other hand, we are a people still under occupation who are expected to control all the different factions while being held accountable for our neighbor. What makes it tragic is that we are being judged all the time by a higher moral standard than anybody else. Our morals are always being tested. We are constantly on our good behavior, and this attitude of patronage in the sense of putting the Palestinians on good behavior all the time to prove that we are of a moral caliber . . . to join the community of nations is inherently racist."

If there is any equality on the West Bank, it is that innocent people are dying senselessly on both sides of the struggle. The day after Hanan paid a condolence call on Rami's family, an incident occurred not far from her house on Radio Street. A twenty-four-year-old Israeli woman, a kindergarten teacher, and a nineteen-year-old Israeli student hitched a ride from Jerusalem with an elderly Israeli couple who lived in the same settlement as they did. They got as far as the neighboring town of El Biryeh when the car had a flat tire. As the two hitchhikers got out to change the tire, a passing car filled with Hamas terrorists opened fire on the Israelis. The kindergarten teacher died instantly, while the student died several hours later at Hadassah Hospital in Jerusalem.

Despite the increase of terrorist attacks, perpetrated by both Palestinians and right-wing Israeli settlers, there is no doubt that Hanan Mikhael Ashrawi achieved exactly what she set out to do when she first appeared on *Nightline* seven years ago. Not only did she successfully change the image of the PLO but she also carved out a place for herself in the current struggle to create a Palestinian state. Even more to her credit, she managed on occasion, throughout her short political career, to act unilaterally and independently of the PLO without paying the ultimate price of banishment or, worse, assassination.

While acting in her official capacity as spokesperson for the organization, she disobeyed direct orders from her chairman and still managed to resign rather than be dismissed. At the same time she also managed to send a message to the world that there were major internal conflicts within the PLO just when the organization needed to show a united front.

Yet, as a reward or perhaps as a way to remove her from the focus of the fray, she was subsequently offered the job of Palestinian representative to Washington. She turned it down, claiming that she wanted "no part in the dirty political in-fighting that was going on."

If Hanan learned how best to seduce the international media and effectively sway public opinion to her side, she has also always had an innate instinct to make the right choices for herself. She somehow believed that any political appoint-ment in what would be a provisional government constructed during a transitional period would never last. For Hanan any commitment to her personal and professional life has always been viewed for the long term. And if Camp David was any indicator of just how "long-term" Hanan's thinking is, it must not be forgotten that it took eighteen months before a detailed peace agreement between Egypt and Israel was signed, and another five years before it was implemented. For such rea-sons she has chosen to step aside temporarily. What she has done while waiting out the end to this nearly half century of struggle is to create an organization that is independent of the PLO. According to Hanan, while she has refused any financial support from the PLO, she has already received some funding from several European governments and influential American benefactors, and hopes to receive more. Hanan's organization will deal exclusively with all human rights abuses throughout the Occupied Territories. "I never in-tended this organization to be in any way connected to the PLO," she states emphatically, "or I could have gotten the funding from Arafat. It is my choice to remain independent." Once again it will be more than a full-time job and afford her little time for her family.

There is also no doubt that such incidents as the one described above, in which an innocent child is killed by the army or when other Palestinians are murdered by trigger-happy settlers, fuel her rage against the horrors of continuing occupation. Curiously, she still appears conflicted when she comments on the violence. In her own words, while admitting the suffering the Jews endured during the Holocaust, she compares that historic atrocity to what the Palestinians suffered as a result of the Balfour Declaration in 1921, which provided for two states, Israel and Palestine, to exist side by side. She could do better. She could compare the terrorist attacks committed by the PLO in the name of liberating Palestine to those committed by the Irgun to create an Israeli homeland. She could do better still. Unlike terrorism committed by the PLO, terrorism committed by the Irgun was never exported to foreign cities throughout the world, where innocent civilians, far from the mecca of the revolution, were maimed and killed.

In her capacity as the guardian of human rights throughout the Occupied Territories, however, there will come a time when Hanan will be obliged to confront issues that have to do with atrocities on the other side of the conflict, specifically when two innocent Israelis are gunned down by Palestinian terrorists in a passing car. Justifying those actions by claiming the world misunderstands the hardships suffered by the Palestinian living under Israeli Occupation is a weak argument. There is no justification or excuse on either side for the murder of innocent people. There is also no justification or excuse on either side for the murder of guilty people. Those accused of a crime should be tried within a legal system and imprisoned, if guilty, under due process of law. What faces Hanan is an enormous task, since she is not someone who is viewing the situation from the outside. After all, she has lived her entire life under two different occupying forces.

When Hanan spoke in abstractions and eventualities on behalf of the PLO, she was unparalleled. When she speaks for herself as it concerns her own experiences or the Palestinian side of the story, she tends to be subjective, justifying the reasons why those atrocities occur. "While I am against violence," she reiterates, "it is too easy to condemn a Palestinian as a terrorist who kills an Israeli without first finding out what happened to him or his family or understanding the accumulation of horror that he has witnessed or endured." It is a difficult argument to convey to any victim or family of a victim—those innocent civilians who have died at the hands of Palestinian terrorists claiming to be fighting for liberation. But it is because of the difficulty of the situation that Hanan was and is crucial to the ongoing struggle for peace. As a Palestinian involved and engaged in the process, she has neither a past connection nor historic complicity with the actions taken by the PLO as recently as yesterday. And while Yasir Arafat has systematically denied his involvement with terror, blaming the attacks on renegade factions, as head of the organization, he is forced to take full responsibility for the actions of its members. The most logical solution for the PLO to gain global confidence, given its changing image, is to replace the leaders whose past records do little to evoke trust. Instead, new leaders who have no involvement in a past that goes beyond that opening peace conference in Madrid should be the pioneers of the emerging Palestinian state.

There is no argument that Hanan has exhibited a profound abhorrence for injustice, articulated with impressive prose the suffering of her people, argued her cause with seasoned American officials, bravely confronted the Israeli Army as an academic as well as a private citizen, and defended herself to the many dissenting voices within her own community. There is no doubt that she has emerged from the hardship of occupation, the violence of the Intifada, and the ambiguity of the Oslo Accord as one of the leading political figures in the Middle East, one of the most prominent women of our time. What remains to be seen is if she will survive in life-and-death terms what she has taken to calling the "pluralistic and democratic traits inherent in the PLO."

As an academic who organized demonstrations and marches, Hanan was criticized as having no grassroots support or definite political goals. In her capacity as spokesperson for the PLO, she was condemned for having more of an affinity for the Americans than for her own people. Now, as one of the most respected and established voices for Palestinian independence, and with a solid grassroots base and a concrete political platform that calls for a Palestinian State led by a newly elected group of leaders from within the Occupied Territories, she is a target of radical groups such as Hamas and the Islamic Jihad. It is no longer a question that Hanan is an obscure academic, a Christian in a Muslim majority, or a woman in a male-dominated society. The problem that Hanan faces from within the hierarchy of the PLO is that her credentials to lead the Palestinian people do not include her participation in the group's past agenda of terror. She has still neither served time in an Israeli prison nor in a UN refugee camp. But she is the one Arafat chose to erase his past. Now Hanan and others like her must carve out a future. Throughout the world, newly elected governments have new leaders; different political parties have diverse policies. If the PLO, as Hanan has represented, is an organization that has changed its basic principles and methods, the time has come for the old guard to step down to make room for those Palestinians who can govern without having to overcome the world's bad memories.

Hanan achieved a twofold goal by legitimizing Yasir Arafat and the PLO for the purpose of a peace negotiation and in the eyes of the world. Now, as the most visible and appealing representative of the Palestinian cause, she must carve out a place for herself in a new Palestinian state. As a voice of reason in an area fraught with conflict, Hanan Ashrawi faces her most difficult challenge.

APPENDIX

THE OSLO ACCORD

Declaration of Principles
on Interim Self-Government Arrangements

The Government of the State of Israel and the P.L.O. team (in the Jordanian-Palestinian delegation to the Middle East Peace Conference) (the "Palestinian Delegation"), representing the Palestinian people, agree that it is time to put an end to decades of confrontation and conflict, recognize their mutual legitimate and political rights, and strive to live in peaceful coexistence and mutual dignity and security and achieve a just, lasting and comprehensive peace settlement and historic reconciliation through the agreed political process. Accordingly, the two sides agree to the following principles:

ARTICLE I

AIM OF THE NEGOTIATIONS

The aim of the Israeli-Palestinian negotiations within the current Middle East peace process is, among other things, to establish a Palestinian Interim Self-Government Authority, the elected Council (the "Council"), for the Palestinian people in the West Bank and the Gaza Strip, for a transitional period not exceeding five years, leading to a permanent settlement based on Security Council Resolutions 242 and 338.

It is understood that the interim arrangements are an integral part of the whole peace process and that the negotiations on the permanent status will lead to the implementation of Security Council Resolutions 242 and 338.

ARTICLE II

FRAMEWORK FOR THE INTERIM PERIOD

The agreed framework for the interim period is set forth in this Declaration of Principles.

ARTICLE III

ELECTIONS

1. In order that the Palestinian people in the West Bank and Gaza Strip may govern themselves according to democratic principles, direct, free and general political elections will be held for the Council under agreed supervision and international observation, while the Palestinian police will ensure public order.
2. An agreement will be concluded on the exact mode and conditions of the elections in accordance with the protocol attached as Annex I, with the goal of holding the elections not later than nine months after the entry into force of this Declaration of Principles.
3. These elections will constitute a significant interim preparatory step toward the realization of the legitimate rights of the Palestinian people and their just requirements.

ARTICLE IV

JURISDICTION

Jurisdiction of the Council will cover West Bank and Gaza Strip territory, except for issues that will be negotiated in the permanent status negotiations. The two sides view the West Bank and the Gaza Strip as a single territorial unit, whose integrity will be preserved during the interim period.

ARTICLE V

TRANSITIONAL PERIOD AND PERMANENT STATUS NEGOTIATIONS

1. The five-year transitional period will begin upon the withdrawal from the Gaza Strip and Jericho area.
2. Permanent status negotiations will commence as soon as pos-

sible, but not later than the beginning of the third year of the interim period, between the Government of Israel and the Palestinian people representatives.

3. It is understood that these negotiations shall cover remaining issues, including: Jerusalem, refugees, settlements, security arrangements, borders, relations and cooperation with other neighbors, and other issues of common interest.

4. The two parties agree that the outcome of the permanent status negotiations should not be prejudiced or preempted by agreements reached for the interim period.

ARTICLE VI

PREPARATORY TRANSFER OF POWERS AND RESPONSIBILITIES

1. Upon the entry into force of this Declaration of Principles and the withdrawal from the Gaza Strip and the Jericho area, a transfer of authority from the Israeli military government and its Civil Administration to the authorised Palestinians for this task, as detailed herein, will commence. This transfer of authority will be of a preparatory nature until the inauguration of the Council.

2. Immediately after the entry into force of this Declaration of Principles and the withdrawal from the Gaza Strip and Jericho area, with the view to promoting economic development in the West Bank and Gaza Strip, authority will be transferred to the Palestinians on the following spheres: education and culture, health, social welfare, direct taxation, and tourism. The Palestinian side will commence in building the Palestinian police force, as agreed upon. Pending the inauguration of the Council, the two parties may negotiate the transfer of additional powers and responsibilities, as agreed upon.

ARTICLE VII

INTERIM AGREEMENT

1. The Israeli and Palestinian delegations will negotiate an agreement on the interim period (the "Interim Agreement").

2. The Interim Agreement shall specify, among other things, the

structure of the Council, the number of its members, and the transfer of powers and responsibilities from the Israeli military government and its Civil Administration to the Council. The Interim Agreement shall also specify the Council's executive authority, legislative authority in accordance with Article IX below, and the independent Palestinian judicial organs.

3. The Interim Agreement shall include arrangements, to be implemented upon the inauguration of the Council, for the assumption by the Council of all of the powers and responsibilities transferred previously in accordance with Article VI above.

4. In order to enable the Council to promote economic growth, upon its inauguration, the Council will establish, among other things, a Palestinian Electricity Authority, a Gaza Sea Port Authority, a Palestinian Development Bank, a Palestinian Export Promotion Board, a Palestinian Environmental Authority, a Palestinian Land Authority and a Palestinian Water Administration Authority, and any other Authorities agreed upon, in accordance with the Interim Agreement that will specify their powers and responsibilities.

5. After the inauguration of the Council, the Civil Administration will be dissolved, and the Israeli military government will be withdrawn.

ARTICLE VIII

PUBLIC ORDER AND SECURITY

In order to guarantee public order and internal security for the Palestinians of the West Bank and the Gaza Strip, the Council will establish a strong police force, while Israel will continue to carry the responsibility for defending against external threats, as well as the responsibility for overall security of Israelis for the purpose of safeguarding their internal security and public order.

ARTICLE IX

LAWS AND MILITARY ORDERS

1. The Council will be empowered to legislate, in accordance with the Interim Agreement, within all authorities transferred to it.

2. Both parties will review jointly laws and military orders presently in force in remaining spheres.

ARTICLE X

JOINT ISRAELI-PALESTINIAN LIAISON COMMITTEE

In order to provide for a smooth implementation of this Declaration of Principles and any subsequent agreements pertaining to the interim period, upon the entry into force of this Declaration of Principles, a Joint Israeli-Palestinian Liaison Committee will be established in order to deal with issues requiring coordination, other issues of common interest, and disputes.

ARTICLE XI

ISRAELI-PALESTINIAN COOPERATION IN ECONOMIC FIELDS

Recognizing the mutual benefit of cooperation in promoting the development of the West Bank, the Gaza Strip and Israel, upon the entry into force of this Declaration of Principles, an Israeli-Palestinian Economic Cooperation Committee will be established in order to develop and implement in a cooperative manner the programs identified in the protocols attached as Annex III and Annex IV.

ARTICLE XII

LIAISON AND COOPERATION WITH JORDAN AND EGYPT

The two parties will invite the Governments of Jordan and Egypt to participate in establishing further liaison and cooperation arrangements between the Government of Israel and the Palestinian representatives, on the one hand, and the Governments of Jordan and Egypt, on the other hand, to promote cooperation between them. These arrangements will include the constitution of a Continuing Committee that will decide by agreement on the modalities of admission of persons displaced from the West Bank and Gaza Strip in 1967, together with necessary measures to prevent disruption and disorder. Other matters of common concern will be dealt with by this Committee.

ARTICLE XIII

REDEPLOYMENT OF ISRAELI FORCES

1. After the entry into force of this Declaration of Principles, and not later than the eve of elections for the Council, a redeployment of Israeli military forces in the West Bank and the Gaza Strip will take place, in addition to withdrawal of Israeli forces carried out in accordance with Article XIV.
2. In redeploying its military forces, Israel will be guided by the principle that its military forces should be redeployed outside populated areas.
3. Further redeployments to specified locations will be gradually implemented commensurate with the assumption of responsibility for public order and internal security by the Palestinian police force pursuant to Article VIII above.

ARTICLE XIV

ISRAELI WITHDRAWAL
FROM THE GAZA STRIP AND
JERICHO AREA

Israel will withdraw from the Gaza Strip and Jericho area, as detailed in the protocol attached as Annex II.

ARTICLE XV

RESOLUTION OF DISPUTES

1. Disputes arising out of the application or interpretation of this Declaration of Principles, or any subsequent agreements pertaining to the interim period, shall be resolved by negotiations through the Joint Liaison Committee to be established pursuant to Article X above.
2. Disputes which cannot be settled by negotiations may be resolved by a mechanism of conciliation to be agreed upon by the parties.
3. The parties may agree to submit to arbitration disputes relating to the interim period, which cannot be settled through conciliation. To this end, upon the agreement of both parties, the parties will establish an Arbitration Committee.

ARTICLE XVI

ISRAELI-PALESTINIAN COOPERATION CONCERNING REGIONAL PROGRAMS

Both parties view the multilateral working groups as an appropriate instrument for promoting a "Marshall Plan", the regional programs and other programs, including special programs for the West Bank and Gaza Strip, as indicated in the protocol attached as Annex IV.

ARTICLE XVII

MISCELLANEOUS PROVISIONS

1. This Declaration of Principles will enter into force one month after its signing.
2. All protocols annexed to this Declaration of Principles and Agreed Minutes pertaining thereto shall be regarded as an integral part hereof.

Done at Washington, D.C., this thirteenth day of September, 1993.

For the Government of Israel   For the P.L.O.

Witnessed By:

The United States of America   The Russian Federation

ANNEX I

PROTOCOL ON THE MODE AND CONDITIONS OF ELECTIONS

1. Palestinians of Jerusalem who live there will have the right to participate in the election process, according to an agreement between the two sides.
2. In addition, the election agreement should cover, among other things, the following issues:
   a. the system of elections;
   b. the mode of the agreed supervision and international observation and their personal composition; and
   c. rules and regulations regarding election campaign, including agreed arrangements for the organizing of mass media, and the possibility of licensing a broadcasting and TV station.
3. The future status of displaced Palestinians who were registered on 4th June 1967 will not be prejudiced because they are unable to participate in the election process due to practical reasons.

ANNEX II

PROTOCOL ON WITHDRAWAL OF ISRAELI FORCES FROM THE GAZA STRIP AND JERICHO AREA

1. The two sides will conclude and sign within two months from the date of entry into force of this Declaration of Principles, an agreement on the withdrawal of Israeli military forces from the Gaza Strip and Jericho area. This agreement will include comprehensive arrangements to apply in the Gaza Strip and the Jericho area subsequent to the Israeli withdrawal.
2. Israel will implement an accelerated and scheduled withdrawal of Israeli military forces from the Gaza Strip and Jericho area, beginning immediately with the signing of the agreement on the Gaza Strip and Jericho area and to be completed within a period not exceeding four months after the signing of this agreement.
3. The above agreement will include, among other things:

   a. Arrangements for a smooth and peaceful transfer of authority from the Israeli military government and its Civil Administration to the Palestinian representatives.

   b. Structure, powers and responsibilities of the Palestinian authority in these areas, except: external security, settlements, Israelis, foreign relations, and other mutually agreed matters.

   c. Arrangements for the assumption of internal security and public order by the Palestinian police force consisting of police officers recruited locally and from abroad (holding Jordanian passports and Palestinian documents issued by Egypt). Those who will participate in the Palestinian police force coming from abroad should be trained as police and police officers.

   d. A temporary international or foreign presence, as agreed upon.

   e. Establishment of a joint Palestinian-Israeli Coordination and Cooperation Committee for mutual security purposes.

   f. An economic development and stabilization program, including the establishment of an Emergency Fund, to encourage foreign investment, and financial and economic support. Both sides will coordinate and cooperate jointly and unilaterally with regional and international parties to support these aims.

   g. Arrangements for a safe passage for persons and transportation between the Gaza Strip and Jericho area.

4. The above agreement will include arrangements for coordination between both parties regarding passages:

   a. Gaza—Egypt; and

   b. Jericho—Jordan.

5. The offices responsible for carrying out the powers and responsibilities of the Palestinian authority under this Annex II and Article VI of the Declaration of Principles will be located in the Gaza Strip and in the Jericho area pending the inauguration of the Council.

6. Other than these agreed arrangements, the status of the Gaza Strip and Jericho area will continue to be an integral part of the West Bank and Gaza Strip, and will not be changed in the interim period.

ANNEX III

PROTOCOL ON ISRAELI-PALESTINIAN COOPERATION IN ECONOMIC AND DEVELOPMENT PROGRAMS

The two sides agree to establish an Israeli-Palestinian Continuing Committee for Economic Cooperation, focusing, among other things, on the following:

1. Cooperation in the field of water, including a Water Development Program prepared by experts from both sides, which will also specify the mode of cooperation in the management of water resources in the West Bank and Gaza Strip, and will include proposals for studies and plans on water rights of each party, as well as on the equitable utilization of joint water resources for implementation in and beyond the interim period.

2. Cooperation in the field of electricity, including an Electricity Development Program, which will also specify the mode of cooperation for the production, maintenance, purchase and sale of electricity resources.

3. Cooperation in the field of energy, including an Energy Development Program, which will provide for the exploitation of oil and gas for industrial purposes, particularly in the Gaza Strip and in the Negev, and will encourage further joint exploitation of other energy resources. This Program may also provide for the construction of a Petrochemical industrial complex in the Gaza Strip and the construction of oil and gas pipelines.

4. Cooperation in the field of finance, including a Financial Development and Action Program for the encouragement of international investment in the West Bank and the Gaza Strip, and in Israel, as well as the establishment of a Palestinian Development Bank.

5. Cooperation in the field of transport and communications, including a Program, which will define guidelines for the establishment of a Gaza Sea Port Area, and will provide for the establishing of transport and communications lines to and from the West Bank and the Gaza Strip to Israel and to other countries. In addition, this Program will provide for carrying out the necessary construction of roads, railways, communications lines, etc.

6. Cooperation in the field of trade, including studies, and Trade Promotion Programs, which will encourage local, regional and inter-regional trade, as well as a feasibility study of creating free trade zones in the Gaza Strip and in Israel, mutual access to these zones, and cooperation in other areas related to trade and commerce.

7. Cooperation in the field of industry, including Industrial Development Programs, which will provide for the establishment of joint Israeli-Palestinian Industrial Research and Development Centers, will promote Palestinian-Israeli joint ventures, and provide guidelines for cooperation in the textile, food, pharmaceutical, electronics, diamonds, computer and science-based industries.

8. A program for cooperation in, and regulation of, labor relations and cooperation in social welfare issues.

9. A Human Resources Development and Cooperation Plan, providing for joint Israeli-Palestinian workshops and seminars, and for the establishment of joint vocational training centers, research institutes and data banks.

10. An Environmental Protection Plan, providing for joint and/or coordinated measures in this sphere.

11. A program for developing coordination and cooperation in the field of communication and media.

12. Any other programs of mutual interest.

ANNEX IV

PROTOCOL ON ISRAELI-PALESTINIAN COOPERATION CONCERNING REGIONAL DEVELOPMENT PROGRAMS

1. The two sides will cooperate in the context of the multilateral peace efforts in promoting a Development Program for the region, including the West Bank and the Gaza Strip, to be initiated by the G-7. The parties will request the G-7 to seek the participation in this program of other interested states, such as members of the Organisation for Economic Cooperation and Development, regional Arab states and institutions, as well as members of the private sector.

2. The Development Program will consist of two elements:

a) An Economic Development Program for the West Bank and the Gaza Strip.

b) A Regional Economic Development Program.

A. The Economic Development Program for the West Bank and the Gaza Strip will consist of the following elements:

(1) A Social Rehabilitation Program, including a Housing and Construction Program.

(2) A Small and Medium Business Development Plan.

(3) An Infrastructure Development Program (water, electricity, transportation and communications, etc.)

(4) A Human Resources Plan.

(5) Other programs.

B. The Regional Economic Development Program may consist of the following elements:

(1) The establishment of a Middle East Development Fund, as a first step, and a Middle East Development Bank, as a second step.

(2) The development of a joint Israeli-Palestinian-Jordanian Plan for coordinated exploitation of the Dead Sea area.

(3) The Mediterranean Sea (Gaza)—Dead Sea Canal.

(4) Regional Desalinization and other water development projects.

(5) A regional plan for agricultural development, including a coordinated regional effort for the prevention of desertification.

(6) Interconnection of electricity grids.

(7) Regional cooperation for the transfer, distribution and industrial exploitation of gas, oil and other energy resources.

(8) A Regional Tourism, Transportation and Telecommunications Development Plan.

(9) Regional cooperation in other spheres.

3. The two sides will encourage the multilateral working groups, and will coordinate towards their success. The two parties will encourage intersessional activities, as well as pre-feasibility and feasibility studies, within the various multilateral working groups.

Agreed Minutes
to the Declaration of Principles
on Interim Self-Government Arrangements

A. GENERAL UNDERSTANDINGS AND AGREEMENTS

Any powers and responsibilities transferred to the Palestinians pursuant to the Declaration of Principles prior to the inauguration of the Council will be subject to the same principles pertaining to Article IV, as set out in these Agreed Minutes below.

B. SPECIFIC UNDERSTANDINGS AND AGREEMENTS

ARTICLE IV

It is understood that:
1. Jurisdiction of the Council will cover West Bank and Gaza Strip territory, except for issues that will be negotiated in the permanent status negotiations: Jerusalem, settlements, military locations, and Israelis.
2. The Council's jurisdiction will apply with regard to the agreed powers, responsibilities, spheres and authorities transferred to it.

ARTICLE VI (2)

It is agreed that the transfer of authority will be as follows:
(1) The Palestinian side will inform the Israeli side of the names of the authorised Palestinians who will assume the powers, authorities and responsibilities that will be transferred to the Palestinians according to the Declaration of Principles in the following fields: education and culture, health, social welfare, direct taxation, tourism, and any other authorities agreed upon.
(2) It is understood that the rights and obligations of these offices will not be affected.
(3) Each of the spheres described above will continue to enjoy existing budgetary allocations in accordance with arrangements to be mutually agreed upon. These arrangements also will

provide for the necessary adjustments required in order to take into account the taxes collected by the direct taxation office.

(4) Upon the execution of the Declaration of Principles, the Israeli and Palestinian delegations will immediately commence negotiations on a detailed plan for the transfer of authority on the above offices in accordance with the above understandings.

ARTICLE VII (2)

The Interim Agreement will also include arrangements for coordination and cooperation.

ARTICLE VII (5)

The withdrawal of the military government will not prevent Israel from exercising the powers and responsibilities not transferred to the Council.

ARTICLE VIII

It is understood that the Interim Agreement will include arrangements for cooperation and coordination between the two parties in this regard. It is also agreed that the transfer of powers and responsibilities to the Palestinian police will be accomplished in a phased manner, as agreed in the Interim Agreement.

ARTICLE X

It is agreed that, upon the entry into force of the Declaration of Principles, the Israeli and Palestinian delegations will exchange the names of the individuals designated by them as members of the Joint Israeli-Palestinian Liaison Committee.

It is further agreed that each side will have an equal number of members in the Joint Committee. The Joint Committee will reach decisions by agreement. The Joint Committee may add other technicians and experts, as necessary. The Joint Committee will decide on the frequency and place or places of its meetings.

Appendix

ANNEX II

It is understood that, subsequent to the Israeli withdrawal, Israel will continue to be responsible for external security, and for internal security and public order of settlements and Israelis. Israeli military forces and civilians may continue to use roads freely within the Gaza Strip and the Jericho area.

Done at Washington, D.C., this thirteenth day of September, 1993.

For the Government of Israel   For the P.L.O.

Witnessed By:

The United States of America   The Russian Federation

GLOSSARY

al-dakhil—PLO leaders inside Occupied Territories

al-Fatah—Yasir Arafat's military arm of the PLO; in 1969 the Fatah leader, Arafat, assumed leadership of the PLO.

al-kharij—PLO leaders outside Occupied Territories

chador—headdress covering the face, worn by Arab women

Democratic Front for the Liberation of Palestine (DFLP)—Marxist-Leninist, pro-Soviet group founded by Nayef Hawatme in 1969

fedayeen—Palestinian fighters willing to sacrifice themselves for the cause of liberating Palestine

General Union of Palestinian Students—Palestinian student group to which Hanan belonged

Green Line—imaginary line that separates Israel from the Occupied Territories as well as the Arab States on its borders

Gush Emunim—Israeli right-wing lobby group that advocates total annexation of the Occupied Territories on religious grounds

Hamas—Islamic fundamentalist/resistance movement, West Bank and Gaza

Hezbollah—a political, social, and military organization that gives focus and general identity in Lebanon to Iran's Islamic regime; the Hezbollah movement was born as a result of the merge of Hasayn Musawi's Islamic Amal and the Lebanese Branch of the Da'wa Party in 1982–1983.

Intifada—Palestinian uprising against Israeli occupation of West Bank and Gaza

Islamic Jihad—Islamic fundamentalist movement

293

jihad—holy war

kaffiyeh—traditional cloth headdress worn by Arab males

Mossad—Israeli secret service

Muslim Brotherhood—an Islamic fundamentalist organization founded in Egypt at the end of the 1920s by a schoolteacher named Hassan al-Banna; it was a religious movement that used terrorist methods against the occupying British Army.

nida'at—orders given by Palestinian leaders during the Intifada for strikes and/or violence by the general population of the West Bank and Gaza

Occupied Territories—those territories captured by Israel after the 1967 Six Day War, including the West Bank and Gaza Strip

Palestinian Democratic Movement for Peace—West Bankers willing to negotiate with Israel

Popular Front for the Liberation of Palestine—formed after the Arab defeat in the 1967 Six Day War by George Habash; the PFLP established itself from the beginning as one of the most violent Palestinian groups, with strong ties to other Marxist revolutionary organizations.

Red Eagles—military arm of the PFLP located in Nablus

Red Panthers—militant arm of al-Fatah in the northern section of the West Bank

Sayaret Malkal—elite Israeli commando unit

Shabiba—Arab name for the "youth" belonging to the PLO

Shakhsiyat—PLO top spokespeople (academics, professionals, etc.), from *al-Shakhsiyat al-'aama*

Shin Bet—Israeli internal security/secret police

sukkah—temporary hut or arbor erected during the Jewish holiday of Sukkoth

Unified National Command (UNC)—Arafat-sanctioned coordinating leadership of Intifada, also known as *al-Qiyada al-Wataniyy al-Muwahhada*

Village Leagues—Menachem Milson's plan that encouraged the election of Palestinian leaders within the Occupied Territories that were pro-Israel

Yediot Aharanot—leading Israeli newspaper

INDEX